British racial discourse

A study of British political discourse about race and race-related matters

FRANK REEVES

CAMBRIDGE UNIVERSITY PRESS

Cambridge
London   New York   New Rochelle
Melbourne   Sydney

Published by the Press Syndicate of the University of Cambridge
The Pitt Building, Trumpington Street, Cambridge CB2 1RP
32 East 57th Street, New York, NY 10022, USA
296 Beaconsfield Parade, Middle Park, Melbourne 3206, Australia

First published 1983

Printed in Great Britain at the University Press, Cambridge

Library of Congress catalogue card number: 83–7273

British Library Cataloguing in Publication Data

Reeves, Frank
British racial discourse.
1. Great Britain – Race relations – Social aspects
2. Great Britain – Race relations – Political aspects
I. Title
305.8′00941   DA125.A1

ISBN 0 521 25554 6

SE

Comparative ethnic and race relations

British racial discourse

Comparative ethnic and race relations series

Published for the SSRC Research Unit on Ethnic Relations at the University of Aston in Birmingham
Edited by
Professor John Rex *Director*
Dr Robin Ward *Deputy Director*
Mr Malcolm Cross *Deputy Director*

This series has been formed to publish works of original theory and empirical research on the problems of racially mixed societies. It is based on the work of the SSRC Research Unit for Ethnic Relations at Aston University – the main centre for the study of race relations in Britain.

The first book in the series is a textbook on *Racial and Ethnic Competition* by Professor Michael Banton – a leading British sociologist of race relations and the former Director of the Unit. Future titles will be on such issues as the forms of contact between majority and minority groups, housing, the problems faced by young people, employment, ethnic identity and ethnicity, and will concentrate on race and employment, race and the inner city, and ethnicity and education.

The books will appeal to an international readership of scholars, students and professionals concerned with racial issues, across a wide range of disciplines (such as sociology, anthropology, social policy, politics, economics, education and law), as well as among professional social administrators, teachers, government officials, health service workers and others.

Contents

Figures

Tables

Acknowledgments

I am indebted, above all, to Professor John Rex, without whose help and constant encouragement this project would never have been undertaken, sustained or completed. Professor Rex acted not only as an academic patron, but went out of his way to help me solve the practical and financial problems arising from prolonged research of this kind. I am also grateful to colleagues at the Research Unit on Ethnic Relations, University of Aston, for providing a stimulating and critical academic environment.

The emotional, intellectual, and domestic support I received from my wife, Melhado Chevannes, was indispensable. While I was attempting to write detachedly about white racial discourse, she frequently found herself on the receiving end of its most pernicious manifestations. The contributions of my baby daughters, Toussaint and Spartaca need also to be acknowledged, but I am uncertain as to whether the interludes they forced on me have added or subtracted from the book. Should I have unduly neglected their constant wish to play, I beg their forgiveness.

I should like especially to acknowledge the help of my old friend, Sydney Peiris. I have spent many enjoyable hours with him discussing race and politics. He also bears some responsibility for locating the more obscure and esoteric references used in the text.

Among the many people who, in a variety of ways, supported my precious project, I should like to mention Ron Cook, the late Frank Noble, and Charles Critcher of the Open University West Midland Regional Office, Jenny Williams, Ivan Henry, Mark Johnson, Trevor and Jackie Coote, Ken and Brenda Purchase, Keith and Peta Wymer, and David and Joan Grabham.

Finally, I should specially like to thank (another) Jenny Williams, Marci Green, Margaret Reeves (my sister), Christine Dunn, Annabel de Meza Arslan and Gwen Morris who, at various stages, contributed to the typing of the manuscript.

Objectivity

A neighbour came to Nasrudin for an interpretation on a point of law.

'My cow was gored by your bull. Do I get any compensation?'

'Certainly not. How can a man be held responsible for what an animal does?'

'Just a moment', said the crafty villager. 'I am afraid I got the question back to front. What actually happened was that *my* bull gored *your* cow.'

'Ah', said the Mulla, 'this is more involved. I shall have to look up the book of precedents, for there may be other factors involved which are relevant and which could alter the case.'

Idries Shah, *The Pleasantries of the Incredible Mulla Nasrudin*, Picador.

Introduction

The overall aim of this book is to provide some explanation for the kinds of discourse used in dealing with racial issues. The central task throughout is to combine the insights offered by a theory of ideology with an analysis of examples of actual discourse about race and related matters. Because of the immensity of the task of trying to account for all kinds of racial expression, the study is confined, in the main, to an examination of political discourse, and further, to the political discourse of a limited number of national politicians belonging either to the Conservative or to the Labour Party.

There are a number of reasons for selecting political discourse about race and race-related issues as a subject for study. Such discourse is related to decision-making or to the absence of decision-making, which gives it a little more significance than that of a casual conversation in a public bar. Also, it is the language of persons who are accustomed to making public pronouncements and are aware, to some degree, of the likely consequences of their utterances. And, because of the ideological setting in which it occurs, political discourse may reveal more consistency and regularity of feature than other kinds of speech. Force of circumstance probably encourages politicans to develop, enlarge upon, and systematise their views on various topics. There is also likely to be variation between different schools of political thought, enabling useful comparisons to be made. For reasons, then, of its association with significant decision-making, its regularity of feature, and the availability of comparative and contrasting data, political discourse was chosen as the focus for the project.

The study is further limited to an examination of what Conservative and Labour politicians have to say about race – thus omitting the more sensational racial declarations of Right-wing groups such as the National Front. For similar reasons (though without implying, in the manner of psychologists such as Eysenck, that Right- and Left-wing attitudes should be classified in tandem), the strong anti-racist stances of communist and Trotskyist groups are neglected. This does not mean that the menace posed to the black community* by the National Front's vicious, Right-wing

* For a discussion of the terminology used in this study to refer to racial minorities, see Appendix 1.

1

propaganda and other action is unrecognised. Rather, the central purpose of the study is to concentrate on the mainstream of British politics in the shape of the Conservative and Labour Parties, which must be held responsible, inasmuch as responsibility can be attributed in this sphere, for making (by inclusion or omission) most of the political decisions that have affected race relations and racial minority groups. This state of affairs is likely to continue to be the case for the foreseeable future. And yet, while there is much literature on fascist ideology, including a recently published *Fascists: A Social Psychological View of the National Front* (Billig, 1978) surprisingly little has been written by social scientists generally, and sociologists in particular, about British Conservative or Labour Party ideology, and even less about those ideologies in relation to racial matters.

One common view is that party political consensus has removed race as an electoral issue, yet within their parties and to their electorate politicians are forced to justify their action or inaction to pressure groups and individuals that challenge them. The aim of the study is to examine the regular features of the justificatory systems adopted by mainstream politicians. Such a study has political relevance: it should provide insights into the relationship between racial and other party values, into the stability of the ideological structure as a whole, and into whether there is much potential or room for further policy initiative in the field of race relations within the present political context.

Despite the decision to limit the study to an examination of political discourse, the task was still sufficiently grandiose to require further focus. This was accomplished by the choice of theory and by the selection of particular cases for analysis.

The explanatory theory adopted was drawn extensively from current sociological studies of ideology with a heavy emphasis on the tradition developed from Marx and Engels's *Feuerbach: Opposition of the Materialist and Idealist Outlooks* (1973). In particular, there is an attempt to relate racial discourse to the general process of capitalist state legitimation described by Habermas (1976). But ideas are also drawn eclectically from the works of Pareto, Gramsci, and Shils, to provide a theory of ideological levels in which the specialist discourse of politicians can be distinguished from the discourse of the general population. It is recognised that the discourse of politicians has an important justificatory function which, in the examination of empirical data, best serves to exemplify its ideological nature.

A series of logical and philosophical distinctions is also employed. The sentences that go to make up an ideological complex are classed as descriptive, evaluative, or prescriptive, while the process of explanation is carefully distinguished from justification. Many arguments in the area of race relations are enthymematic, meaning that they are not stated in full. Premises or conclusions are suppressed because they are already accepted as common knowledge by the population and because enthymemes are often rhetorically more persuasive than full argument.

The empirical data selected for analysis were drawn from the debates on the Immigration Bills, as recorded in Hansard, and the debates on immigration, race relations, and other kindred issues recorded in Conservative and Labour Party Conference Reports.

The book is organised into eight chapters. Chapter 1 examines in detail the meaning of terms such as 'racism' and 'racialism' and whether these concepts are adequate for describing the complexities of discourse dealing with race. The meaning of the term 'racism' is explained and three different usages – a 'weak', 'medium' and 'strong' – are distinguished. There is some discussion of the means by which racist discourse might be identified, and Professor Banton's arguments on this point are subjected to criticism. The critique of the concept of racism aims to show that it is generally inadequate as a means for analysing discourse about racial matters.

Chapters 2 to 4 attempt to locate discourse dealing with race in the framework of the social structure, and for this purpose draw extensively upon various theories of ideology, making use in particular of themes drawn from the work of Marx and Engels. Initially, the meaning of ideology and its relationship with discourse are set out in detail. Then, an economic structural explanation of racial division, postulating a 'square of alienation', is offered for consideration. It is argued that while economic explanations of race relations might throw light on the reason for racial responses generally, they are unable to account for the many complexities of political discourse dealing with race. Specialised political discourse is best understood within the context of the political legitimation process in which the representatives of particular social classes or class alliances seek to persuade the population that they are acting for the public good and in the general interest. Although this might seem a very obvious point to make, it differs from the widely accepted view that 'racism' can be simply explained in terms of action in pursuit of economic interest. While the underlying dynamic of capitalism has to be recognised, the contending classes pursue their interests at different institutional and discursive levels. The actual content of any example of racial or racist discourse is likely to reflect the true complexity of the decision-making process in which politicians seek to maximise a whole range of benefits and to minimise losses.

In Chapter 4 a typology of Conservative and Labour values is devised to describe the specialised political discourse of the two major political parties. The aim is to show that what is said about race issues is tempered by the predominant class values of British ideology as a whole; values that arise from the antagonism between the classes and class alliances of a capitalist society. Racial expression, then, is subject to the constraints of class values, and must avail itself of the forms and categories that Right - and Left-wing class ideologies provide.

Chapter 5 constitutes an attempt to show how the analysis provided in the previous chapters can be applied. The values of Conservative and Labour are paired, and their contrasting ideological and policy implications described. Examples are drawn from the historical legacy of Conservative and Labour classics and from the Party Conference Reports. Conservative traditionalism and organicism is contrasted with Labour rationalisation and commitment to structural change. Nationalism is contrasted with internationalism, imperialism with anti-imperialism, the maintenance of class stability with the pursuit of egalitarianism, social order with social justice, laissez-faire and the rejection of state interference with social ownership and the advocacy of government intervention, the emphasis on self-reliant individualism with welfare collectivism, and the limitations of human nature with the possibilities offered by nurture and education for human improvement. And finally, Right- and Left-wing 'bogies' – communism and 'extremism' of any kind for the Conservative camp, fascism for Labour – are mentioned in respect of their consequences for racial views and policies. Throughout this section, attention is devoted to the ways these values have affected opinions and positions adopted towards black people.

Chapter 6 is concerned with how discourse, which, at face value, makes no use of racist or racial categories, can be used with racial effect or to disguise racial intent. There is the straightforward situation where practices resulting in inegalitarian racial consequences are justified, consciously or unconsciously, by recourse to arguments of a non-racial or racist kind. Alternatively, there is a form of deracialisation, described here as 'sanitary coding', in which persons speak purposely to their audiences about racial matters while avoiding the overt deployment of racial descriptions, evaluations, and prescriptions.

The arguments used by Members of Parliament for justifying Commonwealth immigration control (which had clear racial consequences) are grouped into seven categories: personalised dispositional and agential, abstracted social process, populist, economic, *pro bono publico*, reciprocity and means-orientated, together with accompanying rhetorical modes. In general, deracialised discourse is defensible against the accusation that it is racist, but is capable, nevertheless, of justifying racial discrimination by providing other non-racist criteria for the differential treatment of a group distinguished by its racial characteristics. 'Sanitary coding' is another rhetorical device which provides absolution from responsibility for racial evaluation and prescription, but here the politician self-consciously shares in a conspiracy with an audience. In order to conceal his racial message he uses the techniques of equivocation and stress as well as attempting to project mental images for others to interpret. As a whole, Chapter 7 is meant to illustrate in detail, and by using a specific issue, i.e. black immigration control, how the ideological facade (the claim that various actions are morally justifiable and are not merely undertaken in pursuit of self-interest) is constructed and efficaciously maintained.

For academic, technical, and personal reasons, the present *British Racial Discourse* is not the book I intended to write, nor the lengthy manuscript of 200,000 words that it later became. It was originally conceived as an empirical study of the discourse about race of national and local politicians, but such was the size of the enterprise and the inadequacy of existing analytical and methodological tools, that the work was forced to take an increasingly theoretical bent and, in combination with interpretation of the copious empirical material (drawn from the taped interviews with politicians), to grow like Jack's beanstalk. The correct solution was to prune unmercifully, which may have had the effect in a few places of disrupting the flow of argument.

All major reference to local politics has been omitted, although the interviews with councillors and other officials had such intrinsic interest that I feel the need to do justice to them in a subsequent publication. In addition to this major surgery, a chapter in which I criticise the usefulness of some social psychological approaches (those in which the concept of 'prejudiced attitude' is stressed to the exclusion of other considerations) was extracted and published as a Social Science Research Council Research Unit on Ethnic Relations working paper (No. 17, 1982). Nevertheless, I have continued to make some cursory reference in my conclusion to the inadequacies of examining discourse about race solely with the aid of the concept of race prejudice.

A further chapter analysing the parliamentary debates on the Race Relations Bills, entitled 'The practice of racialism, versus the rhetoric of racial tolerance' has been deleted in another attempt to tackle the persistent problem of length. This has had the effect of reducing the number of convincingly worked examples of deracialisation, although the far more valuable theoretical chapter on that subject has been retained.

Short résumés of some of the arguments advanced in the missing sections have been included in the conclusion which tries to knit together in a more even fashion the various threads running through the book.

The manuscript as a whole is now far leaner and more realistic in the demands it makes on the reader. It aims to provide a partial account of

British racial ideology as it is practically experienced in the form of political discourse, as well as to offer some theoretical understanding of its relationship to the social structure and in particular its relationship to inter- and intra-class divisions. Such a massive undertaking is likely to be inadequate in many respects, and the work, when read as a whole, may appear on occasion to be either repetitive or unsatisfactorily synthesised. Nevertheless, it is hoped that it does attempt to provide an overview of the nature of British racial discourse, and to bring one or two original concepts to bear on the task. There is undoubtedly a need for further extensive academic work to be conducted in this area.

1

The meaning of 'racism': its limitations in the study of discourse dealing with racial issues

Terminological difficulties beset the whole field of race relations and, particularly, the study of racial discourse. Before setting out to describe the characteristics of British political discourse about race, I shall try to explain the meaning of 'race', 'racism', 'racialism', 'racist', and 'racialist'. I shall examine in detail the use of the word 'racism' as this description has been widely applied to the kind of things people say about race. Because of a general vagueness and ambiguity in the meaning of all these terms, the exercise requires a great deal of arbitrary legislation, influenced in part by the needs of the subsequent study. In the course of analysis, various confusions, lurking in everyday and previous social scientific usage, are revealed. It should be stressed, however, that the whole area is a semantic 'battlefield', in which Wittgenstein's analogy of word tools does not come amiss. But the social and political ramifications of 'category legislation' are more akin to the deployment of tanks and barbed wire than to the use of the hammer, pliers, and saw of Wittgenstein's homely tool-box. The use of words has political significance: their application in social context reveals something of a person's scheme for ordering, understanding, and acting in his world.

The reality of race consists in the first instance of perceivable characteristics of groups of people. 'Perceivable' in this context means 'capable of being perceived' ('perceived' = 'made available to the senses'). Pigmentation, physique, descent, historical or geographical origin, dress, language, and cultural norms and expressions are perceivable at what philosophers have called the level of the material field. But although perception by itself would appear to require the capacity to differentiate, the recognition of racial difference requires some form of classification, comparison, and judgment of categorial significance. A recognition of racial difference involves a comparison of different pigmentations, physiques, etc., and their acceptance as indicators of a general racial category that acquires significance in conjunction with a broader system of thinking

7

about the world. Perception of itself does not reveal the existence of race. Perceived differences become imbued with significance inasmuch as they act as an anchorage for a set of beliefs, and individuals have cause to consider their position in the light of that set. This idea is superficially similar to the Kantian idea of an object being conceptually determined or grasped by means of a concept, the concept acting as the condition of experience, although it is not clear whether Kant is referring to the conditions of perception or of understanding. It is the overall framework of ideas into which 'race' is inserted, therefore, which provides it with significance for social existence and understanding.

In its everyday usage the term 'race' is both vague and ambiguous. The limitations to the word's usage are rarely clear, and even if they are it is not always apparent which of the word's recognised usages is being used in a particular context.

Is a race 'a group of people of common origin or descent', 'a division of mankind based on certain physical differences', 'one of the divisions of living creatures', e.g. 'the race of man', or something else again? In zoological literature, stipulative definitions of race have been offered which derive from and may also affect everyday usage if they become popularised. There is obviously a connection between race defined as 'a group regarded as of common stock' and as 'a population within an animal species possessing a distinct gene frequency'. The sociologist's approach has been to study the definition of 'race' in popular usage in a given society. 'Race', then, is seen to be a social classification based primarily on perception of physical differences, although these physical differences need not be demonstrably genetically based.

Lachenmeyer (1971, p. 10) points out that:

> linguistic symbols must at certain points represent observable
> attributes, properties, and relations. A term's referential
> meaning consists of the points of contiguity between it as
> linguistic symbol and the observable attributes, properties and
> relations that it represents. Thus, referential meaning is the
> most relevant 'meaning concept' for a consideration of
> scientific terminology.

The sociologist, then, identifies 'race' not merely by the use of the linguistic symbol but by its referential meaning. I may recognise others' discourse to be about race, when it employs a category which I am able to identify as having a referent corresponding to that designated by my own understanding of the term 'race'. It is not to be recognised solely by the occurrence of one particular linguistic symbol.

This also means that the boundaries that are placed around a given usage must be made absolutely clear if it is to be the arbiter of whether others are 'really' discussing race. Banton (1977, pp. 148–9) provides an example of the difficulties involved in boundary-drawing by distinguishing racial minorities ('created when opposition to the social incorporation of a minority is justified on the grounds of the minority members' hereditary characteristics, particularly those associated with skin colour and nineteenth century doctrines of racial typology'), national minorities ('people who are either citizens of another state or regard themselves as such and want the political map revised'), and ethnic minorities (dependent 'upon a belief among the minority members that the nature of their common descent requires or justifies their coming together'). The classification, he says, 'makes allowance for a minority's being both ethnic and racial and for changes in the relationship of the inclusive and exclusive boundaries'. It serves to distinguish a variety of groupings all of which might previously have been referred to as races: e.g. the black race, the Welsh race, the Sikh race, etc.

Definition must always involve questions of where to draw the line: when the line is drawn too tightly, much that others think about as 'racial' will be excluded, giving rise to a 'reductionism', and when drawn too extensively, it will take in far too much substance, resulting in 'expansionism'. When Cox (1970) distinguishes race prejudice against blacks from intolerance of the Jews, it could be argued that the line has been drawn too tightly. From the point of view of explaining the structural mechanisms of race relations, however, it is undoubtedly a most thoughtful distinction to make. The possibility of subdividing large general categories of diverse phenomena is probably of great importance in developing an understanding of, and providing explanations for, the race relations complex (which seems to suffer more from expansionism than reductionism). However, it involves lexicographical legislation with political repercussions. For example, are the speeches of Enoch Powell to be thought of as concerned primarily with nationhood rather than with race?

One rough and ready method of tackling demarcation disputes is to connect definitions to frequencies of usage in particular historical and geographical contexts. Thus, when British political discourse in the 1960s and 1970s is examined, it becomes clear that the categories that correspond most closely with Banton's definition of a racial minority (in terms of skin colour) – a definition which might usefully be adopted – are 'West Indians', 'Asians', 'coloured immigrants', 'immigrants', 'spades', 'wogs', and 'racial' or 'ethnic minorities'. In this context, it seems that skin colour is the decisive racial feature, despite the fact that the Jewish 'race' is also identified. In another era, however, the linguistic symbol, 'race', might have a somewhat different denotation. It is the referent, not the presence of the linguistic symbol, that is crucial, although there is in fact likely to be substantial correspondence in referential meaning between the sociologist's, and the 'man in the street's' linguistic symbols. The race category adopted here, then, consists of the class of phenomena designated racial by social scientists and referred to in common parlance under this and other designations, as indicated in Figure 1.

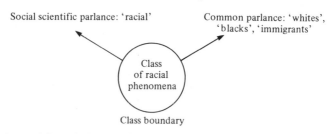

Figure 1. Racial symbol and referent

Racial discourse consists of spoken and written material (e.g. speeches, books, articles, debates, conversation) that makes use of a racial category. Quite how central the race category must be to the discourse, and how frequently it must occur, are matters to be decided by the researcher.

Racial discourse may constitute part of a recognised political ideology. ('Ideology' is defined in Chapter 3.) In attempting to provide a comprehensive map of political affairs, ideologies are likely to find a place for matters of race.

A political ideology such as the national socialism outlined in *Mein Kampf* is centrally concerned with racial explanations of social processes, evaluations, and political prescriptions, and is frequently described as 'racial' or 'racist ideology'. Furthermore, the ideology's adherents might proudly accept the accuracy of a 'racist' label. (But even national socialism deals with issues other than race.) The social observer must not allow the political ideologists' assertions or denials of 'racist' content to play much part in deciding whether the ideology makes extensive use of the racial category: he must decide by reference to content, although the assertions of adherents, particularly those in principal positions in political parties, will qualify as part of that content.

Political ideologies such as British Conservatism, Liberalism, and Labour beliefs, however, are not appropriately described as 'racial' or 'racist'. Very little of the discourse that goes to make up the totality of these ideologies deals in any direct way with racial issues. This is not to deny that the social scientist may be able to recognise the adverse effects of the fulfilment of these ideologies' prescriptions on racial groups. But the ideologies are not accurately described as racial in the sense of making wide use of racial categories, explanations, evaluations, and prescriptions. It is still possible, however, to identify those parts of ideologies which *are* dealing with relations between racial groups and where terms do have an acknowledged racial referent. Ideologies with little overall emphasis on race may make use of racial categories when a sequence of events about which decisions must be made is regarded as racial, or when there is a need to counter a racial interpretation offered by another ideology: e.g. 'immigrants ought not to be repatriated'. They are best described as ideologies in which racial categories, evaluations, or prescriptions appear. This study will be mainly concerned with ideologies such as these.

It is also important to consider the possibility that ideologies from which racial categories are absent from the adherents' point of view, or which remain unrecognised by many of the adherents, may justify practices recognised by the social observer as racially discriminatory. In other words, the effect of the fulfilment of prescriptions contained in the ideology is racialist although the ideology itself is non-racial in that its descriptive, evaluative, and prescriptive content does not make any use of racial categories. What better way to turn a blind eye to racialist practice than to justify it without reference to race itself? I wish to argue that there is a strong tendency in British political ideology to 'deracialise' situations which would appear racial to the social observer, and which may be judged by him to be racially discriminatory in their consequence.

In summary, I distinguish three kinds of ideology that have significance for race relations:

(1) racial ideology with an integral racial element
(2) ideology judged non-racial overall, which nevertheless contains racial elements
(3) non-racial ideology with minimal or no racial content.

Although it is likely that, as a matter of fact, racial ideology will lead to racial practice, it is at least conceivable that racial ideology need not result in racial practice. Also of great interest is the possibility of the existence of non-racial ideologies that exist side by side with racial discrimination – an idea explored at length in later chapters.

In discussion of ideology and discourse dealing with racial matters, the terms 'racism' and 'racialism' are frequently used. As these terms occur again and again in most of the literature in this area, the rest of the chapter is devoted to a detailed examination of their meaning. Although the previous discussion, in mentioning racialism and racial discrimination, understandably hinted at the negatively evaluated consequences of much racial discourse, it is important to recognise that there is no necessary connection between the three kinds of ideology outlined above (racial ideologies, ideologies containing racial elements, and ideologies making use of few or no racial categories) and racism or racialism.

I shall use 'racism' to refer to particular kinds of language configuration and 'racialism' to refer to kinds of act, process, or material effect. This distinction is by no means clear cut: racial abuse, or incitement to racial hatred, might be considered *racist* from the point of view of its verbal form or content, or *racialist* from the point of view of the act committed, the process involved, and the consequences. Nevertheless, it is conceptually most useful to preserve a distinction between 'racist' word and 'racialist' action. I shall deal first and in close detail with the term 'racism', as it is this that is most aptly applied to ideology or discourse.

Racism

There are at least three meanings of 'racism': the 'weak', the 'medium', and the 'strong'. Many a trick lies in the failure to recognise the differences between them. An even more specialised use of 'racism', offered by Banton, is discussed afterwards. The term 'racism' is generally applied to a body of beliefs containing the following assumptions:

(a) that races of human beings exist
(b) that these races differ from one another
(c) that the differences are deeply rooted and enduring
(d) that the differences are significant, possibly because they appear in themselves to be explanatory, or because explanations of other social features may be inferred from them
(e) that the differences have social consequences, for example, for social policy.

This meaning is 'weak' in the sense that it only emphasises the importance of a system of classification, and also, possibly, its explanatory value and social consequences. It does not require the body of belief to include a moral evaluation of racial differences, or prescription of how a person ought to act towards members of a different race. The weak meaning of racism may be given a more specific connotation by providing:

(b-descriptive) precise details of how and in what way the races differ
(c-explanatory) an explanation for the continuing existence of races and racial differences. This might be couched in psycho-cultural terms, but, in the last analysis, it is the persistent nature of the differences and not the explanation for their persistence that is important
(d-explanatory) reasons for the assumptions being thought significant (e.g. (e) in terms of the social consequences that result or have resulted from racial differences or past belief in their significance).

Weak racism becomes medium racism when the assumptions (a) to (e) are extended to include the evaluation:

(f) that the differences between races are of superior to inferior,
     that they occur in some sort of rank order.
Medium racism, therefore, is descriptive and evaluative.

The strong sense of racism goes one step further. It includes all the
characteristics (a) to (f) but holds in addition:

(g) that the superior race(s) ought to be entitled to more
     favourable treatment and the inferior to less.
In extreme cases, the inferior races will scarcely be recognised as human,
and be placed so far down the ladder of development that the policies
adopted by the 'superior' towards them will amount to genocide – a
reflection of their evaluation as 'worthless'.

An example of the weak use of 'racism' is provided by Van den Berghe
(1967, p. 11), when he states that 'the existence of races in a given society
presupposes the presence of racism, for without racism, physical characteristics are devoid of "social significance"'. Abbott (1970) comments
critically that on Van den Berghe's definition 'it would still be racism, if
races were perceived or recognised in a neutral way, or in a favourable or
positive way (e.g. one group might think that another group had
characteristics considered desirable by the first group or that they
themselves possessed desirable characteristics)'.

The weak sense of 'racism' leaves open the possibility of a different
evaluation:

(f-contra) that differences exist but that they are of equal
     importance,
and of a different prescription:

(g – 1 contra) that the races ought to be treated equally.
The medium sense of 'racism' accepts the evaluation that differences
between races are of superior to inferior, but, nevertheless, still allows the
possibility of an alternative prescription:

(g – 2 contra) that the inferior races *ought not* to be treated as such
     by the superior.
We might consider, as an example, the ideas of a ruling race that, while
accepting its genetic superiority and entitlement to rule, exercises a
benevolent paternalism, or even a positive discrimination, in favour of
'lesser mortals'. Lord Acton (1834–1902), for instance, wrote of 'inferior
races' being 'raised by living in political union with races intellectually
superior . . . Nations in which the elements of organisation and the
capacity for government have been lost, either through the demoralising
influence of despotism, or the disintegrating action of democracy, are
restored and educated anew under the discipline of a stronger and less
corrupted race' (1922, pp. 290–300).

Strong racism does not allow of any of these exceptions. Hitler's theory
of an Aryan race destined to conquer and subjugate other races for its own

needs includes the social Darwinist imperative that only the needs of the more advanced race are to be taken into account in the inevitable struggle for survival. Strong racism contains a racist prescription, such as:

> No boy and no girl must leave school without having been led to an ultimate realisation of the necessity and essence of blood purity . . . By mating again and again with other races, we may raise these races from their previous cultural level to a higher stage, but we will descend forever from our own high level.   (Hitler, 1974, p. 389)

One advantage for persons subscribing to weak racism, i.e. a classification based on the descriptive and explanatory significance of racial difference, is that they may deny that their views entail either (f), the evaluation of one race as superior in comparison with an inferior, or (g), commitment to favourable treatment for the superior. This may be a distinct advantage in a situation where there are political disadvantages in being accused of being racist. Eysenck (1971) is quite conscious of the distinction between weak and medium/strong racism when, in a book discussing the difference of IQ between whites and 'negroes', he points out that: 'facts, of course, are one thing; deducing social policies from these facts is quite another . . . it could just as well be argued that negroes required and should be provided with a better system of education to remedy these defects insofar as that was possible' (p. 10). He goes on to claim that the difference of IQ between 'negroes' and whites is partly attributable to genetic differences, and he even hypothesises about how selection (of slaves) might have come to favour the less intelligent: 'If for instance the brighter members of the West African tribes which suffered the depredation of the slavers had managed to use their higher intelligence to escape, so that it was mostly the duller ones who got caught, then the gene pool of the slaves brought to America would have been depleted of many high I.Q. genes' (p. 46).

All the characteristics of weak racism are demonstrated by this work which treats racial differences as significant but claims not to evaluate them. A great deal of attention is paid to the differences, and yet such emphasis is excused on the basis of the hypothetical nature of science. Unfortunately, the persuasiveness and strength of hypotheses do not always coincide and, while the scientist might attempt to limit himself to description, his methodologically less astute audience might supply the missing evaluation and prescription.

Weak racism tends to be a feature of scientific rather than political discourse, and arises from the much-vaunted, objective nature of science, which underscores its concern with description and explanation and rigorously eschews moral evaluations and prescriptions. It is likely that a greater inclination towards strong racism would be found in a survey of racist political discourse. After all, there is a propensity, demonstrated in ideology, for the facts to be brought into line with the political task in hand.

Hodge (1975, p. 11) mentions the need to concentrate on the element of racism which stresses 'the belief that the superior races should rule over the inferior and the attempt to put this belief into practice'. It is not 'prejudice' – 'the belief that some races are superior to others' – that has 'harmful consequences'. 'The harm occurs when a group not only believes in its superiority, but also believes this superiority entitles it to rule and control.' He goes on to define 'racism' as 'the predication of decisions and policies on considerations of race for the purpose of subordinating a racial group and maintaining control over that group'. It should be of no surprise that in explaining the meaning of racism in the political realm, Hodge lays stress on a prescription of control and domination.

In the context of this study, 'racism' is primarily used in a medium or strong sense. Weak racism amounts to the acceptance that racial differences exist and that they help to explain the social world, but it omits any overt suggestion of a moral ranking of those differences. An expression of weak racism is best treated as a descriptive element of racial discourse and is not what is meant in the context of this study (or in most political usage) by 'racism'. This does not mean that under certain circumstances it cannot be used as an effective basis for a medium or strong racism.

Racial discourse is best assessed as (strongly) racist by considering its component racial prescriptions. The prescription must also be of a particular kind: advocacy of positive discrimination in favour of an oppressed group in order that it might achieve equality would not qualify as racist. A racist prescription is one whose fulfilment would be likely to result in deviation from a moral standard of racial equality. The prescription must advocate the inferior treatment of a race, or races, on the grounds of racial difference, by another race considered to be superior. The social scientist recognises (medium or strong) racist discourse because: it uses racial categories (categories that are seen to equate with the social scientist's concept of race), it contains a moral evaluation of the races in terms of superior to inferior, and it contains a moral prescription advocating different and (as a final goal) unequal treatment of the races. The prescription does not always have to be stated, but it does have to be understood. It is often derivable enthymematically from an evaluative premise that indicates a relationship of racial superiority to inferiority and is sometimes justified by reference to such a premise.

The moral prescription

The question arises as to whether racism can be assessed on the basis of racial evaluation alone. Of course, this is a possibility, as I have indicated in discussion of 'medium racism', but it also raises the problem of how to classify expressions such as 'the Germans are militarily superior to other races' and 'negroes are superior at sport'. The ranking of such differences in order of merit would not appear in itself to entail strong racism. It might become so, however, if the evaluation is seen to be *moral* (as opposed to non-moral), rather than technical or aesthetic.

A moral value is related to human conduct and takes 'precedence' over other forms of value. It is not always clear from evaluative expressions whether terms such as 'good', 'bad', 'superior', and 'inferior' are being used *morally*, and, even if it were clear, the evaluation is usually insufficiently precise to give an immediate indication of a person's behavioural orientation to the issue pronounced upon. A claim that a practice is good or bad is not as definite as a claim that it is right or wrong (and, methodologically, it is probably best to select material that is most clearly and explicitly formulated). The *moral* nature of discourse is likely to be most apparent to the observer in the examination of prescriptions. Of course, not every prescription is moral: the rules of games, of etiquette, and technical and aesthetic prescriptions are non-moral.

There is disagreement between philosophers over the criteria for identifying the moral. Many moralists have held the 'right' to be self-evident. From the paucity of comment on the subject in race relations literature, it seems that the moral characteristic of a racist prescription (advocating inferior treatment for members of a race) has also been treated as self-evident.

Ladd (1957) argues that moral prescriptions have special authority in that they have superiority and legitimacy. By superiority, he has in mind the *categorical* nature of the moral 'ought': e.g. '(You ought) never (under any circumstances) (to) trust a Jew.' It is not a hypothetical as in the case of 'if you want a nigger for your neighbour, (you ought to) vote Labour'. (In fact the main racist punch of this slogan seems to derive from the enthymematic categorical 'You ought never to want a nigger for a neighbour.') The moral prescription does not depend on the end in view. No further justification is needed once it has been accepted as 'right', and to justify it non-morally is always logically redundant. The moral prescription also takes precedence over other methods of conduct, that is, over non-moral prescriptions, and ought not to be neglected. It is always sufficient to justify overruling other behaviour, though it does not insist that this must occur.

By legitimacy, Ladd has in mind the *grounding* of a moral prescription. First, possibilities must exist of justifying the prescription. Second, an 'inter-subjective' element – that the moral prescription is intended to be accepted by not only those it is directed at, but by its asserter – is required. And third, the moral prescription must be 'founded on the nature of things':

> This requires that they [i.e. the moral prescriptions] be in some
> way derived from man's conception of human nature or of the
> world, or reality in general (including supernatural reality) . . .
> I suggest that every ethical system must have such a
> foundation, although of course, moral prescriptions cannot
> strictly be deduced from it without committing the so-called
> 'naturalistic fallacy' (the fallacy of deducing a prescriptive
> from a non-prescriptive statement).   (Ladd, 1957, p. 106)

With this last requirement, Ladd secures the moral prescription to the matrix of an ideology consisting of a mass of descriptive, explanatory, evaluative, and prescriptive statements providing a group-centred 'picture' of the world. Although the racist nature of discourse is to be formally identified by reference to prescriptive statements, the other components of discourse are racist inasmuch as they provide a persuasive framework for the *acceptance* of racist prescriptions, and fail to raise questions about, or to suggest other options to replace, current racialist practice. This is one reason why Van den Berghe's definition is not unconvincing, why 'weak racism' is felt to exist, and why non-racial discourse has been accused of racism. But not least for analytical and methodological reasons, a formal way of identifying racist discourse – in terms of moral prescription – is needed.

Even so, the moral prescription will not always be easy to identify and may have to be ascertained by, for example, logical inference (see below). A general characteristic of ideological justification remarked upon by other writers (e.g. Seliger, 1976) is the tendency for moral values, as ends, to be displaced by technical values, as means. In other words, racial discourse is likely to contain a preponderance of technical prescriptions that divert attention from the superior moral considerations on which they must depend for justification. This may be even more marked as a result of the phenomenon of deracialisation, described in greater detail in Chapter 6.

Is it impossible, therefore, for discourse to be formally and strongly racist if a racial prescription is absent? This question is of crucial importance in the identification of racism. There are two commonly held views that lead to difficulties. First, there is the position that, despite the fact that a prescription does not employ racial categories, it nevertheless remains the speaker's intention to be racist. He may be disguising the fact with pious words, but, given our knowledge of his 'real' intentions, his words have another more sinister meaning. This argument is particularly convincing if the blandly non-racial prescription can be shown to have racialist effects. Second, there is the position that a prescription that prima facie does not employ racial categories may be judged racist by an observer on the basis of its effect. These views may be referred to respectively as the intentional and effective considerations.

Intention

The suggested need to take into account the ideologist's intention in order to decide on the racist nature of discourse may be better understood by making a distinction between the mental and verbal aspects of intention on the one hand, and the separation of the private and public spheres of discourse on the other.

Although a person may have racist thoughts, it is only through the use of words, signs, and symbols that he is able to make his thoughts available to others. Racist thoughts (prejudices) undoubtedly exist, but they are only identifiable and attributable through words, signs, and symbols.

It is often difficult to separate strictly the private and public spheres of life, but knowledge of a person's private views (as an example, Chairman Dobson's comments about 'wogs') may offer a yardstick against which to judge the sincerity of more formal public utterances. As politicians specialise in trying to satisfy different audiences with diverse views, it is likely that there will be inconsistency between remarks made to one group and remarks made to another. A judgment of whether a discourse is racist or not will depend on where the boundary is drawn around the discourse, and on an estimate of the relative importance of the different statements made within it. The publicly known, 'off-stage' remarks are ambiguous or unclear.

Intentions, then, are only likely to be known if expressed and publicised. They may constitute part of political discourse if they fall within what has come to be defined as its boundaries. I am not now dealing with intentions *versus* public statements, but with intentions that (admittedly sometimes by accident, and at great cost) become part of a total political discourse and a legitimate means of judging whether it is racist. It is a matter of debate as to how much weight should be placed on public revelations of private asides, particularly as much is now made of the 'right to a private life', but undoubtedly, many people feel that what is said between friends is a better indicator of the truth than what is said to achieve political goals.

This view appears most convincing when a political leader decides that his goals can only be achieved by conspiratorial action, and his conspiracy is made public. The Granada Television *World in Action* programme (3 July 78) revealed that the National Front Chairman, John Tyndall, just before his 33rd birthday, had written a private letter in March 1967 to an American Nazi, which said: 'I do not believe that a movement with an open Nazi label has a hope of winning national power in Britain or the U.S. I have therefore sought to modify our propaganda, though not, of course, the essence of our ideology.'

Nevertheless, it is the political goal expressed in a public prescription that is most likely to affect people's lives, and not the bedroom whisper of an indiscreet politician. Intention, then, is relevant in the assessment of the racist nature of discourse inasmuch as its expression is treated as part of that discourse. Methodologically, however, the 'private secrets' of politicians are rarely available and although they may occasionally – in later autobiographies, for example – reveal the way in which a political potentate generated an idea, or was forced to follow a political strategy, they cannot easily be used in a large-scale, general, and representative analysis of ideology. If the main political ideologies are effectively to influence social practice, they must, after all, either be publicly subscribed to and widely shared, or held by a dictatorial elite.

Tyndall's letter reveals how National Front ideology is to be developed by its inner circle and not what is to be said publicly. If the members of the National Front had already gained power, there might be no need for the subterfuge, but in their attempt to gain power, it is as interesting to study their public ideology as it is their private, because it is their public ideology that must be convincing to large numbers of people. In the example given above, a National Fronter's private discourse, in the hands of counter-ideologists, has become a weapon with which to discredit his organisation.

Effect

It is frequently suggested that the practical effect of discourse might be used to decide whether the discourse were racist. This raises the problem of the relationship between discourse and action. There are (at least logically) the possibilities that: discourse containing overtly racist prescriptions may *not* result in racialist action, discourse without racial categories may have racialist consequences, and racist discourse may lead to racialist practice.

If we were to rely on *effects* alone to judge the racism of discourse, then discourse advocating racially inferior treatment but having no effect would have to be excluded. Furthermore, it would be impossible to distinguish between non-racial and racial discourse that both had racialist effects. It is the interesting cases of non-racial statements justifying and resulting in racial discrimination that make it so important to create this distinction and to limit the category of 'racism' to the overtly stated. In other words, I wish to limit the use of the term 'racist' to 'the study of ideas' and to admit to the criticism that 'the problem of racism disappears as soon as politicians and other change their style of theorising' (Rex, 1970, p. 38). This does not mean that the 'race relations structure or problems' – or racialism – will disappear, however. In seeking to affirm the causal link between any discourse, racial or otherwise, and racialist practice, the expression 'racialist–effective discourse' might be appropriate.

Some bizarre consequences arise from the attempt to identify racist discourse by its effects. There is a tendency to look for 'deep' or secret references to the effects within a discourse that at face value fails to deal with them. Attempts are made to find the hidden unstated racism in ambiguous expression, metaphor, and 'deep structures'. There is a turning away from the discourse itself to the psychology of those voicing it, and investigation into their secret intentions, dispositions, false consciousness, and childhood repressions.

Imputing

However, all this does not rule out the possibility of imputing expressions of belief from action. For example, the Granada *World in Action* programme, in providing a list of racialist attacks by National Fronters on blacks and Left-wingers, sought to establish the National Socialist and racist nature of the Party's ideology. If there is evidence that in other circumstances a mode of practice has been justified by a particular form of ideology, and there are sufficient similarities between present practices and these other circumstances, then the presence of a correspondingly similar ideology may be inferred. The study of ideology, however, should make the researcher extremely wary of using this method alone to establish the presence of racial categories. (Granada Television, for example, provided a great deal of other spoken and written evidence.) Apart from the considerations of intention and effect, the question remains of whether discourse can be racial if racial categories are absent.

Besides the technique of imputing belief from action with the help of circumstantial evidence, beliefs may be discovered by asking questions. Interrogatively acquired beliefs come into being when symbolised for the first time in the process of discussion with the interviewer. Verbal expression utilising racial categories may emerge as a result of questioning about race. Alternative formulations might be suggested until the respondent agrees on the appropriate one. In fact, this is a special example of the eristical method by which ideologies develop. (See Appendix 2.) The danger lies, to use an appropriate expression, in the interviewer 'putting words into people's mouths', and in constructing an ideology that bears little resemblance to the salience of the interviewee's already symbolised beliefs. Yet for the social scientist, this is a useful way of gaining information and standardising responses to particular issues.

Another method of proceeding is by logically inferring further statements from the discourse as it stands. It is quite possible that statements may be logically dependent on presuppositions that are not openly stated in the discourse, or that are even denied. The politician may not recognise or be prepared to admit to himself that his statements have these logical implications. It behoves the social scientist to be wary of attributing statements, particularly to those who expressly deny their existence. There is, after all, no empirical reason why people must be consistent in their pronouncements of belief. Nevertheless, within a given framework such a method is logically justified. If no racial prescription is actually present in a discourse, the context may permit it to be reconstructed (enthymematically). A moral evaluation of a particularly pronounced kind might strongly incline the researcher to classify a discourse as strongly racist.

Sometimes there may be insufficient evidence available to decide whether a racial prescription is directed to achieving a group's disadvantage or not. Unless there were plenty of circumstantial evidence, it would be impossible to judge whether the discourse were racist or not. Similarly, where apparently contrary prescriptive statements coexist, some of them conducive to inequality, some to equality, all the researcher is entitled to do is to describe the equivocal nature of the discourse, or to try to assess the overall position from what is stated. Logical inference within a body of discourse is not only a matter of interest to the social scientist, but may be a source of great insecurity to the politicians who sense the dangers of inconsistency.

Banton's view of racism

The definition of racism outlined in the previous passage does not accord with that outlined by Banton in 'The Concept of Racism' (1970). Banton draws on Ruth Benedict's definition that 'racism is the dogma that one ethnic group is condemned by nature to congenital superiority'. 'The kernel of this doctrine', he says, 'is found in the assertions: (a) that people's culture and psychological characteristics are genetically determined and (b) that the genetic determinants are grouped in patterns that can be identified with human races in the old morphological sense that envisaged the existence of pure races' (p. 17). He goes on to define racism as: 'the doctrine that a man's behaviour is determined by stable inherited characters deriving from separate racial stocks having distinctive attributes and usually considered to stand to one another in relations of superiority and inferiority' (p. 18).

Banton's definition suffers from two related inadequacies and his semi-recognition of their existence. First, according to my account, he has only managed to describe weak racism, or, at a pinch, medium racism, and then only if the expression '*usually* considered to stand to one another in relations of superiority and inferiority' (my emphasis) is interpreted as a *necessary moral evaluation*. There is no sign, however, that the need for the evaluation to be morally based (in addition to being technically or factually supported) is recognised.

As a consequence of failing to recognise fully the evaluative and prescriptive content of racism, Banton is unable to deal with Harris's distinction between scientific racism and folk racism (as mentioned by Banton). Banton gives as his reason that he is 'not persuaded that it is proper to speak of race consciousness or racism in times or places where people do not employ a concept of race'. On this last point, I agree – *racial* discourse can only be identified by the presence of a racial category. But the racial category need only be secured to the perceivable characteristics – frequently, but not always, biologically based – of a group of people. It need not be 'determined by stable *inherited* characteristics deriving from separate racial stocks'. There is a difference between deploying a racial category (the anti-racist uses racial categories, too) and accepting a biological theory as an explanation for racial variation. A category may be anchored to a biological difference – skin colour – but the difference *marked* by colour can also be *explained* in terms of geographical, cultural, class, or other factors. Categorising and explaining are two separate processes.

In terms of the previous discussion, Banton has recognised assumption (c), that the differences between races must be treated as deeply rooted and enduring, but limited it to (c – explanatory), and further, to (c – explanatory), of a solely *genetic* kind. Such an approach is gravely reductionist in effect. It fails to recognise the cultural forms of racism common to the twentieth century. There is no need to claim that racist explanations must be biologically based. Indeed, as Fanon (1970) so wisely points out, 'vulgar, primitive, over-simple racism' justified on a biological basis has long since given way to 'more refined argument': 'This racism that aspires to be rational, individual, genotypically and phenotypically determined becomes transformed into cultural racism' (p. 42).

The second inadequacy of Banton's definition, then, lies in its reduction of 'racism' to a nineteenth-century-based, bio-scientific racism. I demonstrate in later chapters that explanations in terms of what is 'natural to man' are just as adequate for justifying racist belief. And rarely do people stop and consider the minutiae of whether 'natural' means biologically inherent, culturally expected or acceptable, or according to divine ordinance. In other words, biological, cultural, and divine necessity (nature, nurture, and providence) are for most purposes not distinguished from one another in common parlance and are used interchangeably as justifications.

If folk racism contains racial categories, explanations (whether in terms of nature or nurture), and evaluations, can it be distinguished in logical structure from scientific racism? One difference might lie in the stress placed in scientific discourse on 'facts' and empirical procedures (however ill-founded) as a means of justification and persuasion. A second difference, already indicated, is that because of the formal exclusion of moral evaluation and policy recommendation from scientific discourse, scientific racism shows a marked tendency to be 'weak', whereas folk racism, not subjected to these requirements, will occur fully fledged and 'strong'.

Rex (1973) has commented on the political repercussion of the biological reductionism of 'racism' which results in Peter Griffiths's and Enoch Powell's speeches being denied racist status. But Banton has reaffirmed his view in *The Idea of Race* (1977), where he points out that 'Powell has attempted to present race relations in Britain as primarily a problem of immigration' (p. 161) and that his central concern is with what constitutes English nationality. I would argue that if the referent of the term 'coloured immigrant', or just 'immigrant', is seen to correspond with the sociologist's race category, and Powell's discourse is seen to contain prescriptions justifying the unequal treatment of coloured immigrants on the grounds that they are inferior on grounds of culture, etc., then there is a strong case for claiming that the discourse is racist. More difficult to decide is whether evaluations and prescriptions are moral (as opposed to non-moral). But in Powell's speeches racial categories and prescriptions both appear to be present. Another of Banton's mistakes appears to lie in thinking that meaning rests in a particular linguistic symbol, and not in the symbol's relationship with the attributes, properties and relations that it represents (see Lachenmeyer, 1971).

The discussion of Banton's use of the term 'racism' reveals many of the difficulties involved in applying it in any comprehensive way to an analysis of British discourse about race. If the term is to be limited to describing discourse containing assumptions that the differences between races are of superior to inferior, and that the superior should be entitled to more favourable treatment, then much of what is said about race in specialised political and general discourse cannot be labelled 'racist'. Of equal importance are non-racist expressions such as those based on belief in class inequality, which can be used to justify racialist practice, and, of course, anti-racist views. An even greater amount of discourse will be excluded if racism is defined as 'the doctrine that a man's behaviour is determined by stable inherited characters deriving from separate racial stocks' (Banton, in Zubaida, 1970, p. 18). 'Racism', then, is an inappropriate term for describing much, if not most, of British discourse about race, but it can still be accurately used to describe the specific kinds of evaluations and prescriptions mentioned above.

The use of the term 'racist' in social science has also been criticised for its 'emotive' connotations that are felt inappropriate to such a context. I feel this criticism to be misguided and probably based on a failure to distinguish between an actor's evaluation and prescription in favour of racial inequality, and the observer's descriptive account of the actor's views. The observer is able to identify a particular discourse as 'racist', by recognising the use of moral evaluations and prescriptions by the actor. In itself, the identification is descriptive: it entails the application of the various criteria of racism to a situation. If the discourse meets the various criteria discussed above, it is prima facie 'racist'. Of course, in using the term 'racist' to describe the discourse, the observer may simultaneously be making a moral judgment: e.g. that the discourse is racist, *and* that this is morally reprehensible. This is often implied by those who describe a text as 'racist', although, analytically, the descriptive and morally evaluative uses may be separated. The social scientist, however, must attempt to confine himself to the descriptive usage, inasmuch as he has pretensions to be producing social science.

Racialism

Although Webster admits that 'racism' and 'racialism' may be used interchangeably, I have sought to precise the term 'racism' and to apply it to a particular form of the spoken and written word. I reserve the term 'racialism' for effects or outcomes, intentional or unintentional, where one racial group is in an unequal economic, political, or social position vis-à-vis another, and is kept there, advertently or inadvertently, by personal acts or institutional procedures. Racialism, then, is a phenomenon closely identifiable with Rex's race relations structure or problem:

> We shall speak of a race-relations structure or problem, insofar as the inequalities and differentiation inherent in a social structure are related to physical and cultural criteria of an ascriptive kind and are rationalized in terms of deterministic belief systems, of which the most usual in recent years has made reference to biological science.   (Rex, 1970, p. 39)

The identification of racialist practice is in this instance made by the observer who traces out the social mechanisms whereby racially identifiable group(s) are systematically discriminated against by others. The actors in the situation, whether oppressors or victims, are not necessarily conscious of the effects of their actions, although often the unequal treatment is justified by recourse to racial discourse. But in the case of institutionalised racialism, various laws, rules, and mores, often unbeknown to, or ignored by, the practitioners (e.g. the effects of the 11 + on black children's chances of obtaining grammar school places) effectively prevent equality of opportunity. For this to qualify as racialism, first the mechanism and outcome must be analysed by the observer in racial categories, and racial categories must be shown to be significant for understanding the resultant state of affairs. Second, in order to make the situation 'racialist' and not simply 'racial', the discriminating effects must be shown to militate against racial equality, resulting in the disadvantaging of one racial group and (usually) the advantaging of another. In this sense, racialism is to be judged as such against a standard of equality.

This does not mean, of course, that the observer must be morally committed to racial equality. All he need do is to apply the criteria for deciding on whether a situation is racialist, e.g. decide whether it maintains, or results in, racial inequality. As with racism, it is possible for the observer to judge a situation racialist and at the same time to commit himself to a moral judgment that racialism is wrong. Social science, however, is concerned only with the descriptive usage.

A number of conceptual difficulties are raised by the usage of the word 'racialist' and its application to human actors (rather than to effects and practices). Where 'racism' is concerned, it is legitimate to attribute the characteristic 'racist' to a meaningful moral prescription advocating racialist practice. 'Racist' could also, without complication, be used of a human actor who knowingly accepted the racist moral prescription. He might demur at the label 'racist', but the social observer's decision that the actor subscribed to the prescription would decide the matter once and for all. What then is the connection between the racist (in word) and the racialist (in action)?

There are three logically possible relations between prescription and action. (The following distinction is obviously similar to that between prejudice and discrimination.)

First, the accepted racist prescription may be fulfilled when the racialism conforms to it. (A housing officer may advocate that blacks ought to be placed in older property and proceed to rehouse them in this way.)

Second, the accepted racist prescription may be violated when the actor pursues a different policy. (A housing officer may advocate that blacks ought to be placed in older property but then rehouse them in standard or new property despite the fact that older property is available.)

Third, no racist prescription might be accepted at all, but an action judged racialist by the observer might take place. (A housing officer may have no conscious views about how blacks ought to be placed in property, but a later examination of his work might show that the blacks he had dealt with had been rehoused in older property.)

For a racialist to be judged *morally*, the first or second conditions must obtain, in other words, an individual must be racist *as well*. But a person can also be judged 'racialist' in the third sense, and confusion and indignation might arise from the implication that he consciously discriminated or set out to achieve a racialist result. It is important, therefore, to remember that a usage of 'racialist' exists which does not imply moral awareness or blame. If a moral term is needed for the actor, 'racist' is more satisfactory, as it covers both those who subscribe to inegalitarian discriminatory principles but do not discriminate, and those who subscribe and discriminate.

One lesson to be learnt is that observation of a single racialist action is never in itself sufficient to enable a decision to be made about whether a person has accepted a racist prescription. In fact, neither the performance or non-performance of an act can be taken as conclusive evidence of the acceptance or non-acceptance of a moral prescription. Nevertheless, as indicated in a previous section, it is often plausible to 'impute' racism.

In summary, I have attempted to demonstrate the following points. Linguistic symbols are anchored to observable attributes to give referential meaning. In this way racial categories in discourse may be identified. Racial discourse is discourse containing racial categories. The terms 'racial' and 'racist' differ in their meaning. There is a distinction between 'weak', 'medium', and 'strong' usages of the term 'racism', and the moral prescription is the criterion by which 'strong racism' can be identified. Whether moral prescriptions must always be present in racist discourse is a matter for discussion and there may be exceptions. Racist intention and racialist effect are often offered as other ways of identifying racist discourse, but although it is worth examining the possibilities offered by employing these criteria, they are, by themselves, unsatisfactory. Banton's definition of 'racism' probably deals only with weak racism. It is correct in insisting that racial categories must be present in racist discourse, but wrong in confusing category identification with explanation. As a result, the definition of 'racism' is artificially narrowed to the genetically determined. A distinction between scientific and folk racism can still be made, but on the basis of different criteria. As a conclusion to the section on racism, moral and descriptive usages of the term 'racism' are distinguished. Next, 'racialism' is defined. The attribution of 'racism' and 'racialism' to human actors raises questions of the racialist's moral responsibility. One lesson to be drawn is that racialist action cannot by itself be used as evidence of racist prescription. The main conclusion from the discussion on the meaning of 'racism' is that although the term might be used to advantage in describing elements of British discourse about race, it cannot provide anything like a comprehensive view of the subject matter dealt with in this study. A description of British racism (as defined above, and by most of the experts in this area) would exclude many of the important features of ideological complexes dealing with race relations.

2

The meaning of 'ideology' and its relationship to discourse

If, as I have suggested, the concept of 'racism' has been poorly defined and its implications vaguely understood, how then is it best to approach the study of ideas that affect or result from the relationship between the races (or, more specifically in this context, between people allocated to different colour categories)? I claim first, that the study of discourse is the best way of treating ideas about race, second, that 'racial discourse' is a narrower category than 'discourse dealing with race' and third, that discourse is most usefully studied in social context.

First, it is best to accept for methodological reasons that only ideas as expressed in language must constitute the subject matter of the study. This is not to assert that ideas cannot exist independently of a public language, nor is it to deny that communication with others is possible without use of the spoken or written word – natural and conventional signs are frequently available. For the sake of simplicity, however, I intend to confine my attention to ideas as expressed in language, and, moreover, to publicly expressed language capable of being used in communication between two or more persons: what is referred to here as 'discourse'.

Although it is useful to recognise that there are likely to be correlations between linguistic expressions, affective states of mind, and social behaviour, and these are of utmost significance in the field of race relations, discourse – unlike prejudice – is not *defined* in terms of propensities to feel or act in particular ways. Of equal interest is discourse unaccompanied by strong emotion or ineffective in behavioural motivation.

Second, it is worth pointing out that the discourse which affects or results from the relationship between the races is not conterminous with the category of racial discourse. To treat it as such would be to fall foul of the serious limitations arbitrarily imposed on the study of the discourse significant to race relations, by the concepts of 'prejudice' and 'racism' and their theoretical derivatives. The sociological observer is able to distinguish between the speaker's intention, a particular set of expressions, and its effect, if any, on a particular racial group.

An expression is described as racial only if it makes use of racial (or

28

Table 1. *Types of discourse*

Social observer's assessment of			Description of type of discourse
Actor's racial intention	The racial content of expression	Resultant racial effect or act	
1 Present	Present	Present	Intended racialisation – effective
2 Present	Present	Absent	Intended racialisation – ineffective
3 Present	Absent	Present	Strategic deracialisation – effective
4 Present	Absent	Absent	Strategic deracialisation – ineffective
5 Absent	Present	Present	Unintended (institutionalised?) racialisation – effective
6 Absent	Present	Absent	Unintended (institutionalised?) racialisation – ineffective
7 Absent	Absent	Present	Unintended (institutionalised?) deracialisation – effective
8 Absent	Absent	Absent	Non-racialised discourse – ineffective

ethnic) categories: it is usually described as racist if it is felt by an audience to imply hostility towards or to attribute negative traits to a particular racial group. Such expressions are obviously of great interest to the sociologist of race relations, but so also are non-racial or non-racist expressions, (a) that result in or justify behaviour which the observer believes has an adverse effect on a racial group, or (b) that, judging from the context in which they are uttered and the consequences they are likely to engender, show evidence of a racial intention, irrespective of the apparent absence at face of racial meaning. Table 1 gives an indication of the possible combinations of speaker intention, content of expression, and racial effect.

If a thorough account is to be given of the role of discourse in race relations, all these circumstances, except the converse (8), must be examined. In small passages of discourse the categories listed can often be separated, but in larger passages they may occur together. Previous studies have tended to concentrate almost exclusively on small overtly racist passages as in categories (1) and (2). But the 'deracialised' expression of categories (3) (4) and (7), in which racist and even racial meaning is absent, yet where racial intent or racial effect can be detected, are of considerable importance, and these are explored in detail in Chapter 6. So also are categories (5) and (7) in which politicians with little or no racial intent, and with or without the use of racial expressions, manage to justify actions which adversely or otherwise affect racial groups. These possibilities are dealt with in Chapters 5 and 7. The primary concern, then, is with racial expressions, non-racial expressions used with racial intent, and expressions, racial or non-racial, with racial consequences.

Despite a tendency in practice to concentrate here on intentions and expressions that are regarded by the observer as hostile to particular racial foci and damaging in consequence, there is no reason, in theory, why 'positive' intentions, expressions, and consequences should not warrant equal attention.

Third, if the sociologist is profitably to study discourse affecting race, he must place it within a social context in which the reasons for its occurrence can be explained, its meaning explored, and its consequences recorded. It is probably tautologous to say that the social significance of the discourse under discussion will vary in accordance with the social position of the speakers, the things they say, and the circumstances with which they are dealing. In most examination of discourse, whether in the literary or political field, speakers are identified, the circumstances in which an utterance takes place are specified, the full meaning of what is said is spelt out, and its effects, if any, are noted. The who, where, what, why, and wherefore of discourse are perennial questions.

Although it is possible to study discourse in social context in a number of different ways, a traditional social scientific approach has been to centre discussion on the concept of ideology and the rich theoretical insights that may be derived from it. This and the following three chapters are devoted to a discussion of the issues raised in the study of ideology, and the application of the theory thus outlined to a study of British discourse affecting race relations.

Ways of studying ideology

Studies of ideology demonstrate preoccupation with seven separate but closely related issues which I shall mention in turn in the light of my overriding purpose of examining discourse as it affects race relations. The issues are (1) problems of definition and of operationalised definition, (2) the historical genesis of ideology, (3) its ontological status, (4) its function, (5) its truth, (6) its relation to 'interest', and (7) its content.

1. Definition

First, there are questions related to definition: what is an ideology, and more particularly, for the purposes of this study, what is a racial ideology and how can it be identified or operationalised for research purposes? My prime concern, of course, is not racial ideology, as such, but ideology, racial or otherwise, affecting race relations. Racial ideology is that which (a) accounts for events in the social world by making extensive use of racial descriptions and explanations, and assigning major causal significance to racial categories, and (b) utilises racial evaluations and prescriptions in a substantial way. A connotative definition of ideology will isolate certain qualities that are thought to typify ideology, while the denotative definition will attempt to indicate the phenomenon which I intend to call 'ideology'. I make use of both approaches in this chapter.

An ideology is best treated as a set of linguistic symbols or sentences. The category does not include everyday practical activity or skills, such as farming or engineering, and is usually confined to discourse 'corresponding' or 'referring' to the material or spiritual world, to the exclusion of discourse dealing with the consistency of a symbolic system, such as logic or mathematics (see Plamenatz, 1971). The sentences of ideology are selected from the general flow of discourse by the social observer on the basis of certain necessary criteria, the definitional sufficiency or theoretical adequacy of which is much disputed in academic circles. For my purposes here, I identify ideology in terms of (a) its internal logical relations, (b) the kind of substantive cognitive elements that go to make it up, (c) the shared nature of its constituent beliefs, (d) its justificatory purpose, (e) its public availability, (f) its relatively enduring life-span, (g) the social agents that develop, profess, and make use of it, and (h) the social areas in which it is most commonly manifest.

(a) The social observer perceives logical and analogical relationships between the various elements of discourse. The discourse describes real or imagined spatial, temporal, relational, causal, and other relationships in the social and physical universe. Generally, ideology consists of arguments from premises to conclusion, rarely valid in any formal sense, but aimed at persuading and convincing an audience that a past, present, or future state of being or course of action is, or is not, legitimate. Recurring argument forms may be seen as a sign of ideological formation.

Seliger (1976, p. 106) distinguishes six 'interacting components' of ideology: description, analysis, moral prescriptions, technical prescriptions, implements (an account of the means of implementing the prescription), and rejections. I would prefer to classify the formal components of ideology in terms of descriptions, evaluations, general and operationalised prescriptions, their quality (whether they are affirmative or negative), and the argument forms into which they are built; together with the rhetorical techniques of association (bringing separate elements together) or of dissociation (disuniting elements which were originally regarded as forming a unity), and foci (headings under which arguments can be classified, in this case, according to their substantive content, or, in terms of logic, their 'most frequently occurring substitution instances').

(b) What is to constitute an ideology is also decided upon by the cognitive substance of the discourse. Arguments dealing with certain subject matter usually involving disputed values in, for example, the moral, political, and religious realms are frequently considered ideological. In Britain, the subject matter of national politics is regarded as ideological, while mathematics and, in the main, scientific findings will be excluded. Common sense views of what is ideological, however, are unsatisfactory because political debate may suddenly develop over issues that have hitherto remained undisputed. Nevertheless, political/moral/religious issues are frequently referred to in this kind of discourse.

(c) A distinction can be made between an individual's idiosyncratic ideas and the ideas he shares with others. Although it may be developed by the innovation of any one individual, an ideology consists of a set of publicly expressed beliefs held in common by a group of people. It is made up of descriptions, evaluations, and prescriptions, which are subscribed to collectively. Ideologies may spread 'spontaneously' among a given population but frequently possess organisational carriers – groups of people organised with the express purpose of convincing others of the worth of a given set of beliefs. The organisational setting of many ideologies is likely to give them greater coherence, and strengthen them in their resistance to countervailing views. Ideology, particularly when supported by an effective organisation, has a juggernaut effect in that deviant views of a minority are unlikely to prevail in the face of mass adherence.

(d) The reason why moral, political, and religious debate serves largely as the content of ideology is related to what is perceived to be its main purpose. Ideology is a discursive system seeking to justify a particular state of affairs or course of action. Ideology emerges only when human beings have to account for their actions to others. Descriptions, evaluations, and prescriptions are combined together to convince the audience that the means and ends of certain social behaviour and, in particular, political behaviour are right (or wrong). The purpose of ideology may be revealed in the implicit or explicit affirmation of that purpose in the discourse itself, or may be inferred by the observer from the known interests of the speaker, or from the effect of the discourse on his audience.

(e) In order to be effective, a justificatory system must be made public. It is possible, as in the case of the Manson hippy commune, for a unique justificatory system to develop privately in a small isolated circle, but generally, as a consequence of its purpose, an ideology competes for public attention. Nevertheless, the agents of a particular ideology might do their best to silence or suppress a competitor. In twentieth-century Britain, conflicting ideologies compete for popular adherence.

(f) An ideology is a relatively enduring set of publicly expressed beliefs. Although the precise periodisation of ideological types is open to much debate, in many cases it is possible to identify ideological traditions that have lasted for hundreds of years – as in the case of British Conservatism.

(g) The frequency with which ideology is used by certain recognisable social agents – politicians or social theorists, or is accepted as the official or agreed doctrine of a political party or social group – offers a further, if secondary, means of identifying it. In one sense, ideology has come to mean the language of politicians: the commitment to certain analyses of social events, values, and policies, expressed, for example, in speeches or conference resolutions. One of the chief roles of the politician is to convince his audience of the righteousness of the decisions he supports and for which he holds responsibility. Although, conceivably, justificatory systems may be non-political, as in the case of certain kinds of religious, technical, or aesthetic beliefs, in the final analysis these must be subordinated to moral justification, of which political advocacy is an important, though frequently disguised, form. For the purposes of this discussion, ideology will nearly always refer to the justification of action or inaction in a recognisably political context.

(h) Decisions binding on numbers of people are usually taken in formal, institutional, or organisation settings such as the local council chamber and parliament, the party conference or local branch meeting, where at the time of decision, they often require justification along formal lines. Ideology, then, may be looked upon as the kind of discourse arising from the controversy engendered in the decision-making process. It is the language of the political forum, and may be identified, in a secondary manner, by its location. But, of course, justification takes place not merely in the formally designated decision-making arenas, but in almost every social setting. The formal setting, however, may reveal ideology's most formal expressions and their link with prior or subsequent social activity, thus providing for sociological analysis the most readily identifiable examples of ideology.

2. Genesis

The second issue in the study of ideology relates to the reasons for the emergence of ideology either generally or in a specific historical context.

Discussion may dwell on the causal relationship between social conditions and the development of ideology in all societies, or alternatively between social conditions at a specific juncture and the development of a particular ideological configuration. Usually accounts of ideological genesis tend to locate a set of beliefs spatio-temporally, and to suggest that people devised new ideologies when circumstances changed so substantially that the old ideologies were implausible in justifying events, were out of harmony with the values implicit in practice, and gave no prescriptive guidance on action to satisfy the wants and aspirations of sections of the population. Shils (1968, p. 69) affirms that 'ideologies arise in conditions of crisis and in sections of society to whom the hitherto prevailing outlook has become unacceptable'.

The difficulty here is that ideologies are constantly undergoing change and questions arise over how to periodise the ideological stream while it is being continually modified by the requirements of social existence operating on the continuity of patterns of thought. The actual time of an ideology's 'birth' is difficult to pinpoint because an ideology itself has the qualities of a chameleon and because there will nearly always be precursors. The debate about Christianity before Christ is a case in point.

It seems that both validity (in terms of the success with which an ideology explains the nature of the political world and can be technically applied to achieve stability or change) and persuasibility (the ease with which an ideology can be spread to wide sections of the population) are necessary if a new ideology is to establish itself against existing ones. Neither do ideologies compete on equal terms on the descriptive level, for old ideologies have been shaped by, and in turn, shape institutions and culture (by affective behaviour) and superficially, at least, describe the reality they have helped to create. They serve those who are already powerfully and advantageously placed, and those who are content with the status quo, and who have no need to change their views. In a stable, homogeneous, social setting in which economic life remains relatively undisrupted and class relations show little sign of radical alteration, ideologies exist relatively monomorphously for long periods of time.

It is true that twentieth-century Britain has seen the growth of the Labour Party and decline of the Liberals. Change in organisational structure, however, cannot automatically be taken as a sign of major ideological rupture. It has been argued that with the growing power of organised labour on the one hand and the convergence of finance, industrial, and landed capital on the other, the welfarism and trade and economic policies of the Liberals were divided respectively between the Labour Party and Conservatives, who were able to find ways of reconciling them with their previous stances. In other respects Labour Party beliefs and

Conservatism are marked by their historical continuity. As long as cataclysmic situations do not occur there is no need for 'holistic' change. New political situations are dealt with in a 'piecemeal' way, by applying the old, successful interpretations, evaluations, and answers. This can be referred to as 'the historical flow' of ideology. In the following chapters, I hope to show how long-term ideological flow has governed political interpretations of black Commonwealth immigration and settlement in the last thirty years.

3. Ontological status

The matter of ideological genesis is frequently intertwined with a third issue: that of its ontological status: in what way is an ideology related to the social factors, material or non-material, from which it emerged; is it 'determined' by them, or, once engendered, does it possess autonomy; does it 'reflect' social reality or 'misrepresent' it? There is a marked symmetry between the social structure (economic base)/ideology (ideological super-structure) debate in social science and the traditional mind/body relation problem of philosophy. I make no attempt here to elaborate on matters of ontology and am content to accept a crudely dualist approach to the problem, believing that the emergent ideological properties, though dependent on physiological and social configuration for their existence, should not be 'reduced' (when attempts are made to describe them or to explain their effects) to accounts of the consequences of practical economic/class relations.

Ideology as a non-material symbolic entity mediates – at least in many circumstances – between the structures of the physical and social world and the non-verbal behavioural response. Ideology is neither a mere 'reflection' in the mind of the human actor, of the real world, nor does it exist apart from the real world. The capacity to think and modes of thought are to be distinguished from the content of thought, both of which are combined to produce ideology as discourse. It follows that a study of ideology cannot amount simply to a description of the material circumstances with which it seems to match up, for once in being, it possesses characteristics and an autonomy of its own.

This may all seem very obvious, but theories of race relations often simply mention an economic relationship of racial subordination and domination and the social consequences which emerge from it, without dealing with the account the actors give of the circumstances in which they find themselves. Such theories lack conviction inasmuch as they do not explain why the actors' accounts of their actions frequently differ from those offered by the observer. Without a knowledge of the actors' accounts, a persuasive explanation of the relationship between the objectively assessed (economic) circumstances of the actors and the actions they take in furtherance of their collective interests cannot be easily provided.

Worse, although a 'structural' explanation of human behaviour that omits an ideological dimension may appear to have validity on a grand and long-term scale, it deals most inadequately with the details of the shorter term and fails to provide scope for a 'political dimension' of human behaviour. A theory of ideology would help to clarify the relationships between first, the social structure as perceived by the social observer, second, the experiences, knowledge, assessments, and behavioural imperatives collectively generated within that structure by the social actors, and third, the consequences of their resultant behaviour.

One effect of ignoring the intervening ideological variable in race relations is to produce rather crude theories that explain racial discrimination, racialist policies, or racist discourse, simply in terms of British capital's need to maintain a dual labour market in which black labour is forced to fill the most undesirable jobs. Reality is more complex than this. Another effect is to rule out the possibility that people, who are seen as merely instruments of overwhelming social forces, may be persuaded at a political level to pursue policies more equitable to black and white alike.

4. Function

Fourth, there is the question of the 'function of ideology'. This is an ambiguous expression because the term 'function' carries a number of meanings. It may refer to the process or operation which is present in the manifestation of ideology. Just as an axe is a tool for cutting wood, ideology is discourse which serves to justify political action. As used below, 'ideology' is defined in terms of its justificatory function, and in this sense of the term, it makes no sense to ask whether it succeeds in performing its function. But 'function' may refer not merely to a process or operation but to the effect of that process or operation on something else. In this limited sense, it is possible to consider what function ideology plays in the social system without raising questions about whether the effects were intended by any human agent, or beneficial or harmful to the system in any way.

Next, there is the meaning of the term which contrasts 'functioning' with 'malfunctioning' and implies that ideology 'functions' in the sense of fulfilling part of an overall social design. This teleological concept of society which attributes goals, and therefore values, to the abstractions of society, race, or class is frequently criticised, although no doubt it is possible, in a Machiavellian way, for an individual or group consciously to use an ideology to achieve certain goals and to assess such means as functional. But there is no systemic imperative that forces an individual to accept without recourse to his own value system, any particular ideology as

'functional'. In this respect, 'prejudice' or 'racism' can only be dysfunc-
tional from the point of view of a given integrationist value system.

For my purposes, the function of an ideology refers either to the process
of justification manifested in ideology (by definition) or to the effect of that
justification on, for example, a given audience, who, by accepting a given
justification, 'legitimates' a course of behaviour. In this sense, a capitalist
ideology is traditionally seen as legitimating the capitalist relations of
production, without requiring the assumption that the legitimation was
intended. Or in the race field, beliefs about black people's inferior
intellectual capacity may help to sanction the way in which they are treated.
The effects which an ideology has on policy and ultimately on a social
structure, should not be confused with the effect of the social structure on
ideology, although it is clear that each has a reactive relationship with the
other.

The function of ideology as justification may be discussed at a less
general level. Ideology is part of language and its function must be seen as
having effect through the communication process. It has a source and an
intended audience at which it is directed. It may also have an unintended
audience that 'overhears' the message.

The message may be sent or accepted for many different reasons. Where
ideological discourse is concerned, the source outlines argument which he
intends the audience to accept. These arguments consist of descriptive,
evaluative, and prescriptive sentences occurring in complex sets. Gouldner
(1976, p. 55) explains that ideologies require the ' " what is to be done?" side
of the language' to be grounded 'in the "report" side, the side that makes
reference to "what is" in the world'. But the presentation of any set of
sentences may involve different emphases of the descriptive, evaluative,
and prescriptive elements according to the purpose of the source and the
receptivity of the audience. An audience's existing familiarity, partial or
thorough, with an ideological complex (particularly one that corresponds
sympathetically with the prevailing ideological milieu) will enable it to
draw for interpretation on more than the partial presentation made
available by the source at any one time. Ideological presentation can serve a
variety of specific purposes separately, or simultaneously.

Arguments may concentrate on descriptive and explanatory accounts
which help the audience to orientate itself to its natural and social world.
MacIver (1961, p. 4) refers to this function as 'man's way of apprehending
things, his way of coming to terms with his world', Christenson (1972, p.
15) points out that 'The cognitive orientations of political ideology help
men to avoid ambiguity in their lives, and provide a sense of certainty and
security.' In practice, description and explanation are often difficult to
separate from evaluation.

Evaluations about the worth of certain people, actions, and events, offer the audience the opportunity to learn how others think and feel and to order their values hierarchically within the context of a reasonably consistent scheme, and thereby to share common attitudes and goals. An evaluation is a guide to individual and collective judgment by which the individual may sort out internal conflicts between his passions, as well as joining with other human beings in the pursuit of common wants. Parsons (1970, p. 349) describes ideology as 'a system of ideas which is orientated to the evaluative integration of the community'.

Prescriptions are presented to audiences as suitable directives for action on their part or on the part of others. A prescription's *acceptance* involves its adoption as a directive for action. It does not necessarily entail the performance, or non-performance, of the action itself. The fulfilment of the prescription must entail the prior acceptance of the prescription, but the acceptance does not entail fulfilment. People do not always do what they believe ought to be done. Obviously, however, an ideological prescription presented to an audience is frequently aimed at persuading it not only to accept the prescription, but also to act upon it. Indeed this is often regarded as ideology's primary function and test of success. Parsons (1970, p. 350) asserts 'there must be an obligation to accept its [ideology's] tenets as the basis for action'. Ideology, Gouldner (1976, p. 26) claims, 'seeks to gather, assemble, husband, defer, and control the *discharge* of political energies'. Stereotypical studies of ideology have frequently emphasised its effectiveness in persuading large numbers of people to engage in mass political action, e.g. Hitler addressing a Nuremburg rally, but, of course, ideology may be equally successful in persuading people to be inactive and to accept the legitimacy of the behaviour of politicans acting on their behalf.

Obviously, this aspect of ideology brings it into close relationship with rhetoric, the study of the techniques of persuading audiences by means of argument. Perelman and Olbrechts–Tyteca (1969, p. 4) regard rhetoric as 'the study of the discursive techniques allowing us to induce or increase the mind's adherence to the theses presented for its assent'. Rhetorical techniques are discussed elsewhere, but their mention here stresses the importance of considering ideology actively within a discursive context aimed at persuasion, whether that persuasion turns out to be successful or not.

5. Truth

Once ideology has been discussed in terms of its function, the further question of its truth is raised. If it is accepted that power, wealth, and privilege are unevenly distributed in a given society, then it follows that certain political decisions are likely to benefit one group more than, and perhaps at the expense of, another. Justification of action or inaction, therefore, can be seen as a means by which one group of people persuades another to accept a certain version of how things are and ought to be, in a manner which happens to benefit the former at the expense of the latter. At this point, questions are raised about the truth of an ideology and the interests that it serves. These are two separate questions, for interests may be served by truth as well as falsehood. Sorel (1950) recognised that it was not the truth or falsehood of social and political beliefs that mattered, but the way they accorded with and expressed the needs, feelings, and aspirations of a group.

One of the first difficulties in dealing with the relationship between ideology and truth is to decide on the criterion by which truth is to be established. Is truth, as a property of statements, to be established by the statements' correspondence with a state of affairs in the world, or is it a matter of group agreement over the relationship between terms? Even if agreement is reached over the criteria of truth, it should be obvious that only statements have the property of being true or false: evaluations and prescriptions, as the other important components of ideology, cannot be established as true or false by empirical means. It probably only makes sense to talk about 'false ideology' in respect of doubtful assertions of fact, statistical inaccuracy, false cause, unsupported hypotheses, selective presentation of evidence, etc.

Of course, many apparently factual propositions are unlikely ever to be operationalised and subjected to rigorous scientific scrutiny. And science, itself, does not lay claim to absolute truth: propositions are true only in relation to available supporting evidence. The truth or falsehood of statements about the world is not always immediately apparent. The discovery of the truth frequently requires an intense intellectual effort which many people are not in a position to attempt or to sustain. They do not consciously choose falsehood: they themselves simply do not know what is the case, and remain ignorant, rather than wrong, until pursuit of certain values leads them to assume that a particular set of statements is true.*

* As an example, Curtin (1964) describes the influence of Edward Long's *History of Jamaica*, 1774, in which he tried 'to assess the place of the Negro in nature' (p. 43). Long thought Africans had 'a covering of wool like the bestial fleece, instead of hair', were inferior in 'faculties of mind', had a 'bestial and fetid smell', were parasitised by black lice instead of the lighter coloured lice of the Europeans, that Negro women bore children after brief labour and with practically no pain, and that mixed-race children were infertile (pp. 43–4). Long's credentials were that he was a resident of Jamaica and, unlike his readers in England, was thought to be in possession of the evidence for his assertions. His views also fitted into earlier prevailing modes of thought such as the idea of 'the Great Chain of being'. Curtin writes that 'Long's greatest importance was in giving an "empirical" and "scientific" base that would lead on to pseudo-scientific racism . . . Long was more of a pro-slavery publicist than a scientist, but his views influenced even those scientists who believed in a more liberal social policy' (p. 45).

Systematically directed 'distortion of truth', or belief in falsehood when truth is readily available, is undoubtedly of great interest, but it cannot be regarded as the sole indicator of ideology. The distinction in logic between disagreement of belief and disagreement of attitude, or Russell's conjugations (e.g. I am firm, you are obstinate, he is a pig-headed fool), reveal the possibility that propositions with identical descriptive content might be acknowledged in different systems of justification. Nevertheless, comparison of ideological *assumptions* of fact with social scientific measurements of the same phenomenon, particularly at a simple descriptive level (e.g. the number of new Commonwealth immigrants and their descendants in Britain), may, in the examination of their discrepancies, help to lay bare important characteristics of a justificatory system. However, the same example shows that while two people might agree on immigrant numbers, they may variously interpret the numbers as 'too large' or 'of no significance'. Evaluation and prescription play a crucial part in the composition of ideology. The preoccupation of liberal-minded social scientists and anti-racist politicians with race relations' empirical truths is understandable. What is surprising is the way they have been content to dismiss as 'prejudice' the population's lack of concern for the truth. Instead, they could have provided more convincing reasons for its inclination towards 'systematic distortion'.

6. Relation to interest

Whether an ideology is true or false in its descriptive aspects, it is put to use in the service of particular social groups, who use it to justify the world as they would like it to be, at the expense of possibilities proposed by other groups. The need to justify a desired state of affairs reflects a situation in which different groups have diverse and conflicting aims.

In Marxist sociology, the conflict between particular social groupings has been attributed to their underlying difference of economic interest, as observed objectively by the social observer, and also subjectively, by the social groupings in question who come to realise their 'class interests'. Marxists believe there is a fundamental difference of interest under the capitalist mode of production between capitalists who own the means of production and proletarians who must sell their labour power. Careful observation of class relationships, then, should show, at some stage, a social class manifesting an expression, behaviourally or discursively, of its class interest. While this might provide the basis for an ideology's emergence, such a manifestation does not in itself constitute an ideology. To understand how an ideology emerges, a distinction must be made between the structural economic, and the responsive political, level.

Under the capitalist mode of production, the interests of the dominant capitalist class are served at the expense of the subordinate proletariat, a state of affairs that can only continue for any length of time if the dominant class has the means of coercion, or, preferably, the persuasive ability to insist that arrangements favourable to it are generally accepted by society as a whole. In other words, the capitalist class must manage to convince the proletariat that it speaks not just for itself, but for the whole of society, or, as Marx and Engels put it: ' to represent its interests as the common interest of all the members of society . . . to give its ideas the form of universality, and represent them as the only rational universally valid ones' (1973, pp. 52–3).

This presupposes not only a social universe of interests, economic, or otherwise, but a world in which interests are *represented* by members of a given social class to one another, and to other social classes. The political level constitutes the world of the systematic representation of interest to others, a level that must make extensive use of the means of communication: discourse. This 'representation' does not take the form of only descriptive representation, but involves evaluation, interpretation of circumstances, and recommendations for action. Neither is it necessary to assume that the representation of interest is confined to social classes: other social units, both larger in the form of nations or alliances, and smaller in the form of substrata, occupational or racial groupings, or local communities, might represent their interests at a discursive level. While this is undoubtedly true, the representation of class interests in contemporary Britain is probably of paramount importance.

But the representation of interest does not by itself constitute ideology. For this to occur, Marx and Engels thought, the interest must be represented as universal – as valid for all social groups. Groups might express their interests directly without any pretension that the pursuit of those interests served the social entity as a whole, or alternatively, they might claim that they acted in everyone's interest, for the public good. They might talk in terms of ' we want, we need, we shall have ', or alternatively, in terms of ' this is right, everyone wants this, everyone will benefit, everyone ought to follow this course of action '. Ideology, in this latter sense, constitutes the justification of political action for the common good. Sometimes, of course, action may be for the common good, but Marx and Engels were stressing the point that in a class-antagonistic society, exemplified by capitalist socio-economic formations, political action invariably benefits one class more than, or at the expense of, another, and that, therefore, the acceptance by a subordinate group of a dominant group's justification for action hinders the subordinate from directly realising its own interest.

None of this implies that the groups themselves are conscious of the deceptive nature of the justification: this might only be discovered by directly studying the economic, or more generally, the material relations of a society. As Marx and Engels point out, 'whilst in ordinary life every shopkeeper is very well able to distinguish between what somebody professes to be and what he really is, our historians have not yet won even this trivial insight. They take every epoch at its word and believe that everything it says and imagines about itself is true' (1973, p. 55).

One further point that should be mentioned here is Marx's and Engels's recognition that effort has to be invested in the production of ideas, and that it is the ruling class that performs this task. They 'rule also as thinkers, as producers of ideas, and regulate the production and distribution of the ideas of their age' (1973, p. 51). Not only does the subordinate class not have the time to devote to thought, but, because it rarely finds itself in a position to take decisions affecting other people's lives, it does not possess the immediate need or the opportunity to develop sophisticated justificatory systems. This point will be developed further in the section on ideological levels.

Although I am anxious to argue that class politics and, therefore, class ideology are crucial for understanding the form of British racial discourse and its consequences, it is obvious that what has been said in the class context about ideology and interest may also be applied to situations of racial domination and subordination. In Britain, the interests of racial minorities are seldom expressed through the mass media, and black people are rarely in a position to speak with effect on behalf of the common interest of a social whole which includes themselves. 'Black ideology' may be produced but it has little opportunity for establishing itself as a dominant mode of justification. In the meantime, justificatory forms serving the interests of certain sections of the white population remain firmly ensconsed. Rarely will it be admitted, for example, that the white population and British social institutions bear any responsibility for the lowly position of black people: rather their comparative privation is seen to be of their own making.

7. Content

Finally, the content of ideology may be studied in its own right. Predominantly, this must involve an interpretation of the meaning of discourse as intended and understood. Attention must be drawn to recurrent themes that perhaps have remained unnoticed by the source or audience. The techniques of argument and persuasion have to be noted and the intricate connotation of terms and sentences spelled out in detail. Above all, the internal consistency or inconsistency of discrete passages or series of passages has to be emphasised. The relevance of certain expressions in the ideological discourse for the political purpose in hand must be judged against the social observer's knowledge of the social context. The precise hermeneutic involved – that is, the principles by which the meaning of the discourse is to be laid bare – is seldom clearly defined, but seems to be related to the observer's concept of the actor's intent, further explication of the actual meaning, or connotation of the passage, the techniques of expression, and the effects of the meaning on the audience.

The study of the content of ideology cannot be reduced to a formalistic rendering of passage length, sentence form, or techniques of presentation or alliteration. In the final analysis, it is concerned with meaning, and must, if it is not merely to repeat the substance of the discourse under examination, order that material and relate it to a context through the use of significant external categories. Yet the superimposition of categories must clarify existing plausible meanings and avoid distorting the original intension of the expression.

The content of ideology must be studied by giving an interpretation of meaning: it does not consist of studies of the genesis or behavioural effects of ideology or of the motivation of social actors. For example, it is not possible to derive adequate categories for the description of ideology dealing with race from an examination of the economic structure of society or, more particularly, of race relations. I am not asserting that discourse cannot be about economic structure: I point out only that the description of an economic structure is not to be identified with the structure itself. Inasmuch as categories derived in this way correspond at all to the content of political discourse, it is because they themselves are part of that discourse. Although it would seem to be an obvious point, it still needs to be reiterated that categories of meaning (word or symbolic categories) are not the same as, and cannot be reduced to, categories of externalised objects (real categories).

Less obviously, and returning solely to the world of word categories, it is a mistake merely to employ categories used to describe the economy in attempting to understand ideological forms, in the same way as it would be absurd to analyse an economic formation using only classificatory forms derived from linguistics. For the purpose of analysing ideology, I consider it apposite and necessary to utilise classifications derived from logic and rhetoric and to develop substantive categories arising from the subject matter of the discourse itself. In the following account of Conservative and Labour ideology, and of the discourse of the parliamentary debates on immigration and race relations, I attempt to develop those kinds of classification that are necessary to reveal the key structures of the justificatory system underpinning race relations. This is not to deny the importance of economic factors in providing the context for the genesis of ideology or for its maintenance, but only to reassert the duality of economic structure on the one hand, and the ideological 'reflection' (or, as I would prefer to say, 'account') of it, on the other.

3

The economic foundations of racial division

Having briefly hinted at the issues raised by the study of ideology (definition, genesis, ontology, function, truth, interest, and content), I shall now try to sketch out a simple theoretical framework which best accommodates what I have to say about British discourse affecting race relations. What follows is neither profound nor original but is an attempt to make explicit my underlying assumptions so that they may be more readily criticised.

From the point of view of the social observer, certain structures may be picked out as significant for understanding and explaining the responses of social actors. Their perception and knowledge of the structures with which they are faced may be entirely different from the social observer's. Thus, the social observer is able to compare his account of how he thinks structural mechanisms operate with the account offered by the social actors. Although a correspondence between them need not be assumed, prima facie, the reason why these two accounts of the same phenomenon should differ stands in need of explanation.

What then is this social observer's conception of the social structure? I accept that the economic aspect of the social structure plays a dominant part in the lives of all social groups and individuals, although they themselves need not use economic categories in the description and

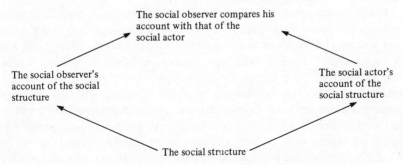

Figure 2. Observer's and actor's accounts of social structure

explanation of that structure. In describing and explaining the economic structure of British society, I make use of the categories and theory of Marxist and Marxist-derived political economy. The prevailing economic structure, in my opinion, is best represented as a capitalist mode of production. The British economy constitutes the basis of a capitalist social formation. The capitalist dynamic imperative resides in an overall capitalist system of production which, irrespective of the responses of individual social actors and groups, creates a relationship that sustains two main social categories: a bourgeoisie and a proletariat. As a class, the bourgeoisie, which owns the means of production, extracts surplus from the proletariat, which must sell its labour power. The proletariat becomes internally differentiated because it possesses different qualities of labour power for which there is a varying demand, and which is sold at different rates.

British race relations must initially be set in this context. In relation to the structure of the British economy, black people originally existed in the relatively poorly developed colonies which were used advantageously by British capital as a source of raw material and as a captive market. British capitalists, if not the British proletariat, benefited from the colonial resources, and created in the process elaborate justificatory ideologies for the political and economic control they exercised over the countries of the West Indies, Africa, and Asia. After the Second World War, a labour-hungry British economy discovered that the colonies might also provide labour power. A migratory process started in which black labour moved from the colonies to a white metropolitan society in order to take jobs which sections of the white proletariat were unable or unwilling to occupy. Industry treated the black colonial migrants only as a factor of production, and held no responsibility for the provision of the goods and services they were bound to need. The migrants themselves, or, alternatively, agencies of national and local government, were held to be responsible for the 'servicing' of the migrant labour force.

The economic ramifications of the migrant colonial labour force on both metropolis and colonies have been explored at length elsewhere (e.g. Castles and Kosack (1973), Jones and Smith (1970), Nikolinakos (1975)), and it is not my purpose to deal with them further. Suffice it to say that black migrants helped fill a labour shortage, took jobs unacceptable to white workers, and, because of their geographical mobility, settled in areas of greatest labour demand. Proportionately to the indigenous white population, they were highly economically active. In addition, black labour was relatively cheap, and, at first, the cost of its reproduction (in terms of education and welfare provision for the family unit) was minimal. Industry benefited in numerous ways. Labour was made available to labour-intensive industries in public and private sectors. Workers willing to undertake unpopular night shifts made continuous working possible, thus rendering economic the installation of expensive new machinery. The state also benefited because, for various reasons, migrants were less reliant on social provision.

Although we might expect the beneficial economic effects of a migrant labour force to affect the way people act towards and speak about black Commonwealth labour – and Sivanandan's account (1976) of the gradual transformation of British immigration laws in the direction of the European model is of relevance here – convincing explanations of ideological configurations are more complex.

It can be accepted with little difficulty that in a capitalist system the fluctuating demand for labour creates conditions that call for the reduction of labour costs, the regulation of labour supply, and the maintenance of particular patterns in the division of labour. These requirements may be widely recognised, especially at a less generally stated level, by employers and government officials who are attempting to ensure the smooth running of the economy and a satisfactory return on investment. If their rational and purposeful management of capital were all that had to be reckoned with, and indeed constituted all that was ever said or implemented with regard to migrant labour, there would be little need for a study of ideology affecting race. But, of course, this is not the case. Even the justification for control of the labour supply is seldom couched in the simple logic of capitalist economics. But, more importantly, economic regulators alone cannot account for the actual decisions taken or their effects, or the singling out of a particular type of labour – black labour – for differential treatment.

Perhaps capitalist economic laws set broad limits to the sphere of possible action and it can be shown that the effects of, for example, migration policies seem always to benefit capitalism, but this is not to assert that capitalists are always purposeful in their actions and sure of their likely outcome. Neither is it to say that the policies that are followed stem only from a crude analysis of profit and loss; certain policies, while damaging to individuals, may have little effect on industry. And capitalism involves more than the successful management of the forces of production. The relations of production develop irrespectively of the wishes of the capitalist and must be met and managed as the need arises, and to the best of its ability by the ruling fraction of the bourgeoisie. The maintenance of a particular capitalist economic formation involves the weighing of other goals, such as the securing of the power to make decisions, against the pursuit of private profit, although, in the long run, the latter must always be paramount. Thus, even a so-called 'economistic' Marxism is likely to accept that policies drawing, for example, on the demand for labour, are unlikely to be decided solely by reference to the job market.

I shall go further and argue that contradictions within actual class-divided societies produce responses which are only accommodated with difficulty by the governments of these societies, and the decisions that are taken are not invariably optimal for capitalism. Furthermore, these decisions result from various perceptions and convictions about the nature of a situation, and are justified in multifarious ways – few of them simply economic. It is these decisions and their justificatory forms that I seek to outline.

My primary concern here is to place the study of ideology affecting race in a structural context, without asserting that these decisions and their justifications are accounted for, in toto, by the underlying economic imperative of capitalism. The intervening processes need to be more fully described and explained. Myrdal (1962, p. 12) is right in warning of the dangers of reducing the ideological forces 'solely to secondary expressions of economic interests'. This would be 'economism', defined by Poulantzas (1975, p. 46) as the belief that 'socio-economic relations are the specific objective of the class struggle'.

The square of alienation

A Marxist structural analysis of society allows for a number of different theories explaining race relations. The status of such theories is rarely made absolutely clear. Certainly, if they aim to explain only a partial aspect of the total reality, they need not be considered universal or complete, and may be reconcilable with one another. With this in mind, I shall explore each theory as an account of the white response to a particular class relationship.

The theories may be reconciled to some extent by considering them as part of a 'square of alienation' in which human beings fail to co-operate with one another as a result of the structural imperatives mentioned in the previous section. 'Alienation' may be understood to refer to the responses, social and psychological, that are likely to emerge in a class-antagonistic economic structure. Clearly, the concept, as used here, is derived from that part of Marxist theory which deals with alienation from other human beings (rather than from the product), and is based on the underlying

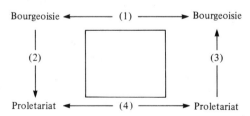

Figure 3. The square of alienation

assumption that social actors desire, or would, in the opinion of the social observer, benefit from the resolution of their antagonism by transforming the economic structure of society.

The square deals with four relations: (1) the antagonism between members of the bourgeoisie, and, in this case, between different national bourgeoisies, (2) the bourgeoisie's efforts to maintain its exploitative relationship with the proletariat, (3) the proletariat's tactics in resisting the bourgeoisie's exploitation and political domination, and (4) the competition between members of the proletariat, in this case white and black proletarians, for scarce resources. If the scheme is to accord more closely with race relations in a country with a colonial legacy and ties, it must be elaborated by the recognition of the importance of metropolitan/colonial relations. The relations between metropolitan and colonial bourgeoisies, and between colonial bourgeoisie and colonial proletariat, are of obvious importance in understanding the economic and political developments of the former independence movement, but the relation (4a) between colonial and metropolitan proletarians is of particular interest in the light of post-war colonial migration to the metropolis.

The consideration of race relations in the colonial context has led to the realisation that the treatment meted out by the metropolitan bourgeoisie to either certain distinguishable sections of the metropolitan proletariat (e.g. US blacks) or to colonial migrants to the metropolis might bear a close resemblance to that perpetrated by the colonial authorities on the native population: the relation (2a) in Figure 4. Rex and Tomlinson (1979) also raise the possibility that the response of the colonial proletariat in the metropolis to the metropolitan bourgeoisie derives its ideological inspiration from the struggle of the national proletariat and national bourgeoisie of the colonies against the metropolitan bourgeoisie. The 'ultimate structural source' of black political movements in Britain, they suggest, 'is to be found in the social structure of Empire and Third World

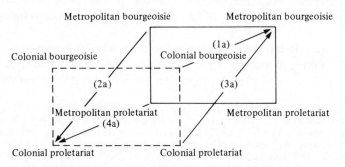

Figure 4. The metropolitan/colonial square of alienation

liberation movements' (p. 293). Black identity groups believe 'that the revolution of the Third World, and particularly the African part of it, is [the black immigrant's] revolution and one with which he should be identified in every way' (p. 292).

Despite the schema outlined here in an attempt to show how various theories of race relations might be reconciled, the theories themselves are generally offered individually and in more detail and applied to specific societies. Below, I give a thumbnail sketch of a number of common theories. My aim is to show how they might clarify the reasons for the development of British ideological configurations affecting race relations.

(1) Competition between national bourgeoisies

Deriving from the work of Hobson, Hilferding, and, more importantly, Lenin, theories of imperialism as a late stage of capitalism can be used to explain how race relations are affected by rivalry between national bourgeoisies. In the nineteenth century, the political interest of the bourgeoisie was expressed in the institution of the nation state, which sought to represent national interests and to define the economic sphere through laws, the control of the monetary system, and restrictions on the movement of the factors of production. Yet in order for capitalists to maintain their high levels of return on investment, it became necessary to expand abroad, and to control politically the territories in which the investment was made. Because other national bourgeoisies were engaged in the same process, rivalry developed between the capitalist states which eventually led to war. 'The war of 1914–18', Lenin wrote, 'was on both sides an imperialist (i.e. annexationist, predatory, and plunderous) war for the partition of the world and for the distribution and redistribution of colonies, of "spheres of influence", of finance, capital, etc.'.

National commitment to overseas expansion and the need to mobilise the British population to fight for the interests of the national bourgeoisie might explain both the jingoism of the British population towards foreigners and their feeling of superiority towards colonial peoples.*

(2i) Relationship of bourgeoisie to proletariat-economic

Oliver Cromwell Cox expounded the theory that 'race prejudice . . . is a social attitude propagated among the public by an exploiting

---

* On a much more mundane level, the dislike of foreign competition is revealed in the attitudes to imported goods and their makers. For example, before the First World War, many German goods carried the letters D R G M (Deutsches Reichsgebrauchs–Muster) which means 'German registered patent'. In Britain the letters were said to stand for 'dirty rotten German make'. More recently, similar attitudes have been shown to all things Japanese: the products, workers' skills, and the people themselves being regarded as inferior.

In the autumn of 1980, British apple growers waged a nationalist 'Save British apples' campaign in the face of competition from continental 'Golden Delicious'.

class for the purpose of stigmatizing some group as inferior so that the exploitation of either the group itself, or its resources or both, may be justified' (1970, p. 393). In other words, Cox saw racial beliefs, together with their manifestations in discrimination, as functioning to preserve the super-exploitation of black people and, consequently, the economic interests of the bourgeoisie.

Cox's theory is often deliberately interpreted as implying a purposeful racial conspiracy on behalf of the bourgeoisie to spread racist propaganda and to maintain racialist practice. Just as easily, it can be seen to refer either to a general desire to perpetuate economic practices that are profitable, or to the actual measurable consequences of racial prejudice. My view is that the differential exploitation of groups of workers on racial lines can be profitable in itself, while at the same time generating the need for a justificatory system which is most likely to be provided by bourgeois ideologists.

But this is not to say that differential exploitation on racial lines is profitable under all circumstances, or that behavioural manifestations arising from an established racist justificatory system cannot severely disrupt production at the expense of the bourgeoisie. Nor is it to say that under certain conditions, the bourgeoisie are incapable of using racial issues in a thoroughly conscious and Machiavellian way. Indeed, it is quite obvious that in Britain politicians representing the interests (on other issues) of the bourgeoisie have done precisely this; but not necessarily for directly economic reasons. It may be felt that discriminatory practices, existing for whatever reason, may help to maintain and provide a predominantly black labour force at lower rates of pay and in substantially worse conditions than white workers would be prepared to accept, in recognition of which fact those employers most immediately involved are unlikely to go out of their way to campaign for less discrimination and higher rates of pay and better conditions for their black workers.

(2ii) Political relationship

Of course, Cox goes further in suggesting that the bourgeoisie maintain antagonistic attitudes between white and black workers in order to facilitate the exploitation of both parties, and to prevent the proletariat organising itself to capture the state and to overthrow capitalism (p. 473). Now in certain historical and geographical contexts, the idea that a regime may deliberately foment dissension between sections of the population fractured on lines of language, tribe, race, religion, colour, or their relationship to the means of production, is by no means far-fetched. Far more likely, however, is the possibility that existing divisions might be astutely used and exacerbated to the disadvantage of the minority groups who possess little power over their own destiny. Obviously, this theory relates closely to the popular ideas of scapegoating and the deflection of responsibility for government failure on to the weak and visible sections of the population.

But Cox's suggestion might appear more plausible when seen in terms of the ideologies that appear to support existing capitalist relations of production. No central dynamic of antagonism towards black people need be postulated, but only a justification for commitment to those beliefs and practices that maintain the various forms of capitalism. Thus, with regard to the colonies, it may be necessary to hold a belief in the civilising mission of the white man and of his general benevolence towards the 'child-like' black man, with the accompanying implication that white people, whether proletarian or bourgeois, are superior to those within their charge. This belief is likely to strengthen the bourgeoisie at the expense of the metropolitan white and colonial black proletariat.

The internal stability of the metropolitan society will also depend on acceptance of justification for the existence of social inequality, a belief that must be actively generated if the bourgeoisie is legitimately going to maintain its privileges. If the inequality in that society partly accords with racial categories, that very same justification will also serve to support racial differentiation. It is not then that the bourgeoisie always actively conspires to produce racially divisive ideology but that the practice of capitalism generates widespread inequality which must be justified. If class and social stratification is accompanied by racial stratification, the justificatory system may utilise class categories, or racial categories, or both. The maintenance, without undue force, of racially exploitative relations will require justification and legitimation.

(3) Relationship of proletariat to bourgeoisie

If a bourgeoisie, or a fraction of a bourgeoisie, differs in racial composition from a proletariat, proletarian struggle against the bourgeoisie may come to be justified in racial terms. Although such racial classification may have at least some empirical base in the actual racial composition of the class in question, by a process of generalisation all members of a particular race, whether they be capitalist or proletarian, may come to be attributed with the supposed qualities of the class. Thus a petit-bourgeois, or managerial, class fraction with whom workers are in close contact may engender racial animosity, by virtue of its class function. Class struggle against capitalism in general may assume racial forms at a real and symbolic level. Such a highly generalised theory could perhaps be modified to explain partially some kinds of anti-semitism, the Rastafarian vision of white Babylon, or the ideology of some black anti-colonial movements.

In a slightly different vein, British workers may be inclined to fight the machinations of management anxious to reduce the cost of labour or commodities by importing foreign workers or goods. Management's attempts to improve relations between workers in order to avoid the disruption of production, may be interpreted as a way of undermining the solidarity achieved by the indigenous workers in their struggle for improved wages and conditions. Indeed, the race relations pietism of those in authority may become closely associated with their class or managerial interests, and be resisted through various anti-authoritarian acts, interpreted by the social observer as racist. Such defiance need not be confined to industry. It has been suggested that various youth cultures may be best explained as anti-authoritarian responses: joining the National Front, 'Paki-bashing', or wearing swastikas possess an anti-authoritarian symbolic value far outweighing the dislike of other races.

(4) Relationships between proletarians

The limited strategies developed by the proletariat for defending itself against capital may stress general worker solidarity or attempt to defend only a section of the work force at the expense of other labour. The dispute in Marxist circles over whether there is such a thing as 'working-class racism' must surely depend on whether a distant or proximate causal explanation is adopted for the conflict that on occasion quite manifestly does occur between sections of the working class. A protectionist strategy on the part of white employees aimed at maintaining the price of labour in a particular plant by refusing to accept black workers who are quite able to fill the shortage can be seen either as a struggle against bourgeois attempts to reduce the cost of labour, or as proletarian competition for scarce resources. The effect may be white racism, but a causal explanation may still be offered in terms of the structural imperatives of capitalism, the need to extract surplus from the worker, and the worker's consequent defensive response against his vulnerability in the market situation.

There remains a possibility that sections of the proletariat might combine along racial lines to safeguard their market position, both as producers or consumers. A typical scenario is outlined by Peach (1968, p. 95):

> It seems to have been almost universally the case that West Indians were taken on as second best. This was not *necessarily* due to colour prejudice on the part of the employer but possibly to fear of it among employees. The situation from the point of view of the employers must have appeared delicate. In their view, they were obliged to take on coloured labour because of the shortage of white labour: they did not want to exacerbate

the shortage by its remedy. Laying aside any overt feelings of colour prejudice, the employees must have felt that any addition to the work force, from whatever source, must weaken their bargaining power. Shortage of labour is, after all, one of the main bargaining tools in attempts to achieve higher wages. Because of the shortage of labour, there was a grudging acceptance of the necessity for coloured labour, but generally on the basis of 'thus far and no further', that is, in colour quotas, in the reservation of certain skills and supervisory categories for white workers and so on.

In dealing with attitudes to post-war foreign labour from the continent, Senior and Manley (1955) point out that the British trade unions took the view that there would be no need to recruit foreign labour if working conditions in the mines and in rural areas were improved to attract natives. The unions also feared a future slump. The interests of the British workers were safeguarded by union agreements which usually kept the volunteer workers in unskilled jobs and prevented them from competing with skilled or even semi-skilled natives (1955, p. 16).

An explanation of race relations in terms of competition between black and white workers in the job market is useful because, in focusing on the productive process, it reveals the more obvious linkages with the overall capitalist mode of production. But capitalist competition is neither limited to nor experienced only in employment. The proletarian finds himself in competition as both producer and consumer, and develops strategies for safeguarding his interests in many different spheres, such as housing, leisure, health, and education, where goods and services will also be in short supply. Although a person may not have the same competitors in every sphere, nor deal with them in the same way, nor recognise any link between one incident and another, there is likely to be an overall tendency to make sense of a totality of experience, resulting in similar responses to recurring stimuli, and eventually perhaps an habituated response in the absence of stimulus. Thus, groups of proletarians may defend an entire way of life which they see as intendant on maintaining a social position relative to other groups. In such circumstances, the smallest change, e.g. in dress or folkway may take on a symbolic importance far in excess of any actual material advantage it has for the group.

Apart from inter-ethnic group competition, alternative, *unifying* strategies can be adopted by fractions of the proletariat wishing to maintain their economic and social status. But the forging of unity will prove difficult if the respective groups do not have or perceive a common interest and have little in common with one another. The differences between groups might be actual or imagined and the evaluation of their importance might vary considerably. Colour, language, religion, historical traditions, previous colonial experiences, social practices, and kinship ties may all contribute to the reasons for treating other groups differently and for finding it difficult to make common cause with them.

(4a) Relationship of metropolitan proletariat with colonial proletariat

A legacy of beliefs arising from colonial class relations is also likely to be of significance in understanding white workers' attitudes to black colonial migrants. These beliefs, though generated in the relationship between metropolitan bourgeoisie and colonial peoples (2a) might have been communicated – particularly in times of jingoistic fervour – to the metropolitan proletariat who, no doubt, would derive some comfort from their perception of their elevated position in relation to the colonial people. Though the metropolitan proletariat were in many ways economically more favoured than the colonial people, the actual material differences were probably of less importance than the symbolic ones: the metropolitan white proletariat actually saw itself as an 'aristocracy of labour' in relation to the inferior black people of the colonies. All this would have been of little consequence for British race relations, had it not been for colonial migration to the metropolis.

The symbolic level

So far, the account of the relationships within the square of alienation has concentrated, without much elaboration, on unspecifically described feelings of dissatisfaction and behavioural strategies. Yet, even in themselves, these responses demand the presence of some level of consciousness, of verbalisation. Nevertheless, it is important to emphasise still further that human beings exist in a symbolic world of words and representations. Their linguistic tools may be developed initially, and continue to enable them, to represent and manipulate the environment in furtherance of their interests, but their language has a facility for detaching itself from objective stabilisers in the real world, and developing relatively independent symbolic associations or even fantastic, idealist universes. This is not the place to attempt a theory of linguistic representation, but to point out only that the symbolic dimension of human existence does not allow a satisfactory analysis of a racial complex to be provided solely in terms of economic alienation. It is not only what blacks are, or do, in relation to whites that matters, but what they come to mean or to represent. Yet the principles of representation are less easy to discover.

Langer's study of symbolism (1976) is frequently cited as providing an insight into the extensive world of myth, ritual, and the arts, which is to be found in every society and not least, it might be added, when examining race relations. Metaphor, she stresses, is the 'law of growth of every semantic. It is not a development, but a principle' (p. 147). It should perhaps be added that metaphorical development, itself, must follow principles.

With the underlying skeleton of the square of alienation revealed, it is important at least to hint at how the flesh of the symbolic interpretation of race relations is attached to the economic bone. Only in this way can the complexities of racial discourse be explained. At this stage, then, but still against a backcloth of social class analysis, it is appropriate to turn briefly to more speculative explanations of the symbolic interpretation of black proletarian migration to a white class society. Sennett and Cobb's *The Hidden Injuries of Class* (1977) might help to provide some understanding of the symbolic significance for white proletarians of the new proximity of black people.

If members of the white proletariat derive some estimate of their own worth by comparing themselves with those they have traditionally held to be their inferiors, then a situation in which colonial migrants – identified by their colour – come to work and live side by side with them and appear to enjoy all the same advantages must challenge that estimate and undermine the white proletarians' conviction that the sacrifices they made to achieve and maintain their standard of living were worthwhile.

Sennett and Cobb develop a general theory of sacrifice as 'the last resource for individualism, the last demonstration of competence':

> It is always available to you, because your desires are always
> part of you. It is the most fundamental action you can
> perform that proves your ability to be in control; it is the final
> demonstration of virtue when all else fails . . . it permits you in
> practice, that most insidious and devastating form of self-
> righteousness where you, oppressed, in your anger turn on
> others who are also oppressed rather than on those intangible,
> invisible, impersonal forces, that have made you all vulnerable.
> (1977, pp. 140–1)

In accepting the historically determined belief in the colonial proletariat's worthlessness, the metropolitan proletarian must make sense of the spectacle of black men working in his factory, living in his street, and drinking in his club. If black men have the same privileges as he, surely he, too, must be worthless, and his many years of sacrifice to keep family and home together, to achieve adequate educational and health facilities amount to nothing. His anger, then, becomes directed at those who are the symbol of the worthlessness of the sacrifices he has made. He has deprived himself only to find his inferiors flaunting the same symbols of success and security on which he has set so much score. If this is the case, then it must follow that the colonial migrants must have cheated in some way, and are guilty of abusing the system as he has experienced it, by, for example, living on social security, making use of facilities to which they as immigrants have never contributed, being allowed unfair access to an undue proportion of council properties, or having a special race relations act passed in their favour.

Sennett and Cobb claim that it was not the blacks so much as the idea of people 'getting away with something I never got away with' that disturbed the workers they interviewed: 'if there are people who have refused to make sacrifices, yet are subsidised by the State, their very existence calls into question the meanings of acts of self-abnegation' (p. 137). Although these suggestions must be treated speculatively, they seem to accord closely not only with some of the actual responses of the white population to the presence of black colonial migrants, but to a theory of proletarian alienation deriving from an economic configuration which produces inter- and intra-class conflict and insecurity.

In brief, I have suggested that hostile white proletarian responses to black colonial immigrants may be explained in terms of (a) white people's perception of the real threat that increased numbers pose to the limited resources of work, housing, social services, etc., (b) the way the presence of black people participating in British social institutions affects whites' self-attributed status (if status or social position is clearly defined with the help of well-established social symbols, then the acquisition of those symbols by a group previously regarded as inferior may be seen as undermining that status), and (c), the meaning invested in individual effort and the apparent ease with which black people achieve comparability without appearing to make the necessary effort. Thus, black people are felt to devalue the proletarian's investment of self-sacrifice – so necessary in helping him to believe he has some control over his own destiny. (This mechanism may explain the source of anger directed against such widely different targets as black people, welfare or social security recipients, council house tenants, students, and other dependants.)

With the postulation of a symbolic level, attention is drawn to the fact that human beings are never simply economically 'determined'. An expression of alienation is not a mere economic reflex but involves a response that is always arrived at with some degree of consciousness. The mention of a symbolic level, exemplified in this case by the work of Sennett and Cobb, is one way of indicating, though fairly unspecifically, that consciousness mediates between economic circumstance and human response. Sennett and Cobb's theory of sacrifice involves the social actor adopting a consciously formulated general cultural and ideological approach to a perceived social reality. Even the apparently basic economic responses mentioned in describing the square of alienation must involve some conscious, if self-interested, pursuit of economic goals.

The point about the conscious pursuit and balancing of values is elaborated in subsequent chapters. Nevertheless, there are certain responses that appear to be more obviously related to the ideally conceived, pure-economic reflex than others. While it must always be acknowledged that human beings operate with some degree of mediating consciousness, it is possible to examine instances that could be described as 'economically basic', in the sense that they approximate to verbal accounts of the self-interested economic strategies that are to be inferred from the square of alienation. In other words, the social actor's account of his motivation closely accords with what is regarded by the social observer as a crudely reflexive expression of economic interest. However, any attempt to offer a simple structural account for the content of remarks made at the discoursive level is always plagued by the dilemma posed by the concept of ideology. If people try constantly to disguise their economic interests behind a facade of ideology, how can any connection be drawn between the 'facades of social structures' and the social structures themselves?

If a connection is to be made between the content of an ideology and underlying economic arrangements, then it undoubtedly lies in some theory of 'relative autonomy', in the sense that an ideology neither accurately reflects the underlying pattern of economic interest, nor exists entirely independently from it in a 'free-floating' capacity. A great deal of ink has been expended on attempts to theorise the precise nature of the relationship between practical relations and ideology and to quantify more accurately the degree of autonomy that ideology commands. In subsequent chapters, it is argued that British racial discourse is best understood in the context of a totality of massive, long-lasting *class* ideological configurations and not in terms of separate *racial* ideological accretions. A distinction is also made between the crude economic response and differing levels of ideological elaboration that might be developed upon it. This quasi-empirical approach which aims, by a series of small-scale plausible connections, to build up a convincing account of how and why certain discoursive forms have been adopted as appropriate in a given social formation is espoused here in preference to an approach which concentrates on more general and abstractly formulated relations between economic base and superstructure, whether couched in terms of dominant or determinant instances, or whatever.

It is sensible to ask whether any of the theories of alienation and general explanations for racial animosity are, or can be, supported by the presentation of data from politicians' responses. If the politicians' discourse is part of an ideological facade, how can any part of it serve to confirm theories aimed at exposing the underlying reality of interest? One simple answer is to point out that the political actor must operate in a real political world and, in his immediate perceptions and descriptions, cannot afford the luxury of total subjectivity. It is also worth mentioning that there are different conceptions of the degree to which the ideas that people hold, are ideologised. The political actor does not *always* need to present his own actions in the best possible light and as operating for the common good, and it may serve his purposes to reveal what he knows about the self-interested motivations of his political enemies. Under certain favourable conditions, some of his remarks, at least, are likely to trace out, often in an accurate and sensitive manner, reasons for racial animosity that accord with those of the social observer.

At this stage, the cynic is likely to argue that the social observer is either himself immersed in the dominant ideological milieu, or merely selecting those elements of another's discourse that are in agreement with his own. The only answer to this criticism is to show, in as convincing manner as possible, the nature of the social actor's interest, as assessed by the social observer, and the meaning of the social actor's discourse – whether it confirms the social observer's assessment or shows a wide discrepancy with it that is clearly advantageous in masking the actor's motives. As ideology in this context refers to *shared* beliefs the 'masking' phenomenon must widely be found within a social grouping and systematic in its effects. Obviously, it is possible to compare the different renderings of social events with the social observer's observations of the same issues.

In this context, the only kind of discoursive evidence that might support the square of alienation would be that which confirmed that black people (a) were perceived as a threat to white people's livelihood, or (b) to their self-attributed status, or (c) were seen as devaluing their 'investment of self-sacrifice'. Occasionally, a frank admission in these terms of the perceived role of black people can be found, although, more often than not, hostility towards blacks will be justified in other ways. Even if a response supports the plausibility of the analysis offered by the square of alienation, it can still be regarded as an element of ideology. Class or other interest may be served occasionally by laying bare the economic foundations of human action.

The belief that black people are somehow inferior to white is often manifested when they are judged individually or collectively to have achieved economic parity or superiority. A recognition that black people are doing well in comparison with certain whites is capable of triggering paroxysms of jealousy. Attention is focused on the possible means by which black people have achieved so much at the expense of whites' self-attributed standing. It is assumed that black people must have been given unfair advantage over whites by government agencies, the courts, employers, etc., in order to have bettered themselves so effectively. This phenomenon may be explained in terms of the traditional symbolic value attributed to the difference of colour (possibly as the means of distinguishing between the aristocrats and plebeians of labour). It is also possible that Sennett and Cobb are right in assuming that white workers become disillusioned and annoyed when they see that their 'self-sacrifice' has been in vain and that, despite all their efforts, they remain on a par with, or even less successful than, those whom they have long considered as the lowest specimens of humankind.

Another idea that emerges in some explanations for racial animosity is that of the threat posed by black people to the traditional neighbourhood regime. It is not only the perceived threat to economic livelihood that is important but the danger posed to the British way of life conceived of as a totality. Change to the merest of folkways takes on a symbolic significance as an attack upon the national heritage as a whole. Minor alterations made in the visible environment might, in themselves, annoy elderly white residents who, for years, have been used to their locality remaining undisturbed. Alternatively, small changes (such as the Indian sweet shop replacing the fish and chip shop, the painting of houses in bright colours) may act as a constant reminder that foreigners are near by, that inferior colonial peoples have presumed to intrude on the sacred environment of a superior British people. The proximity of black people is seen as a form of neighbourhood pollution and self-degradation. The obvious decline of previously respectable inner city areas and, perhaps, even the general malaise of old age felt by the elderly residents who cannot move out may be blamed on the highly visible new factor in the situation – black colonial immigrants. Thus, even the smallest changes to the neighbourhood symbolise an attack upon white status and self-esteem, relative to other groups. In summary, long-term economic rivalry in the field of production and consumption gives rise to status differentials which are strictly delineated by numerous, accreted, cultural symbols bearing an importance far beyond their value (as functionally assessed by the social observer).

4

The state, levels of political articulation, and the discourse of the Conservative and Labour Parties

The inherently unstable capitalist economic system affects the livelihood of the bourgeoisie and proletariat in different ways. Though both classes are in harness to it, the bourgeois is unlikely to see its constraints as irksome: indeed he stands most to gain from maintaining the overall framework and from attempting to control and stabilise its oscillations. With the system of production weighted against him, the proletariat, too, wants economic security but is rarely satisfied with or secure in achieving it. Inasmuch as he feels himself likely to benefit from existing economic relations, or is likely to avoid increased discomfort by conformity, he will accept the status quo. But this support cannot be guaranteed: if conditions worsen or fail to fill expectations, alternative economic relations may promise much more. As the effects of capitalism are uneven, subversive responses to it may be differentially distributed throughout the population.

Responses may be individual or collective, supportive or disruptive of the status quo, involve different levels of organisation and degrees of development of institutions, and take coercive or persuasive forms. The threat to social stability or primary responses to the economic structure has resulted in a secondary response of control, institutionalised in the form of the state.

The state, then, is a secondary, organisational reflex evolving in part from the fear of insecurity generated by primary responses to economic opportunities unevenly distributed among the population. Crudely generalised, the state will be supported most strongly and unquestioningly by those who are likely to benefit from the economic structure it helps to maintain, while its practices will be least attractive to those who are most conscious of the inadequacies of existing arrangements. The harsh realities arising from any form of social disruption result in most groups lending support to arrangements that can guarantee stability, whether or not that stability is at the expense of justice and economic equality. With the state

61

seeking to stabilise existing social relations by coercion and persuasion, the social actor is presented with the stark choice of whether to accept his allocated position in an inegalitarian social order or to risk rejecting it in the face of social coercion and the likely social instability that might result from any action taken. The choice that he makes in the light of his primary economic interests, and the secondary political restraints placed upon him, can be described as the tertiary response or reflex – that of political practice.

This very simplistic and generalised account of the nature of the political state and the economically motivated tensions it seeks to resolve by coercion and persuasion is inadequate in explaining the complexities of an actual socio-political formation. It does, however, give some indication of the way the important political institution of the state arises as a means of controlling class conflict to the greater advantage of those who benefit most from capitalism. In addition, it can be seen that the social responses summarised by the square of alienation will be articulated within the political framework set out by the state.

The generalised notion of 'response' must, of course, be developed. Initially, behavioural manifestations in the form of individual or collective actions and institutional and organisational processes may be distinguished from their linguistic or verbal accompaniment. In dealing with discourse affecting race relations, our concern must be with the latter, but this can only properly be understood within the context of the former.

If we turn from theoretical generalisation to an examination of empirical reality, twentieth-century Britain reflects structurally, and in its political responses, the characteristics of an advanced and overwhelmingly capitalist social formation. Class interest is expressed in many ways, but in relation to the state, a number of institutions (such as the trade unions, the CBI, and political parties at national and local level) are acknowledged as the means of articulating and integrating the interests of the various social groupings. Inasmuch as a class 'in itself' can be said, through organising in furtherance of its interests, to have become 'for itself', it is clear that the two major political parties, Conservative and Labour, while both accepting and operating within the structure of the existing state, are at the same time class-based, and frequently reflect the differences of interest between the two major classes of bourgeoisie and proletariat. Obviously, other class fractions and localised groupings caused by structural variations complicate the situation, but the generalisation is nevertheless worth adhering to.

An acceptance of the essentially class-based nature of British political articulation (which should not be confused with the stronger assertion that the parties always act in the best interests of particular classes or fractions) is crucial for understanding race relations issues. The politics of race relations, even if appearing to possess autonomy, is always circumscribed by class considerations, and indeed must be treated within the context of the long-standing organisational and ideological forms that arise from the divisions of social class. Put crudely, racial responses in Britain originate from the alienation created by inter- and intra-class divisions, and are then generally justified in terms of class ideology by party organisations representing those class divisions; I develop this theme more fully below.

To understand the complexities of racial discourse, however, it is necessary to recognise the varying need of and purpose for verbal response of different groups in the social structure. Alienated proletarians, in no position to make and enforce decisions on their political environment, may merely express their deep-felt animosities, whereas ruling fractions of the bourgeoisie need to persuade the rest of the population of the importance of adopting policies dealing with race that have the effect of maintaining order and avoiding, at all costs, disruption of production. At the same time they will want to satisfy the electorate that they are attending to its problems.

The 'speech acts' of the ruling fraction, when viewed in toto, of necessity, will reveal greater complexity than those uttered by groups deprived of power and in no position to achieve it. Persuasion, of course, is not merely a function of what is said, but of the opportunities available for making what is said widely known. Not only is the power to coerce differentially distributed among the population but so also is the power to persuade. The necessary skills – often developed to a fine art – and the organisational and technical facilities to spread information and to influence its composition will be closely supervised by the more powerful groups in society and, in particular, by the state.

Persuasion, however, does not depend solely on the power of the ruling classes to 'brain-wash' the population by selecting, manipulating, and evaluating information, and controlling channels of communication. Deutsch (1966, p. 52) stresses that to be:

> susceptible to persuasion, men must already be inwardly
> divided in their thought. There must be some incompatibilities
> in the facts they remember, or in the facts that they can be
> induced to accept. There must be some contradictions actual
> or implied among their habits or values. In short, there must
> be something for persuasion to get started on, and something
> substantial for persuasion to maintain its hold for longer
> periods. What matters, therefore, is the distribution of
> individuals and groups that can be persuaded – and kept
> persuaded – within any given time.

From a Marxist perspective, individuals' experiences of alienation (including dissatisfaction, indecision, and inter-personal animosity) arising from the objective class structures in which they find themselves may be dealt with in different ways. Policies may be pursued which maintain existing class divisions and contain and repress alienation. Alternatively, class structures may be undermined and abolished and, in the course of that process, alienation utilised or sublimated in the struggle to remove its structural sources. The containment and repression of alienation is made possible by the maintenance of the contradiction between capital and labour which comes to be internalised within the individual. The individual is placed in a position where he must choose either the improvement of his condition and the securing of justice by opposing the oppressive and coercive organisation of capitalism, with all the sacrifices that entails, or the acceptance of a compromised existence and an agreement to accept things as they are. The ruling fraction, as an agent of the bourgeoisie, seeks to maximise its interests by maintaining, as far as possible by persuasion, the existing state of affairs. Inasmuch as it is successful, the framework which generates alienation remains intact. But because of the inherent contradiction within the system, the state of 'ideological hegemony' is only very precariously maintained through persuasion.

As Habermas (1976) explains, the modern capitalist state faces a 'legitimation crisis', legitimation being the successful culmination of attempts to persuade the population to accept the existing political order. In more traditional political parlance, legitimation is the conversion of power into authority. The modern state has not only increasingly intervened in the market economy, but has extended its tentacles into every aspect of civil life, with the consequence that its actions require additional powers of legitimation. According to Habermas, these have been found in a justificatory system of technical rationality, whereby it is believed that experts such as scientists and technicians know, by virtue of their skills, what is best. Thus politics becomes a matter of manipulation in order to achieve ends that are so far taken for granted that moral and ethical questions are excluded from debate. In a system that is inherently unstable, however, the state – particularly where it has assumed wider areas of responsibility – may not always be able to satisfy its clients, who, in the event of serious disruption, are likely to seek new solutions to their problems. At this stage, the state will have to devote greater effort to persuasion, but, owing to its internal contradictions, its increased scope of responsibility, the population's level of expectations, and its failure to meet them, it is liable to suffer a 'legitimation crisis'.

With regard to race, Habermas's work helps to locate the state's justification for its race relations policies in the general context of capitalist legitimation. The state must maintain its overall control over the population through coercion and persuasion. It is seen to have responsibility for race relations and is expected to take action to deal with the consequences of the alienation of white from black, when it occurs. The kinds of racial policies and justificatory forms that emerge are likely to be compatible with, and indeed part of, those major ideological configurations that provide legitimation for the capitalist social structure as a whole.

But black and white sections of the population experience the effects of capitalism in different and unequal ways. The justificatory forms that satisfy and placate the white electorate may fail to persuade the black population, for whom the legitimation crisis of the state may be far more imminent: this will be particularly so where blacks are affected directly and unequally by racially discriminatory policies or legislation. Of course, the state may make no attempt to appeal to certain minorities who will be seen as 'beyond the pale'. It is quite apparent from a study of British political ideology of the last thirty years, for example, that black people have only recently come to be accepted as part of the political audience and as potential voters. Previously, and with a clearly dehumanising effect on the discourse used to refer to them, they were treated as political 'objects' rather than as agents in the political process, although it is true that, more recently, politicians responsible for the justification of government policies have sought to appeal to both the white and black electorate.

In the course of their development, political blocs, opposed to the economic system that is supported by the state, draw on the experience of the classes on which they are based and produce counter-justificatory systems for those needing to interpret and organise their experiences. In most social formations, therefore, although the ruling ideology will be in the ascendancy for all to draw upon, alternative justificatory systems will be available and strenuous efforts will be made by ideologists loyal to the existing social order to bridge the differences or to incorporate counter-justifications into the prevailing system. This is necessary, if persuasion is to succeed, for it must be presumed that for a counter-justificatory system to come into being, despite the hegemony of ruling ideas, it must accord strongly with the experiences and desired responses of some sections of the population – particularly those who seek to utilise and sublimate their alienation. Thus, there will be a tendency for ideologists who support the status quo and seek to ensure its appeal to wide sections of the population to draw off some element of counter-thought for incorporation into a modified and ubiquitous ruling ideology. This might explain the frequent complaints of opportunism and revisionism made by revolutionaries against ideologies and organisations which at least initially were seen as rejecting capitalist thought.

Because sections of a population respond differently according to their position in the socio-political structure and are involved to a greater or lesser extent with state and political institutions, the justificatory and persuasive content of their discourse is likely to vary considerably. In studying racial discourse, it becomes clear that there are levels of expression and justification ranging from a straightforward expression of a feeling of alienation, to a politically sophisticated, carefully weighed, and plausibly justified statement of racial import. Recognition of these differences has led various writers, in pursuit of diverse objectives, to develop what can loosely be called a concept of ideological levels. If we are to understand the many kinds of discourse dealing with racial issues, it is important to look carefully at what has been said about the existence of 'levels'. The ideas of three writers: Pareto, Gramsci and Shils are of particular relevance.

Pareto (1963) makes an important distinction between action that is performed as a means to an end and action that is not so related. When social actor and observer both recognise the means/end conjunction of an action, it is to be termed 'logical'. When either agent or observer do not recognise end or purpose, it is 'non-logical'. Non-logical actions are actions that are performed prior to conscious purpose: a baby sucking the breast, or having a temper-tantrum, as well as the instinctive behaviour of animals, might serve as examples. Although the baby's sucking may be end-orientated from the point of view of the observer ('the baby is seeking milk'), it is not sucking *in order* to get milk, or with *the purpose* of getting milk (an end-orientated action), but because of some psycho-physiological state of hunger. It is only with conscious thought that an anthropomorphic, teleological patterning is added to an existential world of cause and effect.

Pareto believes that there are many human actions that are non-logical, both from the actor's and observer's point of view. But 'human beings have a very conspicuous tendency to paint a varnish of logic over their conduct' (1963, Vol. 1, p. 79). 'The human being has such a weakness for adding logical developments to non-logical behaviour that anything can serve as an excuse for him to turn to that favourite occupation' (p. 104). By non-logical behaviour, I understand Pareto to mean behaviour for which the actor has not thought of an explanation or justification, while, in contrast, logical behaviour is behaviour for which he possesses an explanation or justification. Just as science undermined the teleological view of the inanimate universe and later, with Darwinism, of the animal world too, Pareto takes a further step of arguing the case for a category of non-purposive human action, which is, however, very difficult to identify because of the propensity of human beings to explain (usually post hoc) their own behaviour in terms of purpose. Such a view is likely to be socially unpopular because it undermines the strongly held moral view that human beings *ought* to act purposively.

Pareto argues that often all we are entitled to say of an action is that we do D *and* believe C, but that we invariably go further and claim that we do D because we believe C. It is, he thinks, more likely that we believe C because we do D.

The distinction between the non-conscious response to a stimulus, and the conscious formulation of a reason for that response is of obvious significance for a discussion of ideological levels. We might have, for example, on the one hand, (1) a near instinctive response on the part of the individual to what is perceived as a threat, while on the other, (2) a mediated response affected by a conscious consideration of elements of a justificatory system. From the point of view of the actor, (1) can not (theoretically at least) be considered to constitute part of a justificatory system, although the actor, no doubt, will sooner or later be expected to explain himself. Perhaps the expression 'I don't know what came over me' may be understood in this context. And from the point of view of the observer, it is likely that an explanation of some sort will be found, such as, 'You behaved like a wild beast.' Where (2) is concerned, the actor, in most cases, will be making use of a justificatory system that is publicly available, widely accepted, and understood by the observer, although with some eccentric groups (e.g. Charles Manson's hippy commune) the ideological framework against which actions must be judged will not be immediately obvious.

The first kind of response (1) might be viewed as the ideal-typical response untainted by purposive consideration, whereas (2), however superficially, has been thought about in the light of a conscious end. In terms of the account of racial alienation given above, we might seek to distinguish some sort of basic economic reflex, from a response to economic conditions that foresightedly seeks to protect and explain the interest of a given group. Although, in reality, it is doubtful that a pure form of (1) exists, we might recognise that (2) could range from a rudimentary 'gut-feeling', closely approximating to (1), to a carefully worked-out statement of purpose which takes into account the likely effect of the expression or action on the community as a whole. A party political ideology might be placed near the end of a continuum as an example of a highly systematised public justificatory system on which actors draw when they are required to give reason for their action. Between the 'non-logical' and fully fledged political there will be many forms and levels of justification. The pejorative term 'economism' might be used to describe an account of ideology offered in terms of economic stimulus and response at or near level (1).

There is no suggestion by Pareto that a reason for action need be given, although, when questioned, the actor will be encouraged to construct one. In this context, it is worth bearing in mind Gouldner's comment (1976, p. 54) that:

> Men are, but are not only, speaking subjects. They are also sensuous actors engaged in a *practice* which may be spoken but is not identical with that speech. Words mediate between deeds and experiences, but there are deeds that overwhelm the capacity for speech, thus imposing silences and dissatisfaction with our ability to communicate or understand our experience.

The experience of racial alienation, then, may not be understood by the actors caught up in the alienating economic system.

Pareto warns us clearly of the pitfalls of assuming any causal link between action and ideology or ideology and action. There is no reason why the 'psychic motivator' must always be exposed in a public justification for action, and, furthermore, there are actions for which a purpose may not be provided by, or known to, the actor. Nevertheless, the pressing effects of actions are prone to encourage the observer to interpret and explain every actor's actions in terms of purpose. As Pareto says, it is much easier to formulate a theory about logical rather than non-logical behaviour (1963, Vol. 1, p. 178). And 'nobody, in practice, acts on the assumption that the physical and moral constitution of an individual does not have at least some small share in determining his behaviour'.

Pareto's observations pose a number of questions for the study of racial discourse. First, it is implied that there need be no necessary connection between the structural determinants singled out by the sociologist to account for practice deemed by the observer to have a racialist effect and the discourse offered as the explanation or justification by the actor for his behaviour. If the explanations do, in fact, tally, then the problem may be hidden: the actor may still not be aware, or may not be able to explain his 'real' reason – should he have a reason – and under such circumstances he may have merely accepted the 'logical' explanation made available to him by the observer. If the explanations do not tally, then the question arises of whether to believe the observer or the actor, particularly if the actor strenuously denies the observer's story.

A second implication that can be drawn is that there may be one explanation for an actor's racial practice and quite another for his racial discourse. It has often been assumed in the theory of race relations that racialist practice and racist belief have the same causal mechanism, or, at least, that they are closely connected, whichever is assumed to be causally prior. But Pareto's observations make it at least possible that they might develop separately. Indeed, in the discussion of ideological levels, it

becomes obvious that the reasons given for the development of rudimentary responses approximating to Pareto's level (1) (offered, for example, by
the theory of alienation) are insufficient to account for more sophisticated
forms of racial discourse which can probably only be explained in terms of
other considerations such as the weighing of values and policies by
decision-makers anxious to achieve a number of different, and sometimes
apparently incompatible, goals. Put in crude fashion, although racial
alienation might explain immediate responses, both behavioural and
verbal, and might provide the basis for explaining subsequent political
manoeuvres to capitalise in some way on the manifestation of that
alienation, the form of the discourse dealing with race will be subject to
political considerations, and can only properly be understood by taking
into account the 'logical' conduct of politicians.

To extend Pareto's point, although an individual X may believe C
because he does D (because he acts out a particular role in a social
structure), a second individual Y may do D because he believes B (which
might include a judgment about X's belief C). The second individual Y's
behaviour and discourse cannot be adequately explained, therefore, in
terms of the reasons for X's behaviour, although it might originally have
been necessitated by it. The situation is further complicated if Y has to take
into account the behaviours and beliefs of any additional persons,
particularly if theirs differ from X's.

In summary, an explanation for racial alienation (whether conceived of
by the actor or observer as primitively non-purposive, or as purposive) and
any rudimentary ideology that might emanate from that circumstance is
unlikely to be adequate in explaining racial discourse considered as part of
a fully fledged political ideology aimed at legitimation. Racial discourse
must be thoroughly described and allocated to a correct ideological level in
order for it to be properly accounted for.

Gramsci offers a further clue to the existence of ideological levels by
distinguishing between three kinds of thought: philosophy as an intellectual order, the common sense of the masses, and religion, which is an
'element of fragmented common sense'. Common sense is defined
negatively as lacking in unity and coherence – in respect of both the
individual and collective consciousness. For the mass of humanity, the
'conception of the world is not critical and coherent but disjointed and
episodic'. Human beings gain elements of consciousness from the multi-
plicity of groups to which they belong:

> The personality is strangely composite: it contains Stone Age
> elements and principles of more advanced science, prejudices
> from all past phases of history at the local level and intuitions

of a future philosophy which will be that of a human race united the world over. To criticise one's own conception of the world means therefore to make it a coherent unity and to raise it to the level reached by the most advanced thought in the world. It therefore also means criticism of all previous philosophy, insofar as this has left stratified deposits in popular philosophy.

(Gramsci, in Hoare and Nowell Smith, 1971, p. 324)

In its unity and coherence, public ideology differs from incoherent, disjointed, and episodic common sense. With regard to racial discourse, we might wish to distinguish an individual's 'gut' response to a given situation (which may be inconsistent with the expression of his opinion at another time and place) from a group's public statement which is likely to have been carefully weighed against other tenets, as well as the likely effect of the 'speech act'. Gramsci's concept of the historical accretion of ideas is also extremely useful in showing both how ideologies come into being and how racial beliefs persist, e.g. as a result of the experience of Empire.

Gramsci is aware, too, that philosophy and common sense can only be analytically distinguished and are never found in a 'pure' state. He writes of 'the healthy nucleus that exists in "common sense", the part of it which can be called "good sense" and which deserves to be made more unitary and coherent'. The different levels affect one another and the more complex ideas of philosophy are likely to 'react back' on their base in 'common sense'. If the philosophy of the intellectuals and the common sense of the masses should become increasingly differentiated then the unity of an 'entire social block' (p. 328) might be threatened.

Indeed the strength of religion of the Catholic church has stemmed from the recognition of the need for 'doctrinal unity of the whole mass of the faithful', and from the church's attempts to ensure that the intellectual stratum does not become detached from the lower.

The Roman church has always been the most vigorous in the struggle to prevent the official formation of two religions, one for the 'intellectuals' and the other for the 'simple souls' . . . One of the greatest weaknesses of immanentist philosophies in general consists precisely in the fact that they have not been able to create an ideological unity between the bottom and the top, between the 'simple' and the intellectuals.   (pp. 328–9)

Education and cultural activity guarantee some continuity between beliefs of the intellectuals and the masses, but it is in the sphere of politics, according to Gramsci, that the relation between philosophy and common sense is assured (p. 331). The masses can only assert their interests by organising themselves with the help of organisers and leaders constituting the elite of political intellectuals who must always justify the party's behaviour to the masses.

In applying these ideas to British politics, we must recognise the continuity between the common-sense culture of social classes expressed in a variety of dissociated discursive responses to the activities of the moment, and the consciously formulated and coherent ideology of the political party, many of whose fundamental premises change very little over the generations. The complexity of an ideological justificatory system arises, paradoxically, from the need to show how a wide variety of political decisions can be founded on a *minimal* set of consistent, or hierarchically ordered, premises. But the continuity between the mass, democratic response to a population's conditions, and a ruling party's policies is always tendentious, as I have already tried to show. Gramsci is wrong in thinking that in politics the relationship between philosophy and common sense is always assured. A bourgeois party may make concessions to the common-sense beliefs of the masses, or, alternatively, over a number of years, work to superimpose its beliefs upon them, while a party serving the proletarian class interest must work to develop the ideological level of the masses, or risk being isolated and misunderstood.

The implications of these ideas for British race relations are clear. Governments must seek to reconcile the differences between their view of the world and that of the electorate whom they rely on to legitimate their democratic pretensions. On the whole, in Britain, the working class has not been convinced by the reasons given by socialists for the existence of social alienation, and the means by which they say it must be dealt with and resolved. Instead, bourgeois parties have successfully persuaded the electorate to maintain the status quo despite the alienation to which it gives rise. Much of the time, alienation is suppressed in its behavioural and verbal manifestations, but occasionally it bursts through the coercive and ideological constraints in ways which threaten existing orthodoxies. In order to maintain its hold on the population, the bourgeois ideology developed by intellectuals must be used to try to suppress altogether, to ignore, to make concessions to, or to incorporate expressions of alienation within its explanatory and justificatory system, without threatening the stability of the existing economic order.

Occasionally, when deviant ideologists have access to the media and manage to put into words the feelings of certain sections of the population, the grip of bourgeois ideas may look dangerously tenuous. Attempts must then be made to repair the persuasive network, by showing that popular ideas are unfounded and illegitimate, or by modifying or isolating them in such a way that adherence to them does not unduly undermine other beliefs necessary for maintaining the status quo. In other words, the population as a whole and its political leaders must never be allowed to become ideologically separated on important issues. Indeed, it is quite obvious that politicians of both parties, like missionaries, are continually working hard to establish their ideological outlook among an heretical and anarchic electorate.

In Britain, the fear of differences arising between certain sections of the population and the government over racial issues, and the possibility that elemental racial reactions might undermine social stability, have encouraged power holders to take various forms of conciliatory action. The formation of the Community Relations Commission whose aim was 'to break down prejudice and intolerance through public education and information' may be seen as one attempt to develop a partial ideology of race relations compatible with prevailing party political viewpoints and in answer to primitive populist responses to racial alienation.

In 1968, Powell's speeches, expressing as they did the level of alienation of sections of the white population, and causing a rash of demonstrations, threatened to upset the consensual line established by the two main political parties. The Conservative leader, Edward Heath, pointed out that his difference with Powell was that Powell discussed racial issues in a manner 'likely to exacerbate relations between the races, rather than lead to their peaceful solution'. Such issues needed to be discussed by the leadership in a calm and rational manner, i.e. within the existing framework of debate.

Powell's immense support was said to spring from the fact that he had dared to express what many people really felt and, by expressing those feelings publicly and from a political position of some importance, had made them acceptable.* He had succeeded in legitimating an alternative and relatively consistent ideological matrix that was able to accommodate the previously dispersed and fragmented elements of common sense about black people. When he was expelled from the Shadow Cabinet this led not only to greater publicity for his ideas, but to a recognition by his supporters of just how difficult it was to make inroads into the prevailing ideological consensus. Powell's position was commonly seen as an anti-authoritarian response to the ideological incursions of the state into the firm bulwark of conventional wisdom possessed by 'the little man'. It was widely held that Powell's unpopularity in establishment circles stemmed from the fact that

---

* A typical letter to the Wolverhampton newspaper, the *Express & Star* (23 April 1968), read: 'Enoch Powell has the guts to voice the opinion of the vast majority of English people of all political parties and creeds.'

he had enabled 'ordinary people' for once to voice their feelings through the medium of his widely reported, public rhetoric. * Of course, ideologies of the Right as well as of the Left are likely to be subject to the hegemonic control of the ruling class, and expressions of alienation repressed. Powell must be regarded as an 'organic intellectual' † of the Right whose success was achieved by developing a Right-wing nationalist ideology which could incorporate the primitive responses of alienated sections of a proletariat lacking in socialist consciousness.

The third writer on ideological levels whom I should like to mention is Shils (1968). Shils, like Gramsci, recognises the need for intellectual endeavour in the formation of ideologies when he claims they are 'the creations of charismatic persons who possess powerful, expansive and simplified visions of the world, as well as high intellectual and imaginative powers'. While not necessarily agreeing with his personalised conception of ideological genesis, we may accept that intellectual input is necessary in order to achieve greater 'explicitness', 'internal integration or systematis- ation', 'comprehensiveness', 'urgency of its application', and 'concent- ration' of 'certain central propositions and evaluations'. In this, *ideology* differs from what Shils calls a 'prevailing outlook' which is vague, diffuse, unsystematic, and lacking 'authoritative and explicit promulgation'.

Apart from these two levels of expression, Shils adds two other possible categories, the *programme* – as an example of quasi-ideology, and *proto- ideology*. The programme is a 'specification of a particular limited objective (e.g. civil rights or electoral reform movements)'. It narrows 'the focus of interest that is implicit in an outlook', but in having only a limited range of objectives, unlike an ideology, does not require a fully comprehensive justificatory system. If political ideology is associated with the political party, the programme may perhaps be identified by its association with the pressure group. The justificatory system of the Anti-Nazi League, or of a Council for Community Relations might serve as examples.

Shils sees the beliefs (expressed in discourse) of adolescent gangs or of

†The following are examples of letters on the Powell issue to the *Express and Star* which express an anti-authoritarian response: 'This is supposed to be a free country, yet a man is "sacked" because he says what he believes and knows to be true. It's about time someone brought to light the feelings of the majority. I'm with Mr Powell every inch of the way.' 'Instead of a democracy, our country is now becoming a dictatorship ruled by a set of people who cannot understand the feelings of the man in the street since they have never bothered to find out.' 'We fought two world wars in the cause of freedom. Now it is being taken from us.' And many more of such ilk.
* Gramsci defines 'organic intellectuals' as the thinking and organising element of a particular fundamental social class. They are distinguished 'less by their profession which may be any job characteristic of their class, than by their function in directing the ideas and aspiration of the class to which they organically belong' (Hoare and Nowell Smith, 1971, p. 3).

military and paramilitary gangs as examples of proto-ideology. Although the closely knit groups assert particular forms of loyalty, discipline, criteria of membership, and reasons for enmity towards outsiders, they do not 'develop or espouse a coherent moral and intellectual doctrine'. Shils attributes this failure to the insufficient intellectual endowment of the groups' members. They lack a fully fledged belief system because of the absence of a 'charismatic ideological personality', 'a founder who is sufficiently educated or sufficiently creative to provide them with a more complex system of beliefs'.

We might wonder how Shils would deal with Charles Manson's hippy group with its elaborate racist cosmology of 'helter-skelter'. Perhaps this point is covered by his assertion that 'such groups lack sufficient contact with both the central value system and the tradition of ideological orientation'. This seems to imply that an ideology is to be identified in the main by its long-standing continuity and setting in mainstream political institutions. As Gramsci (Hoare and Nowell Smith, 1971, p. 341) puts it: 'mass adhesion or non adhesion to an ideology is the real critical test of the rationality and historicity of thinking. Any arbitrary constructions are pretty rapidly eliminated by historical competition . . . constructions which respond to the demands of a complex organic period of history always impose themselves and prevail in the end'.

Aided by the ideas of Pareto, Gramsci, and Shils on ideological levels, we might now seek to distinguish the discourse of politicians in the process of political deliberation from the casual conversation – admittedly sometimes involving ideas of political import – of the common man. The view that it is useful to make such a distinction is shared by Lane (1962, pp. 15–16) who writes:

> Of course, there are differences between the articulated,
> differentiated, well-developed political arguments put forward
> by informed and conscious Marxists or Fascists or liberal
> democrats on the one hand, and the loosely structured,
> unreflective statements of the common man . . . I distinguish
> between the forensic ideologies of the conscious ideologist and
> the latent ideologies of the common man.

On the basis of the preceding discussion, I shall attempt to draw up a dyadic typology of discourse, two ideal types, termed respectively (1) specialised political discourse and (2) general discourse. It is important to remember that the typology is a sociological construct for which there are only approximations in real life. The extent of its generalisability is unclear, but it is conceived with the British political system in mind.

Specialised political discourse is engaged in by social actors, who, in the main, have undergone a lengthy political apprenticeship. For example, a large proportion of Members of Parliament of both major political parties have been to public school (three-quarters of Conservatives and one fifth of Labour) and to university (well over half in both parties). In October 1974, 44% of Conservative and 49% of Labour MPs had professional occupations; 33% of Conservatives and 8% of Labour MPs were businessmen (see Guttsmann, (1963)). Others have been long active in the constituency parties or in the trade union movement.

Specialised political discourse is always verbalised and can be found in oral and written forms. It is communicated through the media and can be closely and repeatedly examined when in print. Words, then, are likely to be carefully chosen in a self-conscious manner and for an instrumental purpose. In making a speech, a politician often reads from notes, and generally his discourse is closely linked with written or printed material. General 'discourse' on the other hand, is sometimes scarcely verbalised. (Rex, in one of his seminars, referred to the 'primitive grunt' of the racist, emotionally overwhelmed, but lacking in words.) It is infrequently written down, and although often supported by television news, newspaper reports, and the like, is not closely linked with reading. Rather, it is an expression of personal experience, of how the individual is immediately affected by an event.

Because political discourse aims at achieving the legitimation of particular policies, it will tend to present them as serving the interests of the whole community. What is done must be seen to be done for the good of the whole, and not for sectional interest. Political discourse, therefore, will have a strong moralistic demeanour in which attempts will be made to reconcile differences of interest by the use of word formulae that emphasise consequences for the public good. General discourse may make use of moral evaluation and prescription but, in making no pretensions to speak publicly in favour of the social whole, can afford to voice individual and sectional interests.

Though both general and political discourse may refer to economic matters, general discourse is often associated with the crudely economic clamour of those who seek to satisfy their needs without taking into account the needs of others. This is not to say that politics is actually concerned with justice in the balancing of sectional interests, but only that politicians must always seek to justify their deeds as serving the general interest. In this way, immediate economic satisfaction is contrasted with politically mediated moral decision-making, the language of the politician laying claim, however falsely, to the latter.

The primary aim of specialised political discourse is persuasion, of getting others to accept the justification of past or future deeds. It is closely linked to action/inaction for a specialised political function and its prescriptive content is usually part of a carefully thought-out strategy. General discourse is part of an ongoing stream of conversation, serving the individual's practical and emotional needs of the moment. It is expressive and indexical (revealing much about the speaker's personality). It need not be linked to political action, or action generally, and, when lacking in a specialised task, merges with other functions and subject areas, e.g. practical jokes, chants at football matches. Whereas specialised political discourse is preplanned and instrumental and performed by agents conscious of why they are involved in particular discourse, general discourse is frequently spontaneous, expressive, and unself-consciously engaged in.

The setting for the kinds of discourse differs, too. Specialised political discourse is to be found in formal debating arenas such as parliament and party conferences, while general discourse is engaged in everywhere, but particularly in the informal groups of family, workmates, and friends.

Where the characteristics of the discursive form itself are concerned, specialised political discourse is structured, integrated, and systematised, showing a recognised degree of consistency, in contrast to general discourse which is weakly structured, less integrated, and unsystematised, with consistency being much less of a priority. Specialised political discourse is conceived of as an overarching system combining descriptive, evaluative, and prescriptive sentences in a totality: not so general discourse, which possesses no overarching or consciously created coherent system, and which does not present descriptive, evaluative, and prescriptive sentences as if they were related, and part of a whole. Specialised political discourse offers a general theory or set of theories for explaining a number of significant events and situations, while general discourse allows of many different and apparently unrelated explanations. Specialised political discourse concentrates on one major theme at a time, while general discourse is syncretic, showing little attempt to divide a 'flowing stream of consciousness' into discrete parts.

Specialised political discourse is based on the premise that political aims are interrelated and that the pursuit of one can affect others adversely. There is a clear and marked means/end distinction. The distinction between means and ends is less obvious in general discourse and the existence of 'intrinsic means' receives more notice.

Both specialised political and general discourse develop eristically – a process in which agents compete for an audience's allegiance by creating new discourse in response to the scepticism, disbelief, and alternative views expressed by others. (This concept is developed extensively in Appendix 2). In political discourse, however, eristic is formalised with a claim being matched against a counter-claim, sometimes in a very regular manner. The formal balancing of dialogue and argument in this way is advantageous to the comparative study of ideologies as it allows the respective weighting given to arguments and counter-arguments in discourse to be quantitatively analysed. Such a technique is not so easily applicable to general discourse unless the researcher employs interrogative methods and matches blocks of discourse for himself, in which case he himself becomes a participant in eristical development.

The policy orientation of those in power is manifested in political discourse in the clear means/end distinction, the concentration on technical means, the preponderance of prescription over evaluation, and prescription's detailed specification and operationalised nature. Argumentation takes on a balance-sheet format, quantification and qualification are present, and, where it suits the policy maker, social scientific material is made use of. In contrast, general discourse does not mark the means/end distinction so clearly and places less emphasis on prescription. Evaluation is often sufficient, but where prescription is present, it may be vaguely specified, difficult to operationalise, and indeed, appear as sheer fantasy. Quantification and qualification are frequently rudimentary and, because agents are not involved in implementing their own suggestions, there is no need for economic or political accounting. 'Folk knowledge' takes precedence over social science, but the folk knowledge of the present is often derived from the social science of the past (Keynes, 1936).

Table 2 summarises the characteristics of the two levels of discourse.

The discourse with which I am primarily concerned in this study is of the specialised political kind. It emerges from the broad matrix of general discourse, or from what Gramsci would call 'the common sense of the masses' and Shils 'the prevailing outlook', and, therefore, can never be totally separable from it. A full study of discourse would have to take such general discourse more fully into account. Here, rather cursorily, I have suggested two possibilities.

The first is that the general discourse dealing with race is an expression of the alienation experienced in the relationship between social classes, where class divisions correspond with racial categorisation. In Lane's terms, the common man's ideology is latent in that his alienation, though experienced, is not always expressed, or, when expressed, uttered in words of his own choosing. The second possibility arrived at by extrapolation from the previous section is that general discourse contains the justificatory forms of the common man who, in his non-specialised political behaviour, must spontaneously develop some political sentiments or alternatively adopt those offered to him by the organic intellectuals of his own or another class. Further, I have suggested that there may be a tension

Table 2. *Differences between specialised political and general discourse*

Specialised political discourse	General discourse
Agents	
Highly specialised groups, long experience of politics	Highly differentiated groups drawn from all occupational categories
Always verbalised: found in oral and written forms	Not always verbalised: mostly in oral form
Closely linked with writing and print	Not closely linked with written form
Often recorded and closely examined	Rapidly fading
Self-conscious choice of words	Spontaneous
Used instrumentally	Used expressively
Aim	
To convince audience that action is taken for the public good – moral justification	Actual reasons – moral or otherwise – frequently stated
Primary aim of persuasion	Primary aim conversational
Justification of past and future action	Serving individuals' practical and emotional needs of the moment – expressive
Linked to action/inaction	Not always linked to action
Often carefully thought-out strategy	Often response to immediate stimuli
Specialised political function	Merging with other functions
Setting	
Formal debating arenas (parliament, party conference)	No formal arena (informal group: family, work, leisure)
Opposition and audience	No necessary opposition or specific audience

Characteristics of discourse

a

Structured, integrated, systematised

High degree of consistency

Conceived as overarching system, combining descriptive, evaluative, and prescriptive sentences in a totality

General theory or set of theories offered to explain events

b

Recognition of relationship between aims and how pursuit of one can affect others adversely

Clear means/end distinction

c

Eristical development, strongly formalised, producing balance of argument against counter-argument

d

Emphasis on policy with the following characteristics:

Clear means/end distinction

Concentration on technical means

Prescription rather than evaluation

Detailed specification of prescription

Prescription operationalised

Balance sheet format of argumentation

Measurability

Use of social science

a

Weakly structured, less integrated, unsystematised

Consistency less of a priority

No overarching or consciously coherent system; descriptive, evaluative, and prescriptive sentences not necessarily related

Many different and unrelated explanations

b

Less recognition of the consequences of particular aims

Distinction between means/end less clear – more emphasis on 'intrinsic means'

c

Eristical development, but not always obvious, and no necessary balance

d

Policy emphasis not necessary

Not always clear means/end distinction

Often fantasy prescription

Often content with evaluation

Prescription often vague

Prescription often vague

No need for economic or political accounting

Qualification and quantification rudimentary

Reliance on folk knowledge (often derived from social science of the past) between the spontaneous expression of his own discourse and the discourse that he is encouraged to adopt by and from others.

The admittedly very general nature and descriptive inadequacy of the account must be excused in the knowledge that my primary purpose is to examine in greater detail what I have described above as specialised political discourse, one of the aims of which is to convince an audience that action has been or is being taken for the public good. The reasons for concentrating my attention at this level are threefold: theoretical, political, and practical.

First, specialised political discourse usually forms part of a major ideological matrix supported by a political organisation. As such, it is not a transient discursive phenomenon, but a long-standing feature of considerable significance in the consciousness of the population and in supporting or undermining the stability of a social formation. Political decisions affecting race relations and, for that matter, the racial complex generally, including the reaction of racial minorities, can be more fully understood and explained by the study of political discourse as ideology.

Furthermore, descriptions of the specific forms dealing with race have invariably been neglected in previous studies where discourse about racial matters has been treated as an immediate reaction to alienated circumstances. As has been repeatedly pointed out, the formulation of specialised political discourse dealing with race often involves the conscious weighing of many factors in the context of already existing ideological formations. Thus, while it might be possible to explain much of general discourse about race in terms of the economic tensions operating on groups of individuals, political discourse must surely be accounted for in terms of the complexities of wielding and maintaining power. Put crudely, explanations for racialist practice are unlikely to satisfy the need for explanations of racist discursive forms.

Second, the idiosyncracy of the discourse I choose to select will be minimised if it also has significance for both the political actor and the groups his decision affects. Political discourse accompanies the political decisions that affect the lives of millions of people and can clearly be seen to be related to action. Almost by definition, it is speech preceding or consequential on action (or inaction) and, as such, acquires a higher status than speech that is not so related. It must be of importance, therefore, to those who seek, directly or indirectly, to maintain or abolish racial injustice.

Third, specialised political discourse is likely to be more formally presented than general discourse, thus facilitating the researcher in his efforts to identify it, to separate it from general discourse, and to develop techniques for its analysis. The circumscription of a topic for study is an important consideration in any research and will depend to some extent on how well the phenomenon, in this case, political discourse, can be separated from its surroundings – from discourse as a whole. To make this task more simple, I have, in this and subsequent chapters, concentrated on the discourse of the two major British political parties, first, by outlining very briefly their general ideological stance, and second, by concentrating on national parliamentary debates on the Immigration and Race Relations Bills. The scope, of course, is enormous but unavoidable if the study is to say anything useful about British discourse dealing with race. It will always be difficult to relate convincingly the general statements of theory to the uncomfortably complex empirical world, but, even at the risk of gross ingenuousness, it is important to make clear the assumed connection between the theory of ideology, on the one hand, and the actual language of current British politicians, on the other. It is not possible in my view to 'operationalise' the concept of ideology, simply by identifying it with political discourse. The identification of a concept with measured data results in reductionism of the concept. 'Ideology' derives its force of meaning not only from some object in the real world that it denotes, but from the complex connotations it has accreted from its use in the many different social theories explaining the relationship between social be- haviour and beliefs. The term 'political discourse' carries few of the connotations of ideology and yet can be used to describe much of the same data.

Only by careful selection of elements from a given political discourse, in which those elements, and the context in which they are uttered, are noted, and conclusions are drawn by the social observer, can the existence of ideology be established. Ideology is a concept that is used to draw attention to various relational characteristics of the raw datum, but cannot, in any strict sense, be constituted by the datum itself, though, for simplicity of expression, an author may not always bother to draw the distinction. This study aims to search for some of the characteristics of ideology in the discourse of the political parties and, in particular, of the British Conservative and Labour Parties viewed against the background of class relations and the black migration to Britain. Inasmuch as a number of those characteristics can be located, aspects of the discourse of the parties may be described as constituting 'justificatory systems' or 'ideologies'. But it should always be remembered that not everything that is said is necessarily ideological, and that party discourse is only ideological inasmuch as it is judged in context to possess ideological attributes.

The discourse under examination here is recognised as belonging typically to the political parties by virtue of the long-term continuity of political theme. Combinations of recognisable 'themes' have endured, with some modification, and with the need for creative application to new events and crises, from the nineteenth century at least. The objective class relations of the time stimulated the growth of political parties representing the interests of classes and class alliances. The actual pursuit of class interest would be obscured by a party justifying its policies as the only possible or plausible course of action for the general benefit of society.

Party 'themes' were developed from, and supported by, a general class discursive milieu which, once systematised by the organic intellectuals of the class, could be spread or superimposed upon a much wider class spectrum. There was competition between party beliefs in the sense that each party strove to persuade the mass of the population of the merits of its policies. In the course of this competition, party beliefs became increasingly systematised into argument and counter-argument, in time, producing opposed justificatory systems. It is in the context of the broad justificatory systems embraced by the Conservative and Labour Parties that political discourse dealing with race has to be examined.

The task remains that of how best to describe the ideological content of the discourse of the two political parties I have chosen to examine. So far, I have loosely referred to political 'themes'. But at this stage, if I am to deal adequately with the contents of Conservative and Labour ideologies, I must develop a descriptive typology of what, in fact, they say and mean. Because ideologies must be successful in accounting for a spectrum of nearly all conceivable events and circumstances, and may be developed originally and unexpectedly to meet most eventualities, the categories employed to describe them must be general in nature.

There is also the danger that the social observer's view of what is thematically significant will differ markedly from that of the political actor. Further, and even more problematically, different political actors within the same party may not agree over what are to be regarded as the most important party themes: politics, as I have argued (Appendix 2) develops eristically, and differences of emphasis are a characteristic of this kind of group discourse. The categories selected are always likely to be 'essentially contested'. Nevertheless, it may be possible to reach some sort of agreement over what themes have, in the past, been, and still are, significant.

One persistent methodological difficulty in attempting to delineate the characteristics of a party ideology is to decide which of the many available discursive elements is to be regarded as typical or representative of its justificatory system. One solution might be to investigate statistically what is said by party voters, and another to concentrate exclusively on the speeches of the party leader. But either course of action poses the questions of who is to be regarded as party spokesman and in what capacity he is to assume that function.

First, because parties are made up atomically of individuals who may make their opinions known on various occasions, and also are composed organically of groups that may speak or pass resolutions collectively, there may be a difference between individual and group expression.

Second, because parties are multifunctional and are organised at local branch, district, constitutency, national, party conference, parliamentary, and government levels, it is not easy to decide which organ represents the party's voice and in what capacity.

Third, because both the social observer and social actor expect to see a structure and pattern within party discourse – and indeed recognise what is typical of a party by the recurrence of a number of themes that supposedly indicate a fairly consistent structure – certain expressions may be held to be representative of the 'real soul' of the party, despite the fact that they are found relatively infrequently when assessed in strict numerical terms. In other words, there is a tendency to select what is typical of party ideology on the basis of preconceived stereotypes, and to neglect evidence that appears to contradict those assumptions, on the grounds that it is *not really* Conservative or Labour.

Fourth, both Conservative and Labour acknowledge the haphazard eclectic manner in which their respective justificatory systems have come into being, and, with somewhat anti-intellectual posturing, unashamedly admit the poverty of theory in the formulation of their principles.

R. J. White (1950), for example, points out that:

> The shape and pattern of Conservative politics have rarely been imposed upon the phenomena of nature, and of human nature, by clever men taking thought. Insofar as Conservatism is a formulated doctrine it is the by-product of real-living, not the fabrication of unimpeded intellect. It has arisen out of nature, out of human nature, like the great spare necessary lines of a landscape seen in the perspective of history.
>
> (In Buck, 1975, p. 175)

Similarly, C. A. R. Crosland, to the question of whether there are socialist first principles, asserts that the British Labour Party was 'not founded on any body of doctrine at all, and has always preserved a marked anti-doctrinal and anti-theoretical bias' (1956, p. 80).

In summary, then, the presentation of what constitutes the essence of a party political ideology is likely to vary because of intra-party eristic (conflict within a party over values, their interpretation, importance, and application), the difficulty of deciding which party official or organ is to be credited with possessing the mainstream party line, preconceived views in the general population of what can be classed as Conservative or Labour, and the haphazard historical development and accretion of discoursive elements. As there is no widely accepted method of solving the problem of which discourse is to be selected as representative, most writers are content to make the selection more or less intuitively. In subsequent chapters, I make use of a range of sources, including manifestos, official policy documents, major political speeches, and, in particular, party conference resolutions and debates concerned with race and immigration. It would, I think, be quite possible to make an entirely different selection, although I am inclined to think that there is some measure of agreement over what sources are of significance and of recurring value for representing party ideology.

The selection of various themes from party political discourse poses further problems. The themes or 'foci' need to be sufficiently numerous to represent accurately all important aspects of the ideological form, yet limited enough to avoid undue complexity. As many of the themes in an ideological complex are, almost by definition, interconnected or hierarchically ordered, the number arrived at must always be a matter of judgment, depending to a large extent on the purpose of the exercise.

As my emphasis throughout has been on the justificatory function served by ideology rather than, for example, on ideology's effect on policy implementation, the themes or 'foci' chosen are probably best described as 'values' because they concentrate on the evaluative, as opposed to the descriptive or prescriptive, content of ideology. A 'value' refers here to the broad heading under which particular evaluative sentences from the selected discourse can be summarised. It is against the background of these values that particular policies towards black people in British society have to be justified to members of the party and to the electorate. Descriptive accounts of events and prescriptions for action may develop independently of the evaluation or, alternatively, may be adopted because of it, but evaluation must take place in the process of justification.

One solution to the difficulties outlined above is to draw up a typology of party values. Ideally, such a typology would have to offer a thorough overview of most of the readily identifiable values that could be abstracted from Conservative and Labour discourse in a variety of contexts, particularly where those values relate to issues of race. In addition, the typology would have to provide a framework against which the respective values of the two main parties could be compared and contrasted.

A fairly high degree of abstraction is required in order to arrive at any simple, comparative typology of this kind. The reality of party discourse is far too complex to be easily reduced to a small number of value headings and, were the values to be formulated, considerable attention would still have to be devoted to explaining the relationship between the value abstractions and the discursive reality they represented. The criticism of the typology must always be that it oversimplifies the reality of discourse. It is for this reason that I have tried to preserve the subtle intricacies of individual responses by quoting extensively. In describing the overall pattern of political discourse, caricature is never easily avoided. A typology, nevertheless, remains a most useful way of classifying the data. I try to support the choice of values with quotations from recognised party classics, but, invariably, the precise formulation of the values and their implications will be open to dispute.

Indeed, the difficulties of developing a typology of values to describe party discourse can never be entirely resolved. Closer inspection reveals that the parties consist of contending factions, each with its separate system of values. There are internal contradictions in the Conservative Party between monetarist, laissez-faire liberalism, and corporatist views, and in the Labour Party between social democratic labourism and socialism. If the proposed typology were elaborated to reflect this complexity, it would begin to lose its heuristic purpose.

Seliger (1976), too, makes an important distinction between the fundamental and operative dimensions of ideology. Political argumentation, he claims, is bifurcated by the need, on the one hand, to maintain 'the centrality of prescriptions based on the commitment to essentially moral principles', and by the need, on the other, 'to devise and justify specific practical measures, and to pronounce on the topical issues of day-to-day politics'. Ideology, therefore, acquires a fundamental dimension 'determining final goals and grand vistas', and an operative dimension consisting of 'the principles which actually underlie policies' (pp. 108–9). The distinction raises questions of how the two dimensions are linked, and of whether it is possible to incorporate both within the typology.

The relationship might be explained in the following way. Party ideologists are able to systematise and refine the values and value hierarchy of a party, by various means, to produce a recognisably 'fundamental' set of first principles. But in the light of existing realities, such as an empty exchequer or hostile electorate, pursuit of first principles is often displaced. Nevertheless, the fundamental values are the raison d'être of the party, and its primary claim to moral consideration.

But when its actions do not appear to accord with its fundamental values, a secondary and supplementary justificatory system is forced into being by the necessity of accounting for the actual, as opposed to the ideal, outcome. In other words, there is a primary justificatory system that deals with ultimate goals, with how the world ideally ought to be, were everything to go as planned, and a secondary justificatory system to account for what the party actually manages to do under less than ideal circumstances. The former can be seen as justification in terms of ends, the latter in terms of means. Put in everyday parlance, it amounts to the difference between aspiration and excuse, between how the social actor thinks the world ought to be, and how he rationalises his behaviour in a world that constrains him. The secondary system invariably attempts to reconcile the actual outcome with the ideal future, by claiming it to be a step in the right direction, as the only way forward in the present limiting circumstances.

Two predictions may be made from this analysis. First, that the more a party is committed to major structural change as the answer to social problems, and the less it achieves in implementing the scale of change considered necessary, the greater will be its need for a two-dimensional justificatory system. Second, the more a party seeks to maintain the status quo, and succeeds in this task, the less will be its need for a dual system of justification. Until recently, therefore, the expectation might be that the Conservatives' essential pragmatism within a fairly static economic environment would allay the need for dualism, while Labour's commitment to a socialism that it never seemed able to achieve would render it more susceptible to a two-fold value system.

Both Conservative and Labour Parties, therefore, have at their disposal two kinds of justificatory discourse. They must first set out their fundamental principles and programmes, and second provide apologetics for the ambiguous actions of their party in attempting to achieve, or in wielding, power, by showing how principles and actions are compatible. The typology offered below cannot easily reflect the complexities introduced by Seliger's distinction, although the difference between word and action and the consequential, secondary justificatory system can be dealt with to some extent in subsequent detailed accounts of the application of party values to matters of race.

Nevertheless, the question may be raised of whether the values offered in the typology are fundamental or operative. The answer must be that they mostly describe the motivating, fundamental dimension of an ideology, which maintains its identity irrespective of the constraining influences of social class and economic and state institutions. Party ideology primarily reflects class aspiration and, only secondarily, class achievement (or lack of it). A justificatory system is concerned first, with optimistically convincing others that an action is right and only, as a last resort, with the defensive business of claiming 'we could do no other'. Although, in practice, the operative dimension might conceivably displace the fundamental, under most circumstances the operative is secondary and arises as a result of trying to uphold the fundamental.

While the claims to fundamental values might be scoffed at by those who are witness to the actual deeds of politicians, the aim of this study is to describe the justificatory forms of political discourse. To persuade another that he is right, a politician always presents his views and deeds in the best possible light. I, in turn, must describe his justificatory system, however great the discrepancy between his word and deed. The operative dimension is required only as a last resort by the embarrassed politician and, although issues of immigration and race relations have once or twice proved mightily embarrassing, the fundamental dimension can still serve to explain the parties' approach to most matters of race.

In abstracting from Conservative and Labour Party discourse, it is probably best to relinquish the position that the resultant values, individually or even collectively, remain party values. The range of values within the two parties, the varying degree of salience with which they are held, and their juxtaposition in contrasting pairs, support the view that they should be construed as a Right-wing/Left-wing frame against which actual examples of party discourse can be compared. Thus, while Conservatism would, on the whole, be congruent with Right-wing values, and Labour views with Left-wing values, an element of overlap might occur. There is no reason to deny that Conservatives, on occasion, favour rationalisation or some form of welfare collectivism, or that Labour embrace an element of nationalism or imperialism, though, in long-term perspective, these values might be deemed out of character. Table 3 sets out the typology of Right- and Left-wing values abstracted from Conservative and Labour discourse.

In drawing up the typology and illustrating the effect that party values have on discourse dealing with a racially defined object, I seek to argue that evaluations of, and facts (including explanations) and prescriptions about, the black presence in Britain are formulated in the light of the long-standing ideological traditions of the two parties, and that their action or inaction on race is justified by recourse to their primary class-based values and derivative secondary values. The justificatory forms affecting race relations are best understood as constituting a minor part of two major class-derived ideologies, the Right-wing orientated of these providing the greatest scope for justification inimicable to black people.

The application of the general value headings provided in the typology to the social phenomenon of black Commonwealth immigration and settlement in Britain helps to explain many aspects of British discourse about race. Responses previously classified as 'racist' or 'anti-racist' can be understood from a political rather than a social psychological perspective, and be seen as a rational extension of a Conservative or Labour world view. They need not be treated as a product of a particular personality type, or sick mind, but as a manifestation of a socially situated ideology that makes sense of the world and guides the behaviour of large numbers of people.

In the chapters that follow, I provide a more detailed outline of

Table 3. *Party values*

Right-wing: commitment to	Left-wing: commitment to
1 Traditionalism and organicism	Rationalisation and structural change (tempered by gradualism)
2 Nationalism	Internationalism – the brotherhood of man
3 Imperialism	Responsible self-government and eventual independence for the colonies
4 Recognition of rank, acceptance of hierarchical arrangements, maintenance of standards	Egalitarianism, implying equality or equality of opportunity
5 Maintenance of the social order and the rule of law	Social justice
6 Rejection of state interference in economic and social life, laissez-faire politics, private ownership	Government intervention in economic and social relations, the mixed economy, social ownership
7 Self-reliant individualism	Welfare collectivism
8 The belief that man is essentially imperfect and that human nature is not easily changed	The belief that man is corrupted by his environment but that he may be moulded and improved by education
9 Opposing 'extremism' of Left and Right, and, in particular, of the traditional enemy, communism	Opposing the traditional enemy, fascism

Conservative and Labour ideologies and try to show how they have affected specialised discourse dealing with racial issues. For the remainder of this chapter, I shall continue to expound the arguments that the two main British political ideologies remain predominantly class orientated, that they cannot aptly be described as 'racial' or 'racist', and that when they do focus on a racial subject, they adopt existing justificatory forms deriving from a traditional class scenario.

The theory of ideological levels developed in the preceding sections enables a distinction to be drawn, in Pareto's terminology, between a 'non-logical' reflex and a 'logical' overlay. These categories allow that, at an ideally conceived, non-logical level, social actors simply experience the social and physical environment, and react spontaneously with it. In transferring to a logical level, the same social actors are able to reflect on their experience and reactions and consciously evaluate them. From a publicly aired evaluation of a common experience and set of reactions, the actors re-examine the context in which they find themselves, and describe it in a way which psychologically supports their evaluation. Non-confirmatory evidence is omitted, and the world is reconstituted in a manner consistent with the evaluation. Thus, the evaluation influences the description which, in turn, fortifies the belief that the evaluation is reasonable. Evaluation of the reaction in terms of its potential for improving a state of affairs judged unacceptable, or maintaining a tolerable status quo, results in the formulation of plans for action: prescriptions about what ought to be done. All this can be represented simply in diagrammatic form (see Figure 5). The important point to note is the – admittedly vaguely formulated – relationship between evaluation and descriptive and prescriptive elements at the logical level.

The model of ideological structure can be elaborated by recognising that, in the construction of an ideological complex able to explain the majority of circumstances in which social actors find themselves, it is necessary to make a *series* of evaluations of different social contexts. At the same time, for ease of comprehension, memorisation, and application, the social actors are likely to employ the two psychological principles of consistency and simplicity, reflected in the tendency to repeat features of description, evaluation, and prescription in the network produced. The isomorphism of its different parts is one of ideology's most notable characteristics. Ideologies seem strongly inclined to develop mono-causal explanations at a descriptive level, common features of evaluation in widely diverse contexts, and universal panaceas as prescription.

On the explanatory dimension, there is also a movement towards self-containment and eventual circularity. Examples can frequently be found of two factors, directly or indirectly related, serving alternatively, or sometimes simultaneously, as both cause and effect of one another.

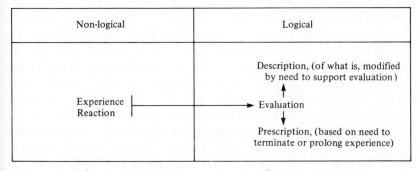

Figure 5. Logical and non-logical levels

Figure 6. Ideological integration

The degree of interconnectedness varies between ideologies. Some ideologies are poorly integrated and inconsistent, others are very tightly knit, and so consistent that, in application to new circumstances, their development is largely predictable. Although there are no satisfactory scales by which to measure what might be termed 'the degree of ideological integration', Conservative and Labour ideologies might intuitively be placed near the middle of a continuum ranging from low levels of integration, exemplified best by general discourse, to high levels, usually caricatured by official Soviet tracts. In order to qualify in the first place as an example of ideology, a particular discourse must demonstrate a certain degree of integration.

One method of classifying ideologies is provided by the recognition that certain kinds of explanation recur more frequently than others. A racial or racist ideology is likely to employ racial characteristics as explanation for a wide range of social phenomena, and to feature race in accompanying evaluation and prescription. Class ideologies are likely to concentrate approvingly or disapprovingly on the hierarchical arrangements in society, in terms of distribution of wealth, ownership, just reward for skills, status, power, and leadership, and the means by which those arrangements might be perpetuated (e.g. law enforcement) or altered (e.g. democratic participation in class struggle).

As an example, a racial ideology might explain a country's economic crisis in terms of the conspiratorial action of some racial group loyal to its own devious ends, rather than to the good of the nation as a whole. Alternatively, it might stress a particular racial group's excessive consumption of resources in comparison with, and at the expense of, others. A Right-wing class ideology, on the other hand, might point instead to the disloyalty and subversive behaviour of employees or trade unionists who demand wage increases from hard-pressed employers seeking to restore the economy and the welfare of the nation. The obvious claim made below is that Conservative and Labour are predominantly class-derived ideologies, and usually account for racial phenomena by utilising existing formulae developed over many years in response to class demands.

In its simplest conception, an ideology provides a verbal association of two categories of phenomena. Leaving aside the precise nature of the association, e.g. whether it be causal, compositional, relational, etc., it is clear that, over time, customary associations or 'constant formulae' come to be established which serve to identify that ideology to a political audience. Thus, the opinions that 'the level of wage settlement is undermining the profitability of British industry' and 'workers are not receiving the level of remuneration they deserve for their productivity agreements' will be recognised, respectively, as constituting, in all probability, examples of Right-wing and Left-wing association. The fact that in any example of ideology a range of associations has long been established is illustrated by the excitement of the political commentators when a politician of significance is felt to have unexpectedly deviated from custom in his utterance.

An established verbal association, or linkage, within an ideological complex is referred to here as a *formula*. Formulae can be thought of as consisting of three parts: the subject, the copula (the linking element) and the predicate. (The choice of terminology from logic is convenient but incidental.) In some ideological formulae, the constituent elements are maintained in traditional form over many years. Where subject, copula, and predicate remain unaltered, the formula may be referred to as a *constant*. Conversely, a *variable formula* is one in which a traditional element is maintained, while one or two other elements are subject to replacement or change. It is also useful to distinguish between two kinds of variable formulae: the *free*, in which the instances of substitution for subject, copula, and predicate do not appear to be limited, and the *restricted* in which, as an empirical fact, there are a noticeably limited number of substitution instances. (The possibility of substitution is not a matter of logic, but of ascertainable empirical fact.) Ideologies, of course, are not static, but the available substitution instances may still be distinguished by making due allowance for the rate of change.

Theoretically, ideologies might have some or all of the following constituents:

(1) centrally placed, traditionally established, constant formulae using race as a causal or evaluative principle
(2) peripherally placed, traditionally established, constant formulae using race as a causal or evaluative principle
(3) traditionally established, variable formulae in which a racial element occurs with noticeable frequency
(4) traditionally established, variable formulae in which a racial substitution instance is one of the many available.

Conservative and Labour ideologies have few traditionally established, constant formulae for dealing with racial issues. Race rarely takes on major causal significance and should it do so, the range of explanation it provides is narrow. Neither has it become frozen within formulae offering no, or few, alternative substitution instances. In both Conservative and Labour ideologies, racial categories have not on the whole been allocated to exclusive positions in the ideological matrix: rather they enter into discourse only when the need to deal with actual racial issues presents itself. At other times, they are scarcely utilised. Nevertheless, Conservative discourse shows a stronger inclination than Labour to use race in certain formulae, and, further, to employ race as one of a handful of restricted variables. Labour, on the other hand deals with racial issues far more pragmatically and, while it has established favoured responses to questions on race, appears more random in the choice it allows.

For each of the value headings mentioned in the typology, I try in the following chapter to show how descriptive, evaluative, and prescriptive expressions, recurring in Conservative and Labour Party circles, are used as formulae for dealing with the selected topics of race relations and immigration. The formulae, derived from a well-tried and trusted ideological matrix, developed to meet a wide range of eventualities, provide the patterns against which racial issues have to be described, interpreted, evaluated, and acted upon. While elements of the formulae have long become fixed by habit and expectation, in most instances the racial substitution instances are far less firmly established. However, there are exceptions.

Some likely examples in Conservative discourse of traditional, constant formulae dealing with race may be found under the value heading of imperialism – although Conservative interest in the imperialist ideal is now very much a thing of the past. But scientific racism, white paternalism, and the importance of white patriality, traces of which still linger in Conservative thought, have, historically, constituted well-established racist formulae in which black people were evaluated as inferior. Most Conservative and Labour discourse about race, however, combines traditional class formulae with racial elements in free, or limited, association.

In the next chapter, the application of party values and more detailed party formulae to British race relations is examined in detail. The argument remains that the two parties' racial policies are nearly always justified along traditional class lines and, whatever the social pressures producing the policies, the policies themselves are invariably presented as conforming in some way with the parties' established values.

5

British political values and race relations

From the mid-1950s, British politicians were confronted with a new and increasingly contentious public issue: the presence in Britain of a conspicuous minority of black people from the Caribbean and the Indian subcontinent. As early as 1949, whites had attacked a black hostel in Deptford, and Reginald Sorenson's vain attempt to introduce a Private Member's Bill in 1950 outlawing discrimination in public places showed early recognition of the conditions that many black people experienced from the moment they arrived. In August 1958, there were racial brawls in Nottingham public houses, and in September, white youths in Notting Hill assaulted black people and damaged their houses. These were only more sensational and overt manifestations of white hostility, the actual dimensions and scale of which are always difficult to decide upon and measure.

Whatever the 'real circumstances', politicians, relying on public support, were forced to take notice of the social issues presented to them through popular means of communication such as the national and local press, radio, and television, and through party organisation. Even so, from the arrival in the late 1940s of the first black people outside of the ports and in any numbers, it took approximately ten years for party officials to recognise the potential political importance of the migration and the white electorate's reactions to it. But, over the next twenty years, their speeches, campaigns, party resolutions, ministerial decisions, and laws made relations between black and white a party political issue in its own right.

Frequently, Members of Parliament were reacting to a series of popularly defined crises, such as the 1961–2 increase in immigration, the Conservative, Peter Griffiths' victory over Patrick Gordon Walker in the 1964 General Election, Enoch Powell's articles and speeches, the possibility in 1968 of a Kenyan Asian immigration, and the arrival in 1972 of 27,000 Ugandan Asians. Sometimes, despite apparent popular and press opposition, ministers actively worked out long-term strategies for implementing the policies which they regarded as necessary – such as the 1968 and 1976 Race Relations Acts.

Black people had come from widely different parts of the Commonwealth to find work in the industrial towns and cities of Britain. The immigrants' skin colour enabled the relatively biologically and culturally homogeneous white British to identify the newcomers and to remain conscious of their presence. Affected by long-standing cultural expectations, some of which derived from the history of Empire, and by their interpretation of the effect that numbers of black immigrants would have on their immediate circumstances, the white population behaved in complex, but predominantly defensive and hostile, ways. The two main white political parties were slowly forced to come to terms with their white electorate.

The novel circumstance of black migration was dealt with by both Conservative and Labour Parties in accordance with their respective long-standing ideological traditions, tempered by the needs of foreign policy and, more importantly, by their recognition and fear of the electorate's apparent hostility towards black people. The Conservatives found it easier to come to terms with the electorate's mood because, on the issue of race, their ideology closely paralleled popular culture and made use of similar justificatory forms. (Indeed, the persistently large Conservative vote, and surveys of beliefs among the working class, indicate that the culture of the mass of the population has never been thoroughly penetrated by socialist thought.) The Labour Party, on the other hand, relied on abstract human notions, such as the brotherhood of man, rather than on a convincing economic class analysis, to justify its early open-door and later cultural pluralist position. At best, this might have appealed to middle-class sentiment, but not to the hard-headed 'economic man' of the working class.

The prospect of widespread racial hostility among their traditional supporters frightened the leadership of the major parties, which both recognised the danger of an Ultra-Right party or pressure group filling the dark political void between the hostile emotional response of the electorate and the initially disinterested policies of the government. The visible black group, and the manner in which it was presented in the media, was beginning to lend greater plausibility to racial explanations for social problems. In order to re-establish electoral support and confidence, to keep a potentially explosive situation under control and to reduce the threat from the Far-Right, both parties moved in a Rightward direction, agreeing to strict control of black immigration and to an informal bipartisan approach to race questions. The move seems to have been undertaken reluctantly: the British political intelligentsia rejected beliefs of racial superiority, and continued to justify their policies in traditional class-political, rather than classical racist terms. In addition, a continuing labour shortage in the early 1960s, together with Commonwealth pressure, played some part in slowing down the Rightward tendency.

The concern in this chapter is to show how mainstream party political values were brought to bear on the issues raised by black migration to Britain. Existing, well-established ideological formulae were employed to provide justification for immigration and race relations policies, partly chosen by, and partly forced upon, the parties in their assessment of the situation. This chapter deals in turn with Conservative and Labour values in the following areas:

(1) The process of change. A comparison is made between Conservative traditionalism and organicism and Labour rationalisation and commitment to structural change.

(2) The nature and significance of nationhood. Conservative nationalism is compared with Labour internationalism, summed up in the slogan 'brotherhood of man'.

(3) The effect of Empire. The rise and fall of Conservative commitment to the British Empire is set against the somewhat ambivalent Labour resolve to guide the colonies to independence.

(4) Class and class mobility. The Conservative Party's satisfaction with existing class relations is compared with the Labour Party's quest for egalitarianism, and the significance for race relations is indicated.

(5) Social justice and social order. The Conservative Party lays great stress on issues of law and order, while the Labour Party shows more concern for social justice. Each produces a distinct pattern of responses in dealing with racial matters.

(6) Laissez-faire versus social ownership. The Conservative Party's rejection of state interference in economic and social life, commitment to laissez-faire politics and private ownership is in marked contrast to the Labour Party's belief in the necessity of government intervention in the economic sphere and the long-term ideal of social ownership of the means of production, distribution, and exchange. Both policy sets have a bearing on approaches to race relations.

(7) Individualism, collectivism, and welfare provision. The Conservative doctrine of self-reliant individualism is compared with Labour Party commitment to collectivism, in regard to the justification of welfare provision for black people.

(8) Concepts of man. The parties' respective approaches to the fundamental nature of mankind affect the way they handle race relations.

(9) Party bogies. Various political figures and organisations come to represent the antitheses of party values. Conservative and Labour Parties seek to distance themselves from their arch-enemies and the various policies with which they are associated, a fact which has significance for race relations.

The general values are described and some evidence offered of their relatively enduring nature. Following this, an attempt is made to show how formulae drawing on these values have been used as justification for and, possibly, as an aid to decision-making in the field of immigration and race relations. Many of the examples are taken from party annual conference reports. The sections that follow offer an impression of the historically enduring nature of two prevailing justificatory systems, and an indication of how they bear on racial matters. They are intended neither as a detailed, all-inclusive history of party policies, nor as a critical comparison of party beliefs with performance in office, nor as a class analysis of party ideologies.

The process of change

The Conservative Party and traditionalism and organicism

The Conservative Party has always seen itself as a party of tradition, believing in the worth of existing social institutions and seeking only to modify them slowly and pragmatically in response to changing circumstances. Lord Hugh Cecil (1912), in restating Burke's contribution to Conservative thought, pointed out that Burke regarded society more as an organism than a mechanism, 'and an organism about which there is much that is mysterious' (p. 48). In accordance with the organic, living nature of society, it behoved politicians to proceed with caution lest they damage the body politic. Change had to be made gradually 'and with as slight a dislocation as possible' (p. 48). Disraeli (1872) saw, as one of Conservatism's great objects, the necessity of maintaining the institutions of the country. L. S. Amery (1945) explained that the Conservative 'is not prepared to place undue reliance on attempts to create a new world order on paper in wishful disregard of the profound differences in national character and ambitions which must impair the efficiency of such a mechanical structure' (in Buck, 1975, pp. 142–3).

The implications for government action and legislation are clear: maintain existing practice and procedure intact as long as they function satisfactorily, make necessary changes by building on past traditions, and interfere with administrative machinery as little as possible, or only to restore the historical status quo disturbed by others. Nowhere is this precept more important than in the economic sphere, where there is strong commitment to the private ownership of the means of production. The

Conservative approach to social and political institutions, says Philip Buck, is to view them 'as the result of a slow and gradual growth of custom, tradition, practice and formal enactment. The stability of state and society is based upon this accumulation of rules and precedents, built up through centuries of experience' (1975, p. 26).

What then should be the role of the Conservative in social legislation such as that aimed at countering racial discrimination? According to Oakeshott (1962, p. 190), 'modification of the rules should always reflect and never impose a change in the activities and beliefs of those who are subject to them, and should never on any occasion be so great as to destroy the ensemble'. In other words, legislation should never precede public opinion, nor interfere unduly with existing practices.

Values of traditionalism and organicism have a considerable effect on Conservative positions on immigration and race relations. On immigration, we should expect commitment – at least initially – to Commonwealth citizens' 'traditional right' of entry to the mother country, and to the honouring of past promises and passports. This would eventually be counterbalanced and undermined by fear of possible changes in white British society caused by the presence of black people and, moreover, of black people with different customs and habits.

A sudden influx of immigrants would be seen as posing a threat to existing social relations and would have to be countered by immigration acts to 'control immigration', to slow down the rate of change, and to give the host community time to 'assimilate', 'absorb', and, perhaps, 'adjust' to the newcomers. There would be strong opposition to 'superior' British institutions being modified to meet the needs of immigrants: if these people were not to be integrated on British terms then, as long as social stability and 'harmony' could be maintained, they would have to live separately, or be encouraged to return 'from whence they came'.

The widespread belief in the superiority of British ways and standards and the threat posed to British traditions through contact with people having 'many merits' but who were 'different' recurred frequently as a justification for immigration control. But immigration control does not provide a solution to the challenge to the British way of life posed by immigrants already settled in Britain. Belief in organicism would seem to dictate that they must be incorporated into the British way of life, in some way or other; ideally, of course, by behaving in exactly the same way as the indigenous British. The 1965 Conservative Conference called not only for firm restrictions on immigration, but for positive and wide-ranging measures for 'the *integration* of existing immigrants in the field of housing, education, employment, and the social services, backed up by the generous resources of the central Government' (my italics).

To the Conservative traditionalist, 'integration' would seem to imply the abandonment by immigrants of all distinctive ethnic languages, institutions, organisations, and cultural practices, and the adoption of the life-style of the British middle stratum. It is only in this way that the traditionalists can be reassured that any challenge immigrants pose to the British way of life has been removed. This interpretation of 'integration' is the thesis to Roy Jenkins's antithesis that it must not be a 'flattening process of assimilation' but 'equal opportunity accompanied by cultural diversity'. The 'atmosphere of mutual tolerance' proposed by Jenkins (1967, p. 267) is scarcely possible if, in Conservative eyes, an immigrant is unable to qualify as a good citizen until he follows British tradition to the letter and conducts himself as an integral part of the body politic. If British institutions are best, then any attempt to modify them constitutes a lowering of standards which must be resisted at all costs.

Two visions – apart from repatriation – are available to the traditionalist and organicist, afraid of the effect of black Commonwealth immigrants on the British way of life and body politic. Immigrants must become culturally indistinguishable from the indigenous British and participate on equal terms within British institutions. Alternatively, they must conduct themselves unobtrusively, and be prevented from influencing British ways, until they decide to 'integrate' on British terms. In this way, the survival of British institutions is guaranteed without concessions being made to foreign influence.

Any concession to non-Christian religions, clothing, and diet is seen as a betrayal of British tradition and 'standards', and attempts to change seemingly minor regulations act as symbolic rallying points for defenders of tradition. The Conservative imperative that British institutions must be maintained and protected from all unnecessary change leads inevitably to a rejection of suggestions that simple modifications might be made for the newcomers. In defence of tradition, even peripheral rules take on symbolic importance. Requests, in defiance of rules on uniform, that Sikhs be allowed to wear turbans to school, or when working on the buses, are seen as undermining standards, as an attack on the British way of life. The mores of a foreign religion take second place to the regulations on uniform of a municipal organisation. Exemption of turbanned Sikhs from the law requiring all motor cyclists to wear crash helmets is regarded as an attack on the law in its entirety and, furthermore, on the principle of equality before it. The Commonwealth immigrant is cast in the role of an iconoclast, of a violator of rules. In common with socialists and criminals, he is credited with having no respect for institutions. Conservative sensitivity becomes even more noticeable when encroachment occurs upon particularly cherished institutions and symbols, such as the family, the police, or the established church.

With regard to anti-discrimination legislation, the traditionalist Conservative might seek to oppose it on a number of counts: it would be an attack on British freedom of speech and association, it would be strongly opposed by the electorate, it would be ineffective and unlikely to make an impression on racial injustice, and it would be an attempt to import American practices which have no basis in British legal traditions. Oakeshott (1962) puts the general Conservative point of view on legislation succinctly, and it helps to provide the kind of justification Conservatives would be likely to offer for the various stances on the Race Relations Acts:

> The Conservative will have nothing to do with innovation
> designed to meet merely hypothetical situations; he will prefer
> to enforce a rule he has got rather than to invent a new one;
> he will think it appropriate to delay a modification of the rules
> until it is clear that the change of circumstances it is designed
> to reflect has come to stay for a while.

The Labour Party and rationalisation and structural change

Attempts within the Labour Party to reconcile socialism's commitment to radical structural change and social democracy's belief in gradual progress towards a fair and rational society, lead inevitably to a diffuse and disparate set of arguments characterised by increasing levels of abstraction and flights of radical rhetoric describing mundane modification of the status quo. Perhaps one reason for the failure of socialism to penetrate popular culture has been the inconsistent message of the Labour Party which fluctuates between fundamental rejection of capitalist first premises and tentative acceptance of suitably modified, highly idealised versions of them.

What has come to be called socialism, in contradistinction to social democracy, advocates an end of the capitalist system, and its class divisions between capitalist and worker, in order to eliminate the economic exploitation of man by man, and to achieve a rationally and humanely run society in which each will contribute according to his ability and receive according to work or need. The socialist recognises that this end is to be achieved by taking into common ownership the means of production, distribution, and exchange, and by ensuring that the state machinery is no longer run for the benefit of the capitalist class. The socialist believes in some kind of *discontinuity* between capitalism and socialism: the capitalist system of ownership with its entrenched economic interests must end before socialism can be achieved, and this is unlikely to occur without an all-out struggle, with or without violence.

Intellectually formulated by Eduard Bernstein in the late nineteenth century, social democracy criticises what it takes to be the cataclysmic nature of Marxian-derived socialism and rejects the idea of irreconcilable class antagonism. A socialist future is still envisaged, but the means by which it is to be attained is through an extension of democratic choice to an electorate whose representatives will gradually shift the balance of the economy in favour of socialism. Capitalism will be modified little by little, until, one day, it will be seen to have metamorphosed into socialism. The social democrat believes in the possibility of a slow, steady socialist advance and *continuity* between the two economic systems.

Whether or not these two strands of thought are logically reconcilable, they are both to be found in uneasy coalition in party resolutions and documents, and in the discourse of Labour politicians. The Labour Party can be said to be committed – if that is not too strong a term – to the principle of structural change if not, as yet, to a programme for its achievement. For example, the definitive Labour Party document, *Let Us Face the Future* (April 1945), which mapped out the post-war reconstruction programme, stated that the Labour Party was a socialist party whose 'ultimate purpose at home is a socialist Commonwealth – free, democratic, efficient, progressive, public spirited – its material resources organised in the service of the people'. But, significantly, it then added: 'socialism cannot come overnight'.

Because of the strong social democratic leanings of many party members – the basic 'economism' of the trade unions, the apparent unpopularity of social policies with the electorate, the opposition of the capitalist press, and many other factors – socialist policies calling for the abolition of the capitalist mode of production have long been omitted from Labour's actual programme when in power.

The alternative policy of maintaining, modifying, and humanising capitalism results in the socialist agenda of common ownership and democratic control being replaced by one of economic rationalisation of existing industrial structures. In addition, the failure to accept the importance of social class analysis and class struggle converts the pursuit of egalitarian social relations into welfarism. The demand for equality is relinquished in favour of the principle of equality of opportunity and a safety net consisting of a national minimum wage and social security payments. Revolutionary activism and urgency of purpose are replaced by quietist gradualism and an acceptance that, far from campaigning to change hearts and minds, the Party should be guided in the name of democracy by existing public opinion.

The overall position was aptly typified by Attlee's personal economic adviser, E. F. M. Durbin in his book *The Politics of Democratic Socialism* (1940). 'It would be difficult to conceive', he wrote, of a more respectable, a more responsible mass movement, than the British Labour Movement today. Extremists of all classes, and particularly intellectuals of the middle class, hate to recognise this historical fact. They struggle to avoid its political implications. But the generalisation remains obstinately true, and any Labour Government that was foolish enough to commit itself to revolutionary action would lose the electoral support upon which it had been formed, would have to fight without an army to lead and would become a sorry company of deluded Jacobins.

The consequences for immigration and race relations are predictable. The Labour socialist ideal is invariably belied by social democratic practice, aimed at maintaining a mixed economy and placating the electorate in order to stay in power. Immigration is controlled in accordance with the demand for labour and/or the racist sentiments expressed by the electorate. Control is justified as an aspect of economic planning. The demand for racial equality is not met by a change in the relations of production and a fundamental redistribution of wealth, but by attempts to increase racial equality of opportunity and to control the 'irrational' workings of the market. In the meantime, the Party continues to voice a confusing and ineffectual rhetoric of racial equality and its commitment to radical measures for alleviating racial oppression. The Labour Right concerns itself with strategies for improving race relations without unduly provoking the electorate. The Labour Left may run the danger of regarding racialist practice as so endemic to capitalism that its remedy must await the coming of the revolution. Nevertheless, the Party is likely to recognise the need for experiment, intervention, and initiative in the area of race relations.

Gaitskell and other Labour MPs opposed the 1962 Commonwealth Immigrants Act, basically on the grounds that it offended against economic rationalisation. Gordon Walker pointed out that the expanding economy created new jobs, 60,000 of which were created between 1955 and 1960. Without importing labour, the service industries (transport and health), so important in the construction of the welfare state, would suffer from shortages. There was, he went on, 'a direct relation between labour demand and immigration' (Hansard, 16 Nov. 1961, p. 710). Gaitskell also believed in the direct relationship between migration and the laws of supply and demand: he argued that 'the movement of immigration is closely related to the movement of unfilled vacancies. If we were to run into a recession we should find the immigration drying up extremely quickly' (Hansard, 16

Nov. 1961, p. 795). It is quite clear that Gaitskell was justifying immigration primarily in terms of the migrants' contribution to economic expansion, i.e. rationalisation, even though the Labour opposition motion was formally worded in terms of the right of free entry, the unity of the Commonwealth, and opposition to racial discrimination. If we accept that social democratic economic rationalisation was likely to remain dominant in this sphere, as it had in others, then it would not be difficult to predict that the Labour Party would be unlikely to oppose control of immigration in a period of economic recession, particularly if other factors such as popular opinion, rendered that course of action expedient.

The cheap labour demanded by the economy in the 1950s was no longer considered as indispensable in the less certain economic climate of the 1960s. The solution was now thought to lie not in making available an adequate supply of labour, but in the mobilisation of scientific research to produce a new technological breakthrough. 'We are redefining and we are restating our socialism', Harold Wilson said, 'in terms of the scientific revolution.' Technical rationalisation was no longer seen simply in terms of steadily expanding the economy by ensuring the necessary ingredients of capital and labour were present. Instead, industry, privately or publicly owned, required the abolition of outdated traditions of production, elitist management and restrictive practices, and merger into efficient units (Harold Wilson, Labour Party Annual Conference Report (hereafter LPACR), 1963, p. 140).

The failure to engage in activist politics generally, and in the politics of race relations in particular, led to the Party's simple acceptance of the electorate's racial animosity. The Party always feared that by pursuing a course that was initially unpopular with the electorate, it would become, in Durbin's words, 'a sorry company of deluded Jacobins' (1940, p. 278). Its acquiescence, in the face of white hostility, to the need to control coloured immigration was well illustrated by both the 1965 White Paper and the passing of the 1968 Immigration Act which subjected to immigration control citizens of the United Kingdom and colonies with United Kingdom passports who had 'no substantial connection' with Britain.

In order to reconcile the racially discriminatory policy of excluding Commonwealth immigrants from Britain with the fundamental socialist principle of equality of treatment for members of all races, a number of rhetorical stratagems were developed, among them the notorious 'balance format'. In February 1965, Crossman noted that 'we have to combine tight immigration controls . . . with a constructive policy for integrating into the community the immigrants who are there already' (1975, Vol. 1, p. 149). The 1965 White Paper spelt out the new dual policy of, on the one hand, controlling the entry of immigrants 'so that it does not outrun Britain's capacity to absorb them', and, on the other, of introducing positive measures designed to 'secure for the immigrants and their children their rightful place in our society'. The racially discriminatory nature of the immigration controls was to be counterbalanced by the Race Relations Acts. By 1968, the Government was able to report to the Labour Party Conference that it had maintained 'a balanced policy by taking a number of steps in the Commonwealth Immigrants Act 1968 to reduce the number of Commonwealth citizens entering the United Kingdom but also introducing increased powers to ensure that immigrants already here are treated in the same way as the indigenous population' (LPACR, 1968, p. 86). The Race Relations Acts could be seen as an ameliorative tactic for excusing the racially discriminatory effect of the immigration controls. The policy was balanced because it combined, in a formula apparently acceptable to the membership as a whole, concessions to Right-wing racial animosity with reaffirmation of socialist commitment to equality of treatment.

The Race Relations Acts might also be understood and explained within the context of rationalisation and structural change. In law, racial discrimination consists of treating another less favourably after having made due allowance for his market position. A person discriminates against another if:

> he applies to that other a requirement or condition which he
> applies or would apply to persons not of the same racial group
> as that other but . . . which *he cannot show to be justifiable*
> irrespective of colour, race, nationality or ethnic or national
> origins of the persons to whom it is applied [my italics].
> (Race Relations Act, 1976)

The Act did not question the already existing economic position of black people, and sought only to remove or lessen the interference of the colour factor in the market mechanism. The Act was not aimed at achieving equality, but of guaranteeing equality of opportunity in the fields of employment, education, and the provision of goods, facilities, services, and premises. This was to be achieved not by mass organisation of the racial minorities or Labour movement exercising pressure from below, but by the due process of law within the courts.

After 1975, there was a marked resurgence and reaffirmation of socialist values in the Party and an accompanying growth of concern for racial equality. New attempts were made to couple theories of the phenomenon of racialism with those of the structure of capitalism and to develop an awareness that racial animosity could only be finally eradicated in the campaign for socialism. Gerry Lerner moved the composite resolution: 'Conference recognises that to end the threat of racialism once and for all requires an end to the system that creates and nurtures it and that the system will use immigrant workers as scapegoats for its inadequacies' (LPACR, 1976, p. 213). At the Conference, socialist fundamentals in the form of a critique of the inevitability of alienation under capitalism were clearly being voiced. The social democratic and socialist strands of Labour thought continued to coexist.

The nature and significance of nationhood

The Conservative Party and nationalism

Political scientists experience great difficulty in defining the multiplexity of ideas contained under the heading 'nationalism'. British nationalism is inclusive of beliefs in the importance of tradition, historical culture, and institutions, but is something far more extensive than these. It is a belief in the entity of the British nation identified through a combination of geographical, racial, linguistic, and cultural criteria. Those who consider themselves members of this entity place considerable importance on its existence and their freedom to decide upon their own nation's affairs without reference to outsiders. Emphasis on nationalism is often accompanied by a fear or dislike of foreigners – those who do not belong to the nation and have no commitment to sustaining it. Loyalty or commitment to the nation is expected of its members, while disloyalty is attributed almost automatically to foreigners, who are regarded as belonging to other nations and, ipso facto, as having other loyalties.

If racial characteristics, membership of kinship lines, or meticulous performance of some cultural activity (the acquisition of which is difficult) are imposed as criteria for membership of the nation, it may be impossible for outsiders to become incorporated in a manner which satisfies the self-appointed guardians of a nation's integrity. The criteria, and enforcement of criteria, for defining nationhood vary according to law, but the law is formulated and interpreted in the context of the prevalent historical and cultural concepts of how the nation is to be identified.

British, or rather English, nationalism,* matured comparatively early in European history. At this stage, lineage, geographical situation, and loyalty to the crown were all distinguishable as criteria for membership of the nation. Richard II's praise of 'this blessed plot' showed that territorial affection loomed large:

> This royal throne of kings, this sceptred isle,
> This earth of majesty, this seat of Mars,

* See Curtis (1968), p. 9.

> This other Eden, demi-paradise,
> This fortress built by Nature for herself . . .
> (Shakespeare, *Richard II*, Act II, Scene I.)

The growth of nationalism was also accompanied by the invention of national myths of racial origin. Poliakov (1974) claims that the English had four great mythologies with which to construct their own myth of origin – the Greco-Roman, the Celtic, the Germanic, and the Hebrew – the last two assuming great importance. He argues that after the Glorious Revolution of 1688, English writers came to regard the constitutional system in Great Britain as the embodiment of liberties derived from Germanic or Gothic sources.

Henry Bolingbroke (1678–1751), statesman and leader of the Tory Party in the reign of Queen Anne, is credited with helping to write:

> Rule, Britannia, rule the waves;
> Britons never will be slaves.

And his *The Idea of a Patriot King* was used to teach George III the principles of kingship. Bolingbroke stressed the traditions of British and Saxon freedom, and admitted 'I feel a secret pride in thinking that I was born a Briton; when I consider that the Romans, those masters of the world, maintained their liberty little more than seven centuries and that Britain which was a free nation above seventeen hundred years ago, is so at this hour' (Snyder, 1964, p. 82).

Edmund Burke, Tory and traditional nationalist par excellence, asserted that, next to the love of parents for their children, 'the strongest instinct, both natural and moral, that exists in man, is the love of his country: – an instinct indeed, which extends even to the brute creation . . . We all know [he continued] that the natal soil has a sweetness in it beyond the harmony of verse. This instinct, I say, that binds all creatures to their country, never becomes inert in us, nor ever suffers us to want in memory of it' (Snyder, 1964, p. 85).

As a creed that reviles theories of internal class division, Conservatism has always placed great value on a unifying nationalism. Arthur Balfour felt that 'no more abominable creed' had ever been preached than that of class war, claiming that Britain's future depended ultimately on 'cooperation, friendliness, mutual good will and service, and all classes working together for one great object' (reprinted in Buck, 1975, p. 128).

Because English nationalism matured early, was long taken for granted, and latterly assumed an imperialist – a 'Greater Britain' – aura, the cultural criteria for deciding on who belonged to the nation were never clearly specified: indeed the criteria changed in accordance with the country's changing relationship with other parts of the world. For example, Charles Wentworth Dilke, writer, traveller, and Liberal MP, gave expression to a highly influential and distinctly racial nationalism in his book *Greater Britain* published in 1869. He conceived of the Anglo-Saxon race conquering the world and eventually displacing the backward coloured peoples. Britain's noble destiny, sustained by an 'instinct of inherited continuity', was also portrayed in the immensely popular work of the imperialist novelist and poet, Rudyard Kipling. By the turn of the century, a concept of British nationalism based on distinctly racial criteria was well established and popularised in the newsprint of, for example, the boys' comics. This was also the golden age of self-congratulatory racial history.

That these ideas were available for use among members of the Conservative Party in the 1920s is well illustrated by Foot (1965) who quotes tellingly from the parliamentary speeches of two Conservative MPs. Mr Charles Crook, in moving a Private Member's Bill for stricter immigration control in 1923, remarked that: 'these four limbs of the race – Saxon, Norman, Dane, and Celt – have given the nation the power that it is today by the mingling of their strength. I am content to maintain our stock as nearly as possible from these four races'. And Mr W. P. C. Greene asserted that 'it is absolutely essential to preserve the purity of our race and to prevent contamination with the riff-raff of Eastern Europe, the stiffs of the Mediterranean, and the dead beats of the world' (11 Feb. 1925, quoted in Foot, 1965, pp. 109–10).

But, despite such earlier trends, the precise nature of British nationhood and the conditions of membership remain ambiguously defined in today's popular culture. It is likely that the requirement of continuity of lineage is reflected in Conservative commitment to their Rhodesian 'kith and kin'. But the actual practice of conferring British citizenship on all those born in Britain – the 'ius soli' – seems to indicate a general acceptance of geographical criteria. The demand that immigrants and others identify with the 'British way of life' draws attention to the importance of cultural tradition in deciding on who is British. Declarations that an applicant is of good character and *loyal* are required of the referees of those applying for citizenship of the United Kingdom and colonies. Most debatable is whether a biological racial criterion is, or ever has been, implicit in the Conservative concept of British nationality. If any generalisation can be made, it would seem that Conservatives place greatest weight on the criterion of loyalty to crown and parliament and to other traditional British institutions. A British citizen is thought of as someone who obeys the law of the land, identifies with his country, and serves it faithfully in times of need – although this is not to say that reference to the British race and to the importance of preserving racial purity cannot occasionally be found.

The effect of Conservative nationalism on questions of race is illustrated by the conception of black people, as an 'alien wedge', which threatens the British way of life. Blacks are thought of as having come from overseas to a place where they do not properly belong. Geographical and cultural, and possibly racial, criteria prevent their being identified as British. They are compared with an army of invasion: they may 'swamp' Britain and irrevocably alter the British way of life. Illegal immigrants are cast in the role of Germans against whom our beaches must be defended. In time 'the black man will have the whip hand over the white' (Powell, 20 Apr. 1968), particularly if his rate of reproduction continues to exceed that of the native British. The British are seen as superior to all foreigners – particularly black foreigners – who have strange habits and customs and lower standards. With an effective Conservative government, the Immigration Acts can keep out the alien horde, dependants can be restricted, and voluntary repatriation encouraged. The Race Relations Acts, however, are seen as aiding the enemy's takeover, as breaking down native defences, and as giving the foreigners privileges over the indigenous white population.

A terrible question is posed by the knowledge that many black children were born in Britain and have no other home: no longer can geographical criteria of exclusion be applied to the new generation, and suggestions that there are cultural and linguistic barriers to nationhood become increasingly less convincing. However, at the present moment, the Conservative is rarely prepared to go further and to countenance an overtly racial concept of nationality.

Conservative nationalism in the field of race is best exemplified in the influential speeches of Enoch Powell before he left the Party to join the United Ulster Unionist Coalition, although he continued to reassert his position, referring, for example, in 1977 to 'enclaves of foreign lands in British cities' (21 Jan. 1977). Powell was concerned to defend his belief in nationalism against an unspecified group of people who 'tell us we must be prepared to contemplate, in fact to welcome, the alteration and alienation of our towns and cities':

> They tell us there is no such thing as our own people and our own country. Indeed there is, and I say it in no mean or arrogant or exclusive spirit. What I know is that we have an identity of our own and that the instinct to preserve that identity, as to defend that territory is one of the deepest and strongest implanted in mankind. I happen also to believe that the instinct is good and that its beneficent effects are not exhausted. (*The Times*, 10 June 1969)

The new and menacing threat to the country's identity arose from the 'foreseeable consequences of a massive but unpremeditated and fortunately in substantial measure, reversible immigration'. Powell presented himself as a latter-day Winston Churchill issuing a clarion call for Britain's defence before the nation completed the work of 'heaping up its own funeral pyre' (*The Sunday Times*, 21 Apr. 1968). He claimed that the future of Britain was as much at risk 'as in the years when Imperial Germany was building dreadnoughts, or Nazism rearming' (speech at Northfield, Birmingham, 13 June 1970). Indeed, the danger was greater because the activity of the invisible fifth column passed unnoticed:

> Race is billed to play a major, perhaps a decisive, part in the battle of Britain whose enemies must have been unable to believe their good fortune as they watched the numbers of West Indians, Africans and Asians concentrated in her major cities mount towards the two million mark, and no diminution of the increase yet in sight.   (*The Observer*, 14 June 1970)

As Winston Churchill recognised, a continuum exists between the lofty defence of the abstraction of nation and the mundane defence of the neighbourhood street. Powell utilised this knowledge in his references to an old lady intimidated by black neighbours and followed by 'wide-grinning piccaninnies'. Indeed, Conservative Party discourse as a whole made great play of the alien threat to homely circumstances. For example, Frank Taylor, at the 1961 Conservative Party Conference, posed the rhetorical question of whether black immigrants could be blamed 'for clubbing together to buy houses, very often over the heads of English residents and thereby, because of overcrowding, driving out the English people and eventually becoming owners of residences in whole streets' (Conservative and Unionist Associations, National Union: Conservative Annual Conference Report (hereafter CACR), 1961, p. 29). Quite apparent are the nationalist themes of the necessity of territorial defence and the threat to the Englishman's freedom of choice.

The questions of nationhood, of national solidarity, and of the national identity of black Britons, are revealed as unresolved Conservative preoccupations.

The Labour Party and internationalism (the brotherhood of man)

In his book, *The Future of Socialism* (1956), C. A. R. Crosland managed to list twelve traditional themes in a summary of socialist doctrines. One source was Christian socialism, which Crosland saw as having a close affinity with Owenism, although the inspiration for Owenism lay in a Benthamite belief in universal happiness, while that of Christian socialism derived from Christian ethics. Both schools, however, held that 'the essential evil was the competitive pursuit of private gain, and the objective [was] a cooperative society of communal ownership in which mutual love and brotherhood would replace the selfish antagonisms inevitably bred by competitive capitalism' (Crosland, 1956, p. 82).

Crosland also isolated the Independent Labour Party tradition, defined by Professor Cole as 'a socialism almost without doctrines . . . a broad movement on behalf of the bottom dog' (quoted in Crosland, 1956, p. 85). According to Crosland, the unique ILP element was not doctrinal or intellectual, but consisted of a 'particularly strong insistence, largely Nonconformist in origin, on the brotherhood of man, on fellowship, service and altruism' (Crosland, 1956, p. 85) that was not only to be found in the domestic context but in relation to the people of other countries. Crosland asserted that the 'internationalist tradition of the Labour Party stems far more from the "international brotherhood of man" appeal of the ILP than from the "workers of the world, unite!" slogan of the Marxists'. 'It is this generous, idealistic, deeply religious emphasis on brotherhood and altruism', he continued, 'which justifies us in identifying the ILP as a separate influence – and one very different in spirit from the Fabian, as may be seen from the contrasted reactions of the two bodies to the Boer war.'

A number of Labour Party traditions, therefore, unite in establishing the 'brotherhood of man' as a commonly recurring value of Labour ideology. The 'brotherhood of man' suggests that the warm friendships and loyalties of close kinship ties should be extended to the universe of human kind.

The slogan may be criticised from a Marxist point of view as 'idealist' in the sense that, at the abstracted level, it can make no reference to the differences of interest that, as a matter of fact, occur between human groups. Other political theorists might question the assumption that there are no important qualitative differences, particularly in industrial societies, between small kinship and larger social groupings. Both criticisms, however, are directed at neglect of the actual political obstacles which are likely to prevent the value being achieved, rather than at the value itself. The Marxist believes that however high-sounding the value, its practical implementarion must take into account the material interests of the respective parties. This is why 'workers of the world unite' differs from 'men must all be brothers', in that the former is related to a theory of common interest in the face of an exploitative enemy. This is only to state the difference of implication of the two prescriptions, but not, of course, to pronounce upon their respective past or future effectiveness, even supposing it were possible for such a thing to be measured.

If the value of the 'brotherhood of man' is intended to affect relations between human beings, however, it must be practically translated and applied. With reference to the Labour Party's incursions into the field of race relations, one criticism has been that the value has kept the Party's conscience intact but has had little effect on policies for the extension of brotherly love to the black neighbour. But, values deriving from, or closely related to, the Christian precept of 'loving one's neighbour' may, like much current Christian ethics, have bearing on personal rather than group behaviour. The Labour Party member may or may not recognise a connection between his decisions in parliament or council chamber and his personal behaviour towards friends, acquaintances, and neighbours. This, of course, is true of politicians of all political persuasions. But the 'brotherhood of man' may become increasingly operative as relationships become more personalised, and, vice versa, 'brotherhood' may be less easily recognised as the relational metaphor is extended to the anonymous multitude, perhaps represented only by statistical data.

Nevertheless, the brotherhood of man is a recurrent theme in Labour Party literature. The famous 1945 document, *Let Us Face the Future*, states clearly that because it is a 'socialist party' the Labour Party 'believes in the brotherhood of man'. The statement of 16 March 1960, from the National Executive Committee (NEC), reaffirming, amplifying, and clarifying party objects, describes the British Labour Party as 'a democratic socialist party', whose 'central idea is the brotherhood of man', and whose purpose is 'to make this ideal a reality everywhere'. Accordingly, it rejects 'discrimination on grounds of race, colour, or creed and holds that men should accord to one another equal consideration and status in recognition of the fundamental dignity of Man' (LPACR, 1960, NEC statement).

But what exactly is meant by the brotherhood and fundamental dignity of man and what political measures have to be taken in furtherance of this value? This question is of particular importance in the light of the Conservative counter-emphasis on nationalism, and of the very logic of national government which is expected to put national interest first. It could also be claimed, for example, that far from contrasting with nationalism, the principle of the 'brotherhood of man' might be extended to encourage co-operation between members of different social classes and consequently undermine the class-based nature of socialist ideology.* Most socialists, however, would understand the brotherhood as extending only to members of the international working class, and as excluding the rich, the capitalists, the exploiters, the militarists, and the anti-democratic

* Herbert Morrison, Minister of Transport in the 1929 Labour Government, gave an indication of this tendency when he said 'I want every business manager to realise that the Labour Government is not their enemy, but that every Minister in this Government wants to take him by the hand, treat him as a man and brother, and help to make his commercial or industrial enterprise more successful than it has been in the past' (*Daily Herald*, 30 June 1929).

elements of the world. Nevertheless, Panitch (1971) has argued that aspects of Labour Party ideology stressing the fundamental unity of society help it to play a nationally integrative role under capitalism. Such a role might detract from the ability to engage in class struggle on behalf of either the British or international working class.

The Labour Party has come under attack both from Left-wing critics who have condemned its class collaborationism and lack of 'international solidarity', and from Right-wingers who have criticised its lack of loyalty to the national interest. But the implications of 'brotherhood of man', though vague, have a significant bearing on Labour justification of policy. This is not to say that commitment to the value is manifest in any obvious way in practice.

At a general level, the Party has sought to suffuse much of its propaganda with the warm glow of compassion to contrast with the Conservatives' ruthless dog-eat-dog philosophy. 'Our appeal is to those who have faith in the capacity and humanity of their fellow men', the 1970 General Election Manifesto asserted, 'and to those who are not solely moved by the search for profit or the hope of personal gain.' More specifically, the internationalist principle is supported by expressions of anti-militarism and of sympathy for developing countries, the poor of the 'third world' and black people from the ex-colonies living in Britain. The politician's commitment to international brotherhood might perhaps be illustrated in his advocacy of policies for increasing overseas aid and improving the treatment of black minorities in Britain.

It is not possible in the context of this study to deal with the subject of overseas aid. Suffice it to say that, in Labour circles, support for overseas aid was frequently regarded as a paradigm test of commitment to international brotherhood, and, further, as many of the recipient countries had black populations, as an example of good race relations.

One area in which Labour supporters often appeal for justificatory purposes to the value of brotherhood is in their expression of opposition to racial prejudice and discrimination. The Party has campaigned for many years against racial injustice and has proved its strength of purpose to its supporters by passing the 1965, 1968, and 1976 Race Relations Acts in the face of vociferous attack from the Right. The value of brotherhood would seem to be avowed in commitment to racial equality, and the themes of brotherhood and racial equality are frequently to be found in close association in Labour discourse.

The apparent suitability of application of a formula mentioning 'brotherhood' (with its associated internationalist connotations), no doubt, stems from the fact that the black worker came from overseas, and was not yet fully accepted as British. In addition, he probably was seen as a standard example of an 'underdog'. Despite Labour worries about the danger to British workers' conditions created by importing foreign labour, both the TUC and the Labour Party, at oratorical level, constantly reiterated the theme of the need for solidarity among workers from different countries.

Reaffirmation of the principle of brotherhood played an important part in the response to the 1968 Powell speeches. R. Burns claimed that 'All we have to do to be a multi-racialist is to believe in the brotherhood of man, the very soul of the socialist movement' (LPACR, 1968, p. 284). S. Gill thought that 'we can easily face Powellism with our honesty of outlook and belief in the brotherhood of man' (LPACR, 1968, p. 285), while Frank Cousins asked the people to unite to stop the exploitation of coloured workers: 'Let us mean it. Let them be our brothers' (LPACR, 1968, p. 286).

The effect of Empire

The Conservative Party and imperialism

Lord Hugh Cecil considered imperialism to be one of the three elements out of which modern Conservatism was formed. He saw it as a way of thinking by which men turned their eyes away from domestic conflict to the part the country as a whole might play in world affairs. He suggested that sometimes this interest originated in fear of foreign aggression and the need for national defence. At other times 'the strong sense of corporate personality which patriotism evokes or expresses . . . seeks to assert itself, to enlarge the sphere of its activity, to guide and control the fate of others' (Cecil, 1912, p. 37).

A plethora of values and policy prescriptions arises out of the close Conservative involvement with Empire, the commitment to which has frequently pulled the party in different directions over questions of race and immigration. Belief in racial superiority or scientific racism arising from empire relations of domination and subordination, paternalism towards the child-like native entrusted to the care of the white man, a view that empire links could best be maintained and fortified by encouraging emigration of white stock, the concept of empire citizenship, the realisation and acceptance of the inevitability of nationalism and independence, and the difficulties of coming to terms with African nationalism in areas of white settlement, are important and closely interrelated themes emerging from Conservative commitment to Empire.

As a result of the division within the Empire between the rulers and ruled, between colonial settlers and 'natives', impetus was given to the development of ideologies of white racial supremacy. The black natives, specifically identified by their racial characteristics, were often regarded as mentally inferior in the fields of technology, science, art, religion, and morals. In the course of the second half of the nineteenth century and early twentieth century, the condition of the native, in relation to the position of the European ruler, was not only rationalised at the level of common sense, but refined by white scholars into a biologically based scientific racism (see Kiernan, 1972; Bolt, 1971; Huttenback, 1976). Groups of men were classified into racial types on the grounds of their physical appearance. Cultural variation and existing power and social relations were then explained in terms of the differential distribution between the racial types of intellectual ability, temperament, moral worth, and aesthetic attraction, etc.

Scientific racism became a central feature of Nazism, and, as a result, was discredited in British intellectual and political circles by 1945. In the 1930s, a number of Conservative politicians openly professed belief in scientific racism, and expressed fascist sympathies (Haxey, 1939), but these views have never been a marked feature of post-war Conservatism at national level, although a faint echo of scientific racism can still be found on the Far-Right of the Party. (For examples see Foot, 1965.) Nevertheless, a strong suspicion lingers that a belief in the differential endowment of the races remains as a folk memory in the breasts of some rank-and-file Conservatives.

It should be pointed out that the distinction between hereditary and environmental factors affecting racial performance is neither made nor understood by large sections of the population. Claims of racial difference and of the inferiority of black standards or ability are frequently presented as a descriptive reflection of reality and no attempt is made to offer explanations for these traits. Nevertheless, with or without a theory of biological racism, whether derived from the work of Count Gobineau (1915) or some other source, a deepseated, unrefined belief in racial difference in performance, and in standards, probably owes its origin to the colonial relationship between white master and black subordinate. This relationship is not confined to the distant past. Much of post-war British colonial history has been concerned with resolving the political difficulties created by the reluctance of white settler minorities to relinquish their power and privileges in the face of black African majorities seeking national independence. The struggle to maintain white domination in Kenya, the Central African Federation (and afterwards in Rhodesia), and South Africa was frequently supported by elements in the Conservative ranks, who identified with their white kinsfolk and British economic interests which they thought would be threatened by 'irresponsible' black nationalism. Anti-democratic stances of this kind would require traditional ideological fortification in the form of belief in the inability, or unreadiness of the 'native African' to control his own affairs. Racial superiority might be deemed either a genetic or a particularly enduring, cultural affair. But whether or not the African might eventually be raised to acceptable British standards, he would continue to need a 'guiding hand' or, in the euphemistic language of the Central African Federation, a 'partnership'.

Opinion varied greatly over the possibilities of civilising the 'primitive peoples' of the Empire, some writers holding to the view that the whole exercise was a waste of time. Others thought, however, that, given time and patience, advancement of the native was possible and desirable. The noble mission of the British was to spread the enlightenment of British civilisation, particularly the advantages of democratic government, to the most humble savage, a duty aptly expressed in Kipling's call to 'take up the White Man's burden'.* 'Our vocation in the world', Lord Hugh Cecil thought, was 'to undertake the government of vast, uncivilised populations and to raise them gradually to a higher level of life' (1912, p. 214), a task that had been partly accomplished in India.

The white man's civilising presence, the need to develop backward nations, the missionaries' vocation to convert the heathen acted as powerful justifications for continued imperial domination. Such ideas deeply penetrated the culture of the British population and survive to the present day.

It was scarcely surprising that many white British manifested a distinctly paternalistic approach to blacks who were seen as needing the generous, but firm, guidance of wiser white counsel. Rejection of such guidance was likely to be interpreted as the thoughtless action of a wayward child. Concern at emergent Commonwealth people's susceptibility to communism and 'irresponsibility' was another symptom of this syndrome.

The Conservative Party's document *Imperial Policy* (1949) stated that the Empire was the supreme achievement of the British people which, if it were to break up, would result in Britain becoming a third-class power unable to feed or defend herself. In the late 1940s, the Conservative Party pledged itself to restore the Empire and Commonwealth to its position as the leader of 'free peoples against the encroachments of world Commun-

---

* From the poem by R. Kipling, *The White Man's Burden*, part of which reads

> Take up the White Man's burden –
> Send forth the best ye breed –
> Go bind your sons to exile
> To serve your captives' need;
> To wait in heavy harness
> On fluttered folk and wild –
> Your new-caught sullen peoples,
> Half-devil and half-child.

ism' by setting up a Commonwealth defence council, by maintaining imperial preference, and by jointly working out a plan for investment, migration, trade, and research.

But by the early 1950s, the Party had been forced to recognise the growth of nationalism in the colonies, and its attendant problems. In his Empire Day address of 1951, Anthony Eden asserted that 'a tide of nationalism has swept over some of the colonies and the demand for constitutional progress will not be appeased with economic food in the shape of national betterment and prosperity'. With goodwill and mutual understanding between races and creeds, and with education and training in the art of government, the colonies could be prepared for independence and Britain would have nothing to fear.

Traditional Commonwealth relations were changing rapidly, as Harold Macmillan publicly acknowledged in his speech to the South African parliament on 3 February 1960 when he talked of the nationalist 'wind of change' blowing throughout Africa. The South African government had no wish to come to terms with black nationalism and was insulted by Macmillan's suggestion that Afrikaner nationalism was simply the first of the African nationalisms to develop. The Sharpeville massacre on 21 March 1960 was followed on 31 May 1961 by the White South African regime declaring itself a republic, and leaving the Commonwealth to maintain its racial policies. Following the example of Ghana in 1957, a spate of African and Caribbean countries prepared for independence.

The 1960 Conservative Party Conference chose to debate not the problems of immigration, but the difficulties of guiding the colonies to self-government. Concern was expressed at the tribulations besetting Conservative kith and kin (who were seen as the representatives of European Christian civilisation in heathen lands) and the unhealthy speed at which the colonies were approaching independence. Ian Macleod, Secretary of State for the Colonies, managed to reconcile differences of opinion in his statement of the Party's four duties: there was a duty to build a society in which men had full rights, a special duty to those 'of our own blood' who had made their home in those territories, a duty to her Majesty's Overseas Civil Service, and a responsibility to the native minorities. How these differences were to be reconciled was not clarified, but the speed of political decolonisation did not slacken. The Conference pledged its support to the Prime Minister and his colleagues 'in their responsible task of guiding the Colonies towards self-government so that legitimate rights are protected and legitimate aspirations fulfilled' (CACR, 1960, p. 12).

Two quotes from the debate on the colonies at the 1960 Conservative Party Conference might be used to illustrate the surviving Conservative pride in Empire and paternalism. Mrs H. M. V. Barrington declared she was sick and tired of the attitude that the colonial record was something of which to be ashamed. On the contrary, 'we can be proud of the part our own people have played in the transformation of our colonies' (CACR, 1960, p. 13). Patrick Wall, MP, claimed that the colonial problem arose not from differences in colour, but from differences in standards. 'What we have to do', he suggested,

> is to work as hard as we can by raising the standards of the black Africans to ensure that we level up and do not take the easy way out by levelling down . . . Progress in Central Africa . . . depends on the maintenance of standards and I believe we owe it, not only to our kith and kin, but to the vast mass of as yet uneducated black Africans for whom we are trustees, to see that the existing standards in Central Africa are not debased.   (CACR, 1960, p. 17)

Similar remarks may be found in Conservative discourse on the future of Southern Rhodesia, now Zimbabwe.

At first, the Conservative Party continued to hold sacred its belief in the traditional freedom of British Commonwealth subjects to come to Britain, although not without some private, if ineffectual, discussion in the Cabinet, as early as 1955, on the possibility of immigration control (see Deakin (1975) for discussion of the delay, intentions, and eventual passage of the Act). Despite Norman Pannell's successful resolution at the 1958 Party Conference opposing unrestricted immigration, 'Social Issues – Some Social Problems' (9 Feb. 1959) reaffirmed the traditional right of the British subject to come to the Mother Country, but asserted that the great majority of coloured immigrants were doing useful work in Britain, were not drawing National Assistance, and were not engaging in criminal behaviour.

The Government's awareness of the political sensitivity of the race question among Commonwealth nations and of the pressure placed on South Africa to leave the Commonwealth may be offered as one reason for its initial reluctance to accept proposals for immigration control. Paul Foot (1965) also mentions an alliance in opposing Commonwealth immigration control between Conservative radicals who recognised the beneficial effect on the economy of immigrant labour, and Conservative traditionalists committed to the greatness and majesty of the British Empire. Not until the 1961 Party Conference, at which a resolution – one of forty – calling on the Government to take action on immigration was passed by a large majority, did R. A. Butler admit that the Government might follow Conference advice. But a number of prominent Conservatives urged the Government and the Party to think again. Nigel Fisher asked whether the problems of immigration were really enough to change 'our whole concept, so important to the Commonwealth, of the principle of free entry of British citizens' (CACR, 1961, p. 28), while Christopher Barr opposed the motion saying 'there are binding Commonwealth agreements: the United Kingdom's word should be its deed' (CACR, 1961, p. 30).

Control in the form of the Commonwealth Immigrants Bill was announced in the Queen's speech in October and the Bill received its second reading in November. As Butler had foreseen, and to the disquiet of what Foot (1965) called 'the traditional right' of the Conservative Party, a number of Commonwealth governments objected not only to the Bill but to the Government's failure to consult them.

Paradoxically, the pragmatic acceptance of nationalism in the Empire which resulted in the colonies achieving political independence from their white colonial masters, and the commitment to the creation of a multi-racial Commonwealth, freed the Conservative Party not only from its imperial mission but from its duty of safeguarding the status of the British subject. *Sans noblesse pas d'obligation.* As 'Empire' began to lose its firm reference to a political reality, so also did the ideological baggage of 'Civis Britannicus Sum'. The justificatory props of Empire were no longer necessary.

However, vestiges of the beliefs outlined in this section survived into the late 1960s and 1970s and required refutation or reassertion as political circumstances demanded. Quintin Hogg felt himself obliged to justify the 1968 Immigration Act by arguing that there was no unqualified right of entry for permanent settlement in other Commonwealth countries. 'Whatever else the Commonwealth bond means', he said, 'there is no evidence that it can be made to mean that.' At the 1969 Conference, Robert Apps remarked that 'The habit of Empire and civis romanus sum die very hard.' Even so, 'we should not shrink from bringing together the laws relating to Commonwealth immigrants and aliens' (1969, p. 93).

Despite the increasingly stringent restrictions on immigration, a reluctant Conservative Party in 1972 was forced to admit the Ugandan Asians. In the face of a Right-wing onslaught, the older imperial justificatory forms were put to work once more. Robert Carr, the Home Secretary, reaffirmed commitment, not to the Ugandan Asians, generally, but to those of them who were United Kingdom passport holders: 'We sought to make sure', he said, 'that no one who had been one of our citizens or protected persons before independence, in the days of the British Empire, should have to suffer the fate of becoming stateless. This was part of our Imperial heritage and our Imperial responsibility. We did do it deliberately and we knew quite well what it was we were doing' (CACR, 1972, p. 78). Later, he took up the imperial refrain again: 'We put a great deal into our Empire and we also took a lot out. We have our imperial heritage and our obligations, and to those we will stick. I know that our party would never forgive a Conservative Government which broke that faith.'

But the forced Ugandan Asian immigration was likely to be the last occasion on which there was a need to express Conservative commitment to the responsibilities of Empire. In reference to the Ugandan immigration, Roy Galley in 1976 said 'We cannot afford grandiose gestures and cries of "Civis Britannicus Sum". We have no debt to our imperial past, a past of which, on balance, we should be proud' (CACR, 1976, p. 41), a faithful reiteration of the now famous remark made in the context of the immigration debate by William Whitelaw: 'The British Empire has now paid its debts' (Leicester, 21 July 1976).

The Labour Party and responsible self-government for the colonies

In a letter to Kautsky dated 12 September 1882, Engels wrote 'You ask me what the English workers think of colonial policy? Exactly the same as they think of politics in general: the same as what the bourgeois think. There is no workers' party here, there are only Conservative and Liberal-radicals: the workers merrily share the feast of England's monopoly of the world market and the colonies' (quoted in Lenin, 1969, p. 143). After quoting Engels approvingly, Lenin (1916) went on to explain how the English colonial monopoly enabled the capitalists to make super-profits out of which they could afford to bribe their own workers in order to create a national alliance between workers and capitalists against other countries: a strategy which reached its logical conclusion in the First World War.

Two main tendencies within the Labour movement were revealed by the war between the imperialist nations for economic advantage. Hyndman's group sided with the other chauvinistic political forces, whereas the Independent Labour Party, headed by MacDonald and Keir Hardy, steadfastly opposed the war. As a result of early ideological inclinations, and the lessons drawn from the war, the Labour Party eventually came to place great emphasis on international peace and goodwill, the end of the exploitation of one nation by another, the policy of granting full autonomy to the white dominions,* and the need to guide colonial peoples, † in time,

* The designation 'dominion' was adopted in 1907 to denote a status different from that of a colony. Full self-government was not achieved until 1919 when Britain relinquished control of foreign policy. The Balfour Formula drawn up as a result of dominion demands at the 1926 Imperial Conference finally defined the dominions as 'autonomous communities within the Empire, equal in status, etc.'.
†'Colonies' is employed loosely to cover all dependencies including colonies, protectorates, and trust territories.

towards self-government and independence within a 'commonwealth of nations'.

But, despite this apparent clarity of principle, reflecting belief in the brotherhood and equality of man, the actual ideological configurations produced by Labour have been extremely complex. Once again, the Labour Party has been faced with an operative dimension on which an actual colonial policy had to be implemented in the face of strong commercial interests: of nationalism and jingoism at home, and of political rivalry and white settler interest abroad. Furthermore, the Empire, being a most heterogeneous grouping, consisting of autonomous white dominions as well as dependencies (including colonies, protectorates and trust territories), generated, over more than half a century, a vast number of disparate political responses.

For the purposes of this study, it is only necessary to draw attention to a limited number of the many strands of thought in the Labour ideology of Empire. I mention only the desire for peace and for peaceful transition to responsible government, the commitment to the 'bottom dog' and the ending of exploitation, and the atmosphere of self-satisfied complacency with regard to political advancement of Empire with accompanying moralistic paternalism. I try to show how orientations developed towards the Empire have application to domestic immigration and race relations.

Labour's heartfelt desire for world peace and equality between nations was illustrated by its dream of world government. Arthur Henderson (1918) recommended a League of Nations for the purpose of preventing war and in order 'to create a common mind in the world, to make the nations conscious of the solidarity of their interests, and to enable them to perceive the world as one'. A number of Labour writers glowingly set out the advantages to world peace and prosperity of a world government.

J. H. Thomas (1920), for example, claimed that the League would be the right medium for 'keeping the industrial balance as well as the political peace of the world' (p. 194). But to do so it would have to become a world parliament with representatives of 'all free peoples' upon it. As long as it was composed only of the victorious nations of the First World War, it would be little better than an alliance. Thomas envisaged his 'League of Peoples' Parliament' as something more than a debating club or advisory committee. It would have power to legislate, and in strong Liberal vein he offers it as the means by which free trade is to be achieved. There is a noteworthy and far from accidental parallel between Labour ideas for co-operation between the different peoples of the world and plans for the development of a 'British Commonwealth of nations'. Both can be seen as a means of restoring the nineteenth-century stability shattered by the Boer and 1914–18 wars.

Labour literature always presented an ideal of world peace and economic co-operation, but invariably neglected to offer a realistic appraisal of the obstacles in the form of national, imperial, and class interests to its achievement. The charge of operative naivety in the formulation of socialist international policy gives an indication of the Labour Government's likely performance in power. When no practical means have been devised for reaching a goal, conservative inertia and class collaboration are likely to establish themselves with accompanying secondary systems of justification. (Nevertheless, the 1924 Labour Government did make moves towards establishing the League of Nations.) With regard to Empire, the Labour Party reaffirmed its opposition to economic exploitation and argued the need to develop economic, educational, and democratic infrastructure for the social advancement of the colonial peoples. Ramsey MacDonald (1907, p. 102) declared that 'the native should be protected from the blighting exploitation of white men's capitalism'. J. H. Thomas (1920) wrote that 'both in regard to Africa and other dependencies, Labour has its principles, and the first one is that there should be no economic exploitation of the native by the white man' (p. 132). The Labour Party would aim at the establishment of native representation upon governing councils with a gradual 'deepening of the responsibilities of government' (p. 134). Eventually, the interests of the dependencies would be supervised by the League of Nations. Labour rule would aim at conditions in which the native took 'his place as a free man in the economic system, utilising for himself the riches of his own country' (p. 134).

The Trade Union Congress of 1925 stated its complete opposition to imperialism and resolved to support the workers in all parts of the British Empire to organise trade unions and political parties to further this interest.

After the experience of the First World War, the Marxist Left laid great emphasis on the immense profits British capitalists could draw from the super-exploitation of the Empire and described the appalling conditions of the colonial populations suffering from disease, starvation, low wages, or forced labour. Strong indignation was expressed over the suppression of trade union organisation and activity in many of the colonies. The rivalry between the imperialist powers for wider colonial markets, sources of raw materials, and opportunities for investment was seen as a constant danger to world peace. As the aims of imperialists were to force down the wages of British workers and to pacify the colonial people's independence movements, the Labour movement had to work for solidarity between British and colonial workers to end all forms of exploitation and to free the colonies from the imperialist yoke. But in the general jingoistic climate of the 1920s, the view of the Left did not prevail.

In contrast, the Labour Right acknowledged the Empire's economic and political potential. Following the 1923 Election, a Labour Commonwealth group was set up with W. S. Royce as chairman, succeeded in June 1924 by George Lansbury. The group decided to hold an Empire – in reality, an inter-dominion – Conference in London on 17 September 1924, at which Lansbury advocated more bulk buying from the Empire, and increased emigration. The Right accepted the need for greater democratic participation in the running of Empire, but recognised the ambiguity of expressions such as 'self-determination' which could describe a wide range of relations with the metropolis.

One popular idea of the process of colonial development was that of 'the ladder of ascent' by which each colony passed through a series of stages, each giving the native leaders slightly more responsibility, until dominion status, i.e. complete self-government, was reached. With a belief that it would take the colonial peoples a long time to achieve the sophistication needed for dominion status – for, after all, the dominions had had the advantage of British culture to begin with – the question of Empire became translated into the question of Dominion.* Influenced by 'greater British nationalism', many Labour thinkers sought to reaffirm the bonds of Empire. Development of the Empire would be to the economic benefit of the metropolis and of the colonies and, as with the dominions, would eventually lead to their closer voluntary incorporation in a world-wide Imperial Union, thus providing an economic justification for the continuation of Empire. Even in 1948, Ernest Bevin was arguing that it was essential that Commonwealth resources should be jointly developed and made available in this way (Hansard, Foreign Affairs debate, 22 Jan. 1948).

The British public and many members of the Labour Party tended to look upon the Empire in a favourable and uncritical light. Whatever the reasons for the existence of Empire, it was argued that the British Government had acquired a moral responsibility towards the colonies that had to be exercised by the provision of good government and the

---

* In reading through a number of Labour speeches on Empire affairs in the 1920s, I was struck by their emphasis on dominion, in preference to colonial, conditions. Of course, this was related in part to the dominions' relatively greater economic importance, yet in all discussion on the merits of Empire, there was a strong tendency to generalise about origins, conditions, processes, and policies, and to neglect the important differences between the white dominions, the areas of white settlement, the Indian subcontinent, and the black colonies. Convincing statements purporting to represent the universal conditions of imperial rule, yet listing only the freedoms enjoyed by a country with dominion status, might obscure the oppressive policies experienced in the black colonies and perform a useful justificatory function. So prevalent was this tendency that Leonard Barnes (1939) felt it necessary to preface his remarks on imperialism by pointing out that he spoke not of the self-government of the dominions, but of the forcible subjection to British rule of India, Ceylon, tropical Africa, the West Indies, and the rest of the so-called dependencies and mandated territories.

maintenance of law and order. Abdication of the powers of government to people incapable of exercising them properly might result in the destruction of property and loss of life. The estimated 400,000 deaths in India and Pakistan after partition could later be used as a reason for condoning prolonged British rule elsewhere.

The most commonly expressed opinion was that although occasional excesses might have besmirched the British record on Empire, it was, on the whole, something of which the country could be proud. If the age of colonisation was bound to come, its British form had been the most humane, and the colonial peoples had benefited greatly from the experience. British imperialism was not oppressive because it sought to raise the standards of subject peoples and prepare them gradually for the independence that was rightfully theirs.

With regard to the Labour concept of colonial imperialism, Creech Jones (1945) probably summed up the more common assessment of the British role when he claimed that 'British control is generally tolerant and easy going and the majority of the people are consequently acquiescent and embarrassingly loyal to Britain' (p. 12). This generally entrenched complacency towards colonial conditions and policy was only to be shaken (if it has as yet been shaken) by the spread of nationalism in the colonies.

But there were British socialists who held a more sceptical view. Bernard Shaw (1928) had pointed out, many years earlier, that the British had always pretended that they were in foreign countries for the good of the inhabitants and not for their own sake. In the long run, however, these pretensions could never be made good because however noble the aspirations of imperialist idealists, capitalist traders were there to make as much profit out of the inhabitants as they could, and for no other purpose. Shaw described the capitalist traders posing as:

> weary Titans shouldering the public work of other nations as a duty imposed on them by Providence; but when the natives, having been duly civilized, declared that they were now quite ready to govern themselves, the capitalists held on to their markets as an eagle holds on to its prey, and, throwing off their apostolic mask, declared their annexations with fire and sword.   (1928, p. 158)

Leonard Barnes (1939), in a Left Book Club edition, wrote that it was essential to understand the Empire as 'fundamentally a class interest', strengthening and consolidating the power and privileges of the groups which were already dominant in the economic and political life of the country. The structure of the Empire, he claimed, constituted 'an immense obstacle to British progress in the only valid meaning of the term – namely the reorganisation of British society in the interests of the unprivileged' (p. 100).

On the fundamental dimension of principle, it was quite obvious that the Labour Party was bifurcated. The Left minority saw the negative effects on Empire and wished to see its exploitative structure demolished as rapidly as possible. A Right majority, neglecting any form of economic analysis, sought to maintain the ideal of an evolutionary process of colonies advancing towards dominion status, with their eventual voluntary participation in some Commonwealth parliament.

In two minds over Empire, the Labour Party never adopted a Leninist economic analysis, nor ever favoured imperial union. It combined commitment to the eventual independence for the colonies with belief in the Englishman's duty to enlighten the uncivilised. It opposed exploitation of colonial people, yet sought to further British economic development of the colonies. And it favoured independence, but independence only under 'responsible' leadership. Labour's confused ideology on colonial peoples evolved against the background of an existing Empire, the absence of a class-based economic analysis of imperial relations, and the acceptance of the moral duty of 'humanely developing' and 'responsibly preparing' the colonies for independence ('trusteeship').

As quotations above from Ramsay MacDonald and J. H. Thomas illustrate, colonial people had to be protected from the worst excesses of capitalist exploitation. This meant, of course, not an end to capitalism in the colonies, but only an amelioration of its harsher effects on vulnerable sections of the population. Furthermore, it was believed that the colonial people needed to be raised from a condition of savagery, albeit noble savagery, to a position in which at some future date they might be permitted to govern themselves wisely. They were frequently seen as innocent and gullible children to be protected from capitalist exploiters and, in what appeared to be the best tradition of libertarian free-school philosophy, they were to be given a degree of latitude in their waywardness.

There was an accompanying danger that when colonial peoples showed reluctance to relinquish their old ways, or idiosyncratically adapted the new ways to their needs, this would be interpreted by Western 'cultural missionaries' as evidence of 'the natives' natural inferiority'. The Westerner was so convinced of the superiority of his way of doing things, that failure to act on his advice was seen by him as stupidity. The thwarted ambition of the paternalist that fell short of producing the results required could quickly generate the need to explain away the perceived deficiency of others in terms of their inherent lack of ability (see Woolf, 1945, p. 93).

Labour's view seemed to be one of a benevolent political paternalism that accepted that the colonial peoples needed some protection from the rigours of capitalism, that they had to be excused for their ignorance of the modern world, and that the British politician's duty, like that of the Christian missionary, was to initiate policies that would enlighten the innocent and bewildered. Essentially, they were considered incapable of conducting their own affairs – until they had reached 'adulthood'.

The Labour Party accepted the need for all peoples to acquire independence and freedom, but acknowledged that this could not be achieved overnight. 'Political and economic domination by one people over another', Creech Jones (1945, p. 12) believed, was 'preposterous today and contrary to all our professions.' According to Leonard Woolf, Secretary to the Labour Party Imperial Advisory Committee, the primary duty of the Colonial Office and of British administrations in Africa was 'to train the native inhabitants in each colony in democratic self-government' so that they could 'take over the administration of their own countries' (Woolf, 1945, p. 94).

Probably, J. R. Clynes (1948) summed up the mood admirably when he claimed that 'the Labour Party did not frown upon tendencies towards independence when others claimed it, and it preferred to let peoples have some practice in the art of self-government to fit themselves for it' (Vol. 1, p. 25). Labour politicians were always 'delighted to know of any advance in colonial peoples' education, social and economic affairs, and greater knowledge in the art of how to govern themselves wisely' (Vol. 1, p. 24). But stress on the need for practice in government might have fortified belief among the British that black colonial peoples were scarcely fitted for the task, that the imperial power had to have the final say in deciding on their readiness for independence, and that external intervention was justified if things went wrong.

All this simply amounted to a rather stifling moralistic paternalism, which, as colonial independence became increasingly inevitable, fitted in well with the prevailing belief that British rule had accomplished its great civilising mission and justice was being done. There was, of course, the countervailing Marxist analysis laying stress on the exploitative and anti-democratic nature of imperialism and the continuity of economic dependence long after the granting of political sovereignty, but this was never a dominant theme in Labour thought. In general, the overall position was aptly served by the formula of 'trusteeship'.

Labour's approach to black immigration and race relations in Britain may have been influenced by its policies towards Empire. The assumption of responsibility towards colonial people abroad was replicated in Labour attitudes towards black workers in Britain.

In the early 1950s, the Labour Party Conference pledged its support for 'the maintenance and development of co-operation in the Commonwealth and its progressive enlargement as a free association of peoples of different race on a footing of complete equality' (LPACR, 1953, p. 150). Recognising the danger to unity of the doctrine of racial superiority in East and Southern Africa, the Labour Party endorsed the view that the essential basis of the Commonwealth had to be equal respect for people of all races, and committed itself towards the progressive elimination of racial discrimination.

In 1958, Hugh Gaitskell, the Party leader, outlined four Commonwealth ideals: the first, belief in democracy and self-government, the second, racial equality, the third, economic co-operation (involving aid from the richer to the poorer countries), and the fourth, non-aggression. In a group of multi-racial states, any idea that one race was superior to another was bound to be unacceptable, and where the principle of racial equality was openly flouted, it caused strain upon the Commonwealth.

Labour's support for the concept of a world-wide multi-racial family was illustrated by its frequent condemnation of apartheid in South Africa as a dangerous and immoral doctrine which set certain races apart as inferior human beings and restricted them to 'a life of servility' (LPACR, 1955, p. 186). Apartheid was incompatible with the British Commonwealth of Nations and a violation of human rights. When parliament debated the withdrawal of South Africa from the Commonwealth in 1961, the Party expressed its total 'abhorrence' of South African policies (Hansard, 22 Mar. 1961).

The strength of commitment to the future development of a multi-racial Commonwealth was demonstrated in the 1958 parliamentary debate on Commonwealth economic problems. Labour speakers claimed that the Conservative Government had gravely damaged the Commonwealth economy. The steep decline in inter-Commonwealth trade was loosening 'the ties which bound our free and equal nations together' and the failure to stabilise commodity prices had impoverished millions of Commonwealth citizens and deprived them of the ability to buy British goods. The Labour Party 'had always maintained that the development of this new, multi-racial, free and equal community bestriding the five continents of the world, was vital to the cause of peace' (Hansard, 2 Feb. 1958; LPACR, 1959, p. 78).

Against the background of this previous, passionate commitment to the multi-racialism of Empire as a foreign policy, it is much easier to understand Labour's moral indignation at the 'bare-faced open racial discrimination' (Gordon Walker, Hansard, 16 Nov. 1961, p. 706) of the 1962 Commonwealth Immigrants Act. In effect, Labour's idealist search for world peace, the brotherhood of man, and its feelings of responsibility for the welfare of colonial peoples had made it the Party of Empire when Empire was on the wane. It remained strongly committed to the propaganda of 'the great multi-racial family of nations'.

It might also be argued that the Labour colonial traditions of benevolent paternalism and of seeking to end the excesses of racial oppression within the framework of capitalist exploitation were perpetuated in subsequent race relations legislation.

Members of the Labour Party sought to outlaw the colour bar not only in Africa, but in Britain. Fenner Brockway, in 1953, attempted to abolish the colour bar by moving a motion opposing 'all discriminatory practices based upon colour throughout the British colonies, protectorates and trusteeship territories' (Hansard, 1 May 1953, p. 2505). After Fenner Brockway had spent ten years campaigning unsuccessfully for a bill outlawing the colour bar to be put on the statute book, Harold Wilson eventually promised him that should a Labour Government come to power, it would adopt his bill (*The Times*, 17 Feb. 1964), a promise repeated in the October 1964 Labour Manifesto.

The first Race Relations Act of 1965 was followed by two more pieces of Labour Party legislation introduced in 1968 and 1976. Significantly, one long-standing criticism of the acts and their resultant institutions of education and enforcement has been their paternalistic philosophy and function. The 1968 Act was justified on the grounds that unless some placatory action was taken the blacks in Britain might become as restless as they were in the cities of the United States.

Downing (1972) claimed that people at the centre of British politics, liberal Tories, Fabians, and Liberals, agreed on the policy that had to be followed: 'But it had to be done *to* the oppressed and not by them, and *without* denting the granite structures which originate poverty and racism in the first place' (p. 329). Other writers drew attention to the paternalistic provisions of the 1968 Act itself. If the Race Relations Board formed the opinion that a coloured worker had not suffered unlawful discrimination, he was not allowed access to the courts himself.

Sivanandan (1976), under the heading 'to domestic neo-colonialism', took the analysis still further. The purpose of the 1968 Act was to educate 'the lesser capitalists in the ways of enlightened capital' (p. 362). With the availability of a new reserve army of labour in the form of European migrant workers, and bearing in mind the social costs of possible racial violence, the state deemed that the exploitation of colonial immigrants through racial discrimination was no longer acceptable. The purpose of the Race Relations Board was to carry that lesson to employers and local oficials, a function reflected in the structure and personnel of the Board and conciliation committees, which were marked 'by the presence of local firms and interests (and token blacks) and the absence of black workers from the factory floor' (p. 362). The Board succeeded in justifying the ways of the state to local and sectional interests and in creating in the process 'a class of coloured collaborators who would in time justify the ways of the state to the blacks' (p. 362).

Without interfering unduly with the existing status quo, yet with an eye on the likelihood of future racial unrest, the Labour Party sought to organise, control, and make decisions on behalf of the black community, to encourage limited reform and the end of overt discrimination, to develop a 'responsible' black middle class and to incorporate a rising and indignant black intelligentsia in various government-sponsored welfare schemes. Thus domestic race relations legislation duplicated many of the effects of colonial policy. It would appear that, in dealings with colonial immigrants, well-worn ideological paths, established in transactions with those same colonies, have been tried yet again, either because they were available and were thought suitable and/or because the economic configurations at home and abroad were sufficiently similar to elicit an identical response.

Class and class mobility

The Conservative Party and recognition of rank, acceptance of hierarchical arrangements, maintenance of standards

As Conservatives are concerned with maintaining tradition and preserving the economic institutions of capitalism, they are also prone to believe in the inevitability of existing class distinctions and in the futility of pursuing the socialist goal of equality. Lord Coleraine (1970) remarked that 'the Conservative no more believes in the possibility of equality than he believes the moon is made of green cheese' (p. 104). But the explanations and justifications offered for the existence of inequality and its universal inevitability vary considerably as also does Conservative opinion on the desirability of alleviating poverty. This might be expected of a party unsure of whether to turn from its nineteenth-century paternalist protectionism, either to the laissez-faire liberal conservatism of Hayek, or to a form of welfare corporatism.

A man's wealth, Lord Hugh Cecil wrote, is acquired by lending his exertions or his possessions, i.e. by selling labour power or risking capital. Where free market forces are allowed to operate, 'Ethics are beside the point; desert is irrelevant; the pecuniary value of exertions is determined by wholly non-ethical economic causes. What economists call "the law of supply and demand" regulates earnings' (1912, p. 124). Similarly, the gains of those who lend their possessions are altogether unrelated to merit. Because, in the eyes of the law, justice does not require that a man be charitable to another, but only that he keep faith with him, there is no commitment on the part of the state to grant relief to the poor. 'Where there is no convention, where there is, that is to say, no implied promise, neglect to help the deserving or the suffering, however cruel or however ungrateful, is not unjust' (p. 175). In other words, the laws of supply and demand decide on the distribution of wealth, and the state should interfere as little as possible in their operation.

An older Conservative view, exemplified by the oft-quoted hymn 'All things bright and beautiful', is that the hierarchical relations between human beings are a reflection of divine ordering. In the late nineteenth and early twentieth centuries, this view was supplemented by various popular theories of elites: some classes were best fitted to rule by virtue of inherited characteristics or superior upbringing. Sir Geoffrey Butler (1914) claimed that the 'vital energy' and 'efficiency of a governing class' consisted in the fact that 'the vast majority of its members have passed through a specialised preparatory training'. To a large extent, the class into which one was born provided the social context in which that training took place. The class system constituted 'a moral and a real necessity' and represented 'the effect of selection by the capacity to govern' (in Buck, 1975, pp. 148–9). Public school and Oxbridge were mere glosses on a well-laid, social-class foundation.

The genetic endowment of social classes and their ability to reproduce themselves effectively were issues raised in the new, nineteenth-century study of eugenics founded in the 1860s by Darwin's cousin, Francis Galton. The word 'eugenics', coined by Galton, in the 1880s, meant 'the science which deals with all influences that improve the inborn qualities of a race; also with those that develop them to the utmost advantage' (1905, p. 35). Before Darwin's *Origin of Species*, it had been generally held that the inherited qualities of a species were fixed, but the new eugenics accepted that the human species was not only changeable, but that there was a moral duty to improve the human stock. 'What Nature does blindly, slowly, and ruthlessly, man may do providently, quickly, and kindly . . . The improvement of our stock seems to me one of the highest objects that we can reasonably attempt' (Galton, 1905, p. 50).

Eugenic arguments became increasingly popular in the early twentieth century and were taken up by many groups, including the campaigners for birth control. The assumptions that various 'higher' human qualities, such as intelligence, were found in greater abundance in the upper social classes, that there was a danger of their being diluted through intermarriage or through the more rapid rates of reproduction among less worthy representatives of human stock were of obvious concern to politicians anxious to preserve the quality of the British way of life, its standards, genetic endowment, and class structure.

Keith Joseph, in 1974, showed that the Galtonian theme, suitably modified by the use of modern sociological categories, was still present in Conservative thinking on social class. Joseph claimed that 'The balance of our population, our human stock is threatened.' The nation was moving 'towards degeneration' for a number of reasons, one of which was that young mothers from unskilled and semi-skilled social backgrounds were giving birth to an undue proportion of the nation's children.

> Many of these girls are unmarried, many are deserted or
> divorced or soon will be. Some are of low intelligence, most of
> low educational attainment. They are unlikely to be able to
> give children the stable emotional background, the consistent
> combination of love and firmness which are more important
> than riches. They are producing problem children, the future
> unmarried mothers, delinquents, denizens of our borstals, sub-
> normal educational establishments, prisons, hostels for drifters.
>
> (*The Observer*, 20 Oct. 1974)*

Conservatives would never crudely claim that there were no able working-class children, but only that fewer able children were to be found within the working class. For this reason, Conservatives would probably support provision for the screening out of working-class children, so that their talent would not be lost to the nation. For example, the provision of a limited number of scholarship places or of similar means of access to a number of the professions would satisfy Conservatives not only that the class system did not waste the nation's human resources, but that the excellence of the middle class was being preserved by its continual recruitment of 'new blood'.

Conservatives are in favour of equality of opportunity in the limited sense of approving of the channels of access to middle and upper strata, providing that the recruitment process does not unduly interfere with the existing social order, that market forces continue to operate, and that no egalitarian measures aimed at standardising environmental influences are undertaken. The Conservative is more than convinced that economic adversity is unlikely to prevent realisation of potential, and that, in the final analysis, 'brains will out'. He feels that the opportunities given to the individual and the freedom of the British way of life guarantee that the truly able will excel. For him, the danger lies in the introduction of regulations furthering egalitarianism by closing down existing avenues of social mobility.

---

* *The Sunday Times* (27 Oct. 1974) examined in detail the inadequacy of Keith Joseph's factual information and pointed out that just under one third of the population of Britain came from families where the husband was engaged in unskilled or semi-skilled work.

The Conservative's belief in the existence in Britain of a fair degree of equality of opportunity, makes him appear unsympathetic towards the complaints of those who claim they have unfairly been denied the facilities to better themselves. He feels that, with the necessary persistence and single-mindedness, immigrants could succeed within the present opportunity structure. The fact that they have failed is a sign to him that they are insufficiently prepared or simply unfit to enter the ranks of higher social strata. It is not the class system that is at fault, but the calibre of the lower orders. To defend standards, class barriers and exclusive practices need to be defended at all costs against pressure from the swelling numbers of the 'lumpen' and from socialist iconoclasts.

Conservative approaches to inequality and social class manifest themselves in a number of ways in the field of race relations. Where black immigration is concerned, it is sometimes felt that the social hierarchy will be undermined by the number of black people entering the country. They are thought of as adding substantially, through immigration and their higher rates of reproduction, to the lower social classes, with the overall effect of lowering standards of health, hygiene, morals, education, and accommodation. Poor standards of attainment in schools with a high proportion of black pupils are blamed on their lower ability or IQ. Also blacks alter what is deemed the just order of priorities in the allocation of scarce resources.

Justification in terms of the preservation of the social hierarchy, as with other Conservative values, may operate in the opposite direction. The status quo can be threatened not only by the numerical extension of the lower orders but by a shortage of their particular kind of labour power. The fear of numbers is counterbalanced by the need for menial workers, aptly expressed by Christopher Barr's claim that 'we need someone to sweep the factory floors' (CACR, 1961, p. 29). Alternatively, continued immigration may be justified by pointing out that particular immigrants do not belong to the lower social strata. 'We are told', Mrs M. Hogarth said, 'that these Asian people are educated and are skilled' (CACR, 1972, p. 74), while Councillor Robert Atkins asserted that 'These people from Uganda are independent, educated and, for the most part, professional – the very stuff of which Tory votes are made' (CACR, 1972, p. 79). Much more frequently, however, black immigrants are associated with the lowest and least socially useful (if not wholly parasitical) stratum of society, and the rate at which they 'breed' in comparison with white stock is a cause for grave concern (see Enoch Powell, 1972).

With regard to anti-discrimination legislation, Conservatives are often inclined to reinterpret the systematic deprivation of the human rights of black people in terms of a justified inequality of treatment arising from blacks' alleged lower standards of education, hygiene, or moral behaviour. For example, it is sometimes thought right that blacks be excluded from certain kinds of housing in much the same way as it would be right to exclude tramps, alcoholics, pimps, or prostitutes. This is not seen as race prejudice, but as a correct assessment of blacks' social status and likely behaviour.

Arising from this interpretation, the Race Relations Acts are regarded as a socialist measure aimed at reducing what, in Conservative eyes, are legitimate or inevitable differences of treatment, in an effort to achieve an unwarranted equality. The Race Relations Bill 'is concerned solely and exclusively with the intention to achieve social equality' (Hansard, 23 Apr. 1968, p. 102), claimed Ronald Bell. In a society deemed legitimately inegalitarian, such measures give black people more than their just deserts. 'The 1968 Race Relations Bill', K. G. Reeves asserted, 'will create a privileged and protected minority' (CACR, 1968, p. 65).

The most notorious exponent of the position was Enoch Powell who, while agreeing with Edward Heath that there had to be equality before the law, pointed out that this 'does not mean that the immigrant and his descendants should be elevated into a privileged or special class' (Birmingham, 20 Apr. 1968).

A more fundamental belief in the fairness of market mechanisms in allocating rewards probably lies behind much of Conservative scepticism about state interference in economic relations between the races. It is believed that blacks are discriminated against, not so much because they are black, but because, for whatever reason, they are inadequate in their market behaviour. If they had ability, opportunities would be there for them to make use of. Their alleged inability to make use of the opportunities extended to them is taken as confirmation of their poor mental calibre.

The Labour Party and egalitarianism (implying equality or equality of opportunity)

'The central socialist ideal is equality' argued Hugh Gaitskell, leader of the Labour Party. He explained that he did not mean by this identical incomes or uniform habits and tastes, but a classless society in which the relations between all people were similar to those existing within one social class: a society 'in which though there are differences between individuals, there are no feelings or attitudes of superiority and inferiority between groups . . . one in which though people develop differently, there is equal opportunity for all to develop' ('Public ownership and equality', in *Socialist Commentary*, June 1955, reproduced in Bealey, 1970, p. 198).

The continuous tension between the socialist and social democratic forces within the Party is reflected in its ambiguous position on the principle of equality. Gaitskell, for example, in explaining what he had in mind by equality, mentioned on the one hand a future of objective egalitarianism in a classless society, and on the other the possibility of a subjective assumption of egalitarianism in a society that operated on the principle of equality of opportunity: and at the same time, his audience was reassured of his commitment to individualism.

Tawney (1964) described how the inequalities of the old regime in Europe had been unacceptable because they resulted not from differences of personal capacity, but from social and political favouritism. In contrast, the inequalities of industrial society were seen as the expression of individual achievement or failure to achieve, and were also economically beneficial for they acted as an incentive to work. It was widely believed that ability could be fully realised in the unbounded field of economic opportunity providing the individual set his mind to the task. If, in the process, inequality arose, it was attributed not to the arbitrary nature of a divinely ordained class system, but to the great differences in personal quality that existed within the population. Thus, economic inequality was explained as the necessary consequence of legal equality and economic liberty. But such bourgeois reasoning could not readily satisfy those sections of the population who experienced the narrow circumscription of their lives and the brunt of capitalist economic exploitation. 'Most social systems', Tawney claimed, 'need a lightning conductor. The formula which supplies it to our own is equality of opportunity' (1964, p. 103).

The doctrine of equality of opportunity has both a descriptive and prescriptive form. It may be used to claim in a self-satisfied, Conservative fashion that individuals all have an equal chance of making use of their abilities to achieve the most desired values of a given society, or, alternatively, in a discontented Labour mode, that individuals must have such chances made available to them. The Labour Party has embraced the view that the general life-style of the working class in the areas of employment, education, housing, and health, must be substantially improved to guarantee to it the same opportunities as other classes.

But, as Tawney pointed out, equality of opportunity obtained 'only insofar as each member of a community, whatever his birth, or occupation, or social position, possesses in fact, and not merely in form, equal chances of using to the full his natural endowments of physique, of character, and of intelligence' (p. 104). As long as differences in social environment have a telling effect on personal development, equality of opportunity is unrealisable. Shaw (1928, pp. 93–4) put it more graphically: 'many people who call themselves socialists [will tell you] what they want . . . is equality of opportunity, by which I suppose they mean that Capitalism will not matter if everyone has an equal opportunity of becoming a Capitalist, though how that equality of opportunity can be established without equality of income they cannot explain'.

While accepting the value of equality of opportunity, the socialist critique focuses upon the impossibility of achieving greater self-realisation without greater actual social equality. The insistence on the necessity of developing human potentiality to the full can be used to justify the provision of a limited number of opportunities to the few at the expense of the many who may, as a result, be deprived of the elementary requirements of civilisation and remain incapable of scaling the ladder of success. The socialist believes not simply in an equality of opportunity that enables a few competitive individuals to excel over others and to be rewarded by riches or fame, but in a greater measure of collective equality that increases the social well-being of the whole community. Where socialists are likely to disagree is over how this is to be achieved.

The social democratic wing of the Labour Party acts as if institutions under capitalism can be modified in a piece-meal way to achieve a much fairer society. If equality of opportunity is ensured, it is argued, members of the working class may rise into positions previously monopolised by the bourgeoisie, thus helping to erase class privilege and the social disadvantage and conflict that accompany it. The comprehensive provision of housing, education, and health facilities will reduce the differences in life chances between social classes to such an extent that equality of opportunity will prevail. People will then be able to move easily from social class to social class in a manner that makes obsolete traditional theories of class conflict.

'British socialists', C. R. Attlee (1937) claimed, 'have always recognised the conflict between classes but have not generally adopted the class war as a theory of society.' Instead, they have concentrated on providing a safety net of welfare provision in an endeavour to abolish debilitating poverty and to guarantee equality of opportunity. The socialist principle of equality, it was implied, would come about gradually as institutional reforms ensured increasingly equal access to jobs, political positions, and social resources. In the words of the 1970 General Election Manifesto, the Labour Party believed:

> that all people are entitled to be treated as equals: that women should have the same opportunities and rewards as men. We insist, too, that society should not discriminate against minorities on grounds of religion or race or colour: that all should have equal protection under the law and equal opportunity for advancement in and service to the community.

In contradistinction to the social democratic wing of the Party, the socialist might argue that in a capitalist market economy, the pursuit of equality of opportunity, as an alternative to a commitment to equality per se, would have the effect of intensifying individual competition and legitimating class differences by ensuring that the particularly able members of the lower placed strata were upwardly socially mobile. Far from destroying the bastions of privilege built on the basis of the private ownership of the means of production, the quest for equality of opportunity could lead to the acceptance of class exploitation and class differences (by presenting the possibility of individual, rather than collective, advancement).

With the social democratic tendency to the fore, the two approaches to the value of equality help to explain some aspects of Labour Party justification of immigration and race relations policies. Great play is made of the necessity of treating black and white equally and of ensuring equality of opportunity in the process of migration and in accommodation, employment, and education. In commenting on the 1965 White Paper (Cmnd. 2739), the Labour NEC Report (LPACR, 1965, p. 80) emphatically asserted that it was 'a cardinal principle of Government policy that Commonwealth immigrants should have exactly the same rights and responsibilities as any other citizens'.

At face, discrimination on grounds of colour offends against the principle of equality of opportunity, and the Race Relations Acts can be seen as attempts to ensure that equality of opportunity is extended to black people. In his speech to the voluntary liaison committees of the National Committee for Commonwealth Immigrants, Roy Jenkins (1967) high-lighted equal opportunity in his definition of 'integration' and went on to stress the importance of satisfying the second generation of 'coloured Britons' who were looking for the same opportunities as the rest of the population. 'The more talented ones', he said, would have 'full, normal expectations for professional, for white collar, for scientific and technological jobs' and vast trouble would accrue if these expectations were disappointed (23 May 1966).

The Race Relations Acts' immediate object was not the achievement of equality between black and white, but the extension of equal opportunity to black people to whom it had previously been denied. The more naive social democrats thought that, by legislating in favour of equal opportunity, obstacles to black advancement might be removed and that, in time, black people might become evenly distributed among the social classes. But, in a labour market in which black people had been introduced to fill jobs that the white labour force was unable or unwilling to take, legal equality could not guarantee economic equality. There were, Alex Lyon acknowledged, 'two parts to solving the problem of ensuring satisfactory race relations in Britain'. One was to 'eliminate racial discrimination', the other to 'eliminate racial disadvantage' (Hansard, 4 Mar. 1976, p. 1667). Recognising the already existing de facto inequality of black people in Britain, the Labour Party responded in the manner in which it had been accustomed to dealing with inequality among the urban poor. It tried to find ways of directing welfare benefits towards the newly discovered class of black 'socially deprived'.

The scene had already been set by a series of well-publicised reports produced by Government Commissions of Enquiry into housing, education, and the social services. For example, the 1965 Milner Holland Report had called for a comprehensive attack on areas of bad housing; the 1966 Plowden Report, for extra resources to be channelled to schools in deprived areas; and the 1968 Seebohm Report, for the designation of areas of special need. The idea that comparatively minor geographical areas of social deprivation could be identified and treated amelioratively was common to them all. The terms 'social deprivation' or 'social disadvantage' adequately reflected the underlying assumption of a minimum living standard, below which a welfare safety net had to be extended and only at and above which equality of opportunity was possible.

In 1968, the Labour Government embarked on an Urban Aid Programme of expenditure on housing, education, health, and welfare in areas of special social need. These areas were identified by the stigma of 'multiple deprivation', revealed collectively by poor and overcrowded housing, above average family size, unemployment, a high proportion of children in trouble or in care and, significantly, 'a substantial degree of immigrant settlement' (*Urban Programme Circular*, No. 1, Oct. 1968). Two other area-based schemes were also set up, both including 'immigrant problems' within their terms of reference: the national programme of Educational Priority Areas, and the National Community Development Project. The special difficulties of the amorphous black population were conveniently subsumed into the general programme of welfare provision in housing, education, health, and other facilities. The planners reduced poverty to manageable proportions by agreeing to confine measures to deal with it to small geographically defined areas.

In seeking to extend welfare facilities, the Labour Left and Right were united in the pursuit of equality and equality of opportunity, but the Left was still able to criticise the Right's failure to recognise the endemic nature of inequality under capitalism. The explanation of inequality in terms of 'social deprivation', and the attempts to eradicate that deprivation by compensatory programmes, ignored the wider structural imperatives and probably encouraged the belief that personal deficiencies were responsible for poverty. (The fact that the very number and concentration of black people living in an area was seen as a factor which qualified that area for welfare provision only perpetuated the view that it was black people themselves who constituted the problem.) As Tawney recognised, equality of opportunity depended not only upon 'an open road, but upon an equal start' (1964, p. 106), which, as a result of competition between unequals in the Labour market, did not exist. Black people had never had an equal start in Britain.

Social justice and the social order

The Conservative Party and the maintenance of social order and the rule of law

Conservatives have always emphasised that the successful working of society depends, above all, on each individual performing his duties in accordance with the law of the land. As Burke (1910, p. 57) put it, 'society requires not only that the passions of individuals should be subjected, but that even in the mass and body, as well as in the individuals, the inclinations of men should frequently be thwarted, their will controlled, and their passions brought into subjection. This can only be done *by a power out of* themselves.'

The rule of law is treated as a fundamental basis of British society stretching back at least as far as Magna Carta. Within the limits of the law the basic British freedoms are made secure. Those who offend against the law are seen as undermining the social fabric and contributing to the state of anarchy, best exemplified, in Burke's opinion, by the French revolution. In Conservative thought, law is nearly always coupled with order, indicating the perceived relationship between a stable set of social relations and the legal bonds that guarantee their continuity. The existing just social order is maintained by the rule of law, the socialist antithesis of which is the conception of an unjust class society supported by 'class laws'.

It would not be difficult to show, with numerous examples, how important the ideas of the rule of law, and respect for law and order, have been to generations of Conservative thinkers, and how, at different periods, they have responded to what they have perceived to be attacks on the social fabric. One of Churchill's main objectives for Conservatism was 'to uphold law and order and impartial justice administered by courts free from interference or pressure on the part of the Executive' (Conservative and Unionist Central Office, *The Conservative Approach*, 'The Faith We Hold', May 1949, p. 1), thus combining the tradition of respect for the law with the principle of a minimum of state interference. If maintenance of the present law assures the continuity of the status quo, and there is a strong desire for things to be left as they are, then it is clearly best that the executive arm of government does not interfere with the law. According to L. S. Amery, 'the main foundation of British freedom is what is known as the "reign of law", that is, of the equal submission of all, executive or ordinary citizens, to the same laws' (in Buck, 1975, pp. 144–5).

In recent years, Conservatives have been much concerned with upholding the rule of law against the various elements they felt were working – consciously or otherwise – for its destruction. In 1970, the Conservative Election programme stated that a '*prime duty* of government' (my italics) was the protection of the individual citizen from 'the serious rise in crime and violence' (Election Manifesto, 1970, p. 26). Fanned by constant press reports of crime to property and persons, the fears of many voters for their safety were harnessed to the traditional value of respect for law. Again, in 1979, the Conservative Manifesto stated that 'the most disturbing threat to our freedom and security is the growing disrespect for the rule of law . . . respect for the rule of law is the basis of a free and civilised life. We will restore it, re-establishing the supremacy of Parliament and giving the right priority to the fight against crime.'

To ensure the effectiveness of 'the fight against crime', the police were to receive better pay and conditions, greater attention would be paid to crime detection and prevention, and violent criminals and thugs were to be given 'really tough sentences'. As the bulwark of law enforcement, the institution of the police force is particularly sacred to Conservatives and any criticism of the police is looked upon, not only with disbelief, but as a dangerous attack upon the stability of the country itself. He who fails to give his unconditional support to the police is thought to be against them, and on the side of the criminal element.

Respect for law and order, then, is a central and long-standing tenet of Conservative thought, and the Conservative makes it his business to be on the look out for those subversive forces engaging in crime, industrial action, political sabotage, or other unacceptable behaviour, and intent on undermining the existing social order.

As with the other Conservative values, the preoccupation with law and order has had a marked effect upon the justificatory forms and policies pursued by the Party in the field of race relations. There is a heavy emphasis on the illegal aspects of black behaviour, which from being a subsidiary or side issue is elevated into the main political concern.

Prohibition on the entry of immigrants who have a criminal record and deportation of those who commit crimes is placed high on the political agenda. Norman Pannell's resolution, carried by a substantial majority of Conference delegates in 1958, contained the suggestion that 'those immigrants who are convicted of serious criminal offences should be subject to deportation' (CACR, 1958, p. 149). Pannell went into considerable detail about the 'undesirable elements' among Commonwealth immigrants, illustrating his point by reference to convictions for living on immoral earnings. He believed 'they should all be deported'.

By 1968, Conservatives had begun to recognise a new threat posed by blacks to law and order: the 'problem of illegal immigration'. A statement issued by the Shadow Cabinet (21 Feb. 1968) demanded a mandatory entry certificate procedure for non-voucher holders so that credentials could be checked in the country of origin, and the establishment of proper machinery for tracing the identity and locality of immigrants during the whole period before they could acquire United Kingdom citizenship.

Another significant law and order issue related to the black presence was that of urban violence, seen as a massive threat to a traditional law-abiding public. In August 1958, there were fights of a racial nature in Nottingham public houses and in September, white youths attacked black people and their property in Notting Hill. Although the perpetrators of these incidents were white, the distinctive causal factor, isolated by the media, was race. As the new addition to the situation, the recent black immigration might easily be blamed for the violence.

Ten years later, in 1968, by a curious stroke of fate, the announcement of plans for a new Race Relations Bill coincided with Martin Luther King's funeral which was marked by looting, arson, and stone throwing in Baltimore, Pittsburgh, Cincinatti, and other American towns. Inevitably, the press and politicians presented the Bill as a means of ensuring that the 'black versus white agony now shaking America doesn't happen here'. It was, of course, against this Bill that Powell's speech on April 20 was directed. Powell saw the Bill as 'throwing a match into gunpowder', a result many thought he himself had come near to achieving at the time of his dismissal by Edward Heath from the Shadow Cabinet. Quintin Hogg reported that the Conservative Shadow Cabinet was split three ways over the Bill. As parliamentary spokesman, he himself was concerned to re-establish party unity and to avoid conflict between the government and opposition, which might lead to bitterness and 'a threat to public order on a scale quite incommensurate with the value or demerits of the legislation as such' (Hailsham, 1975, p. 231).

The association between urban violence and the black presence soon came to be well established. The news presentation focused in the main on two issues: on the crimes of 'mugging' and on the danger of race riot conceived as occurring on the lines of the American experience, although the civil disturbances of the last ten years in Britain have had little in common with the US situation. Among politicians of the Right who offered any political analysis or policy recommendation, the inner-city deprivation thesis, coupled with a tautologous breakdown of law-and-order account was popular in the late 1960s and early 1970s, to be replaced in the late

1970s, among Conservative circles, by explanations in terms of extremist exploitation of the race issue.

The build-up of mugging as an exemplar of the breakdown of law and order is well documented in Stuart Hall *et al.*'s *Policing the Crisis* (1978), a book which grew from the campaign on behalf of three youths, of whom one, Paul Storey, a fifteen-year-old Handsworth youth, was given two concurrent sentences of twenty years for assault and robbery. (See Paul, Jimmy and Mustafa Support Committee, 1973.) The growing concept of mugging as a black crime is well illustrated by Enoch Powell's reference to it as 'racial' (in a speech at Cambridge, April 1976) and by his suggestion in an interview about the black population, that British people no longer dared 'to step out of their front doors after dark because thugs will steal their wallets' (*New Statesman*, 13 Oct. 1978).

One Conservative position at present (1979) in the ascendancy, is to argue for better detection of crime, stricter enforcement of the law, and heavier punishment. In a phone-in programme in November 1978, Mrs Thatcher called for greater emphasis to be placed on the punishment of young criminals. She was tired of being told that it was not the youngsters' fault that they were in trouble and that society was to blame. 'Instead of handing the problem over to social workers, we have got to provide the proper detention centres.' The police force would have to be strengthened and tougher detention sentences introduced (27 Nov. 1978). For William Whitelaw, Conservative Opposition Spokesman on Home Affairs, 'punishment' would be a Conservative Government watchword. Speaking in Solihull, Whitelaw said that, unless due regard was paid to the principle of maintaining the sanction of discipline, 'the very boundaries which separate order from disorder, discipline from indiscipline, and lawful from unlawful behaviour, would inevitably be eroded' (23 Mar. 1979; *Express and Star*, 24 Mar. 1979).

These policies are to be directed against all who are guilty of undermining the law, but if black people are thought of as law breakers, or are forced to assume the role of law breakers, a role which in the case of illegal immigration, mugging, and various civil disturbances, the press has indeed cast them in, then the Conservative pressure to preserve law and order may fall disproportionately upon them. A Conservative concerned with law and order and its converse, crime, may regard blacks as undesirable – not solely because they are black, but because he assumes, albeit falsely, that they are more prone to criminal activity. In addition, however, the Conservative may be anxious to uphold the law as it stands and to oppose any violence or illegal behaviour directed against black people, individually or collectively. Even though he may be unenthusiastic about the presence of blacks in Britain and be committed to strict control of immigration and voluntary repatriation, he is likely to believe that, irrespective of colour, all people should receive equal treatment before the law. And, despite evidence to the contrary, as a fervent believer in British justice, he is likely to maintain that they always receive it.

The Labour Party and social justice

Rawls (1979), in attempting to establish a close association between equality and social justice, expresses his general conception of justice in the following simple way before going on to elaborate his principles:

> All social values – liberty and opportunity, income and wealth and the bases of self-respect – are to be distributed equally unless an unequal distribution of any, or all, of these values is to everyone's advantage. Injustice, then, is simply inequalities that are not to the benefit of all. Of course, this conception is extremely vague and requires interpretation.
>
> (p. 62)

This may describe the underlying moral value or justificatory principle of justice, but leaves unanswered the way it is to be practically implemented. A great deal must turn on beliefs about what is to everyone's advantage or disadvantage and about what degree of equality or inequality is necessary to achieve what is advantageous. The Conservative might, of course, reject out of hand Rawls's principle of justice as fairness, as well as asserting that existing social arrangements, inequalities included, actually produce – to put it in utilitarian terms – the greatest happiness of the greatest number. The socialist, however, is likely to be both sympathetic towards Rawls's principle, and to accept that the inequalities and injustice that exist under capitalism must be eradicated.

It appears that, in its pursuit of egalitarian measures, the Labour Party also reveals its commitment to the value of social justice. There is a close relationship in Labour thought between equality and justice as illustrated by the statement approved by the NEC to reaffirm, amplify, and clarify party objects (16 Apr. 1960). This declared that Labour stood for: 'social justice, for a society in which the claims of those in hardship or distress come first . . . Where difference in rewards depends not upon birth or inheritance but on the effort, skill, and creative energy contributed to the common good, and where equal opportunities exist for all to live a full and varied life.'

Socialism, in questioning the existing social order, challenges the justice of its rules, both legal and non-legal, and the way they are enforced. It is frequently argued in socialist circles that the laws are made by the rich for the poor, and serve the interests of their makers. The laws protect property at the expense of humanity. And before the law the rich are able to afford justice by being in a position to hire the best lawyers and to pay fines and damages. Jurors are likely to be prejudiced in favour of those with high social status and against those with low. In addition, the law is seen to operate in a social context in which certain people, brought up under unfavourable conditions, are more prone to become offenders. Their culpability, it is felt, must be judged, not in relation to an objective standard of the law, but to a relative standard formulated in the light of the life opportunities that have been granted to them. Historically, the existence of unjust, oppressive laws that have borne down onerously upon particular social groups and classes has made socialists wary of automatically assuming that existing laws and the order of society they support are just.

The spontaneous anger arising from overwhelming frustration in the face of legal injustice can be resolved politically by adopting the naive anarchist view that all laws are unjust and that human beings will only be able to coexist in a fair and happy state in which there are no legal codes. Although there has been a strong anarchist tendency in the development of socialism, some highly modified theory of 'class law' has generally taken precedence in British socialist thought. Yet the Left has preserved marked libertarian inclinations, believing in the values of individual freedom of choice, and the spontaneous enjoyment of 'natural' human energies. The Labour Party has traditionally opposed restrictive and puritanical pressures on the life of the individual, and has sought to liberalise, for example, laws on divorce, abortion, homosexuality, and liquor licensing, and to implement penal reform. R. H. S. Crossman (1970, p. 15) claimed that 'the test of socialism is the extent to which it shapes a people's institutions to the moral standards of freedom – even at the cost of a lower standard of living or the surrender of an empire'.

Despite the element of libertarianism, the Labour Party has always been anxious to reaffirm its respect for the rule of law. In the absence of Labour ability or willingness to mobilise the working class, the law has been seen as the chief means of bringing about social reform. In power, the Labour Party has upheld the principle of obeying even unjust laws until they are repealed. The Marxist conception of the courts and police as forming part of a repressive capitalist state apparatus has never attained much credibility in Labour quarters. On the contrary, the theory of the class nature of the state has been rejected in favour of a belief that it may act as an impartial arbiter of a Labour Government's will, and be used as an agent for social transformation.

The disparate tendencies outlined above: the principle of justice as 'fair shares', the idea of 'class law' (one law for the rich and another for the poor), the questioning of injustice, libertarian leanings, countervailing respect for the civilising rule of law, and the belief in state impartiality have affected the Labour stance on immigration and race relations in different ways.

The principle of justice as fair shares is most obviously manifested in the Labour demand for equal treatment of black and white. This may be summed up simply in the words of Joan Lestor (LPACR, 1972, p. 158): 'For our socialist philosophy, our commitment to social justice includes the black worker just as surely as it includes the white worker.' The rather obvious demand for racial justice through equality of treatment would need no further illustration, but for the fact that it is open to different practical interpretations. Equal treatment of black and white can be simply understood if black and white are alike in the respects that justify their equal treatment. But, if Labour supporters think black and white are different in certain crucial respects, social justice may require inequality of treatment. It might be held that if whites are considered to be in a less favourable position than blacks, and justice is to obtain, they should be preferentially treated. Or, alternatively, black people should be preferentially treated if they are in a less favourable position than whites. From time to time, both assumptions have been found in Labour circles.

In the debate on the 1965 White Paper, Bob Mellish (LPACR, 1965, p. 217) showed indignation at what he believed was a social injustice being perpetrated on the citizens of Lambeth by continued immigration. He asked rhetorically whether the Conference was telling him, as Parliamentary Secretary of Housing, to go to Lambeth, 'who have a waiting list of about 10,000 of their own people', to instruct them to give a housing preference 'to these coloureds who have come in without any measure of assistance before'. 'If you ask me to do that and you say this is a socialist approach, I say to you frankly and firmly that I shall be asking Lambeth to create the most grievous racial disturbances we have ever seen in London and this is a fact' (LPACR, 1965, p. 217). Mellish obviously believed that a necessary criterion for equal treatment was not only need but length of residence and long-term contribution to the welfare state.

A belief in the injustice perpetrated on the white population by black newcomers' entitlement to equality of welfare treatment with whites is in total contrast to one premised on the injustice of the existing structural inequality of the black population in Britain. One solution that has been proposed in Left-wing political circles to remedy the existing injustice arising from the inferior position of the black population is that of 'positive discrimination'. At the 1976 Labour Party Conference, Sardul Singh Gill suggested that 'we should positively discriminate, for the time being at least, in favour of special dispensation towards the underprivileged in this society' (LPACR, 1976, p. 219). Formulated originally in the United States, 'positive discrimination' is an ambiguous expression, drawing much of its power from the juxtaposition of the term 'positive' with the generally negatively conceived '(racial) discrimination'. In this way, it hints that the reversed 'discrimination' may be at the expense of white people. Positive discrimination in the field of race relations is a proposed policy for achieving a more even distribution of black people through the social structure, but the means by which this is to be achieved are rarely spelt out in terms of practical policies.

They may amount to little more than a compensatory welfare programme aimed at achieving equality of opportunity for black people; they may involve measures to give blacks more opportunities than whites of a similar social status; or they may require wholesale reconstruction on an egalitarian basis of existing class society. If black people, distributively, were all worse off than whites, then a distinction could be made between the first two possibilities: as it is, the direction of resources to black people per se, rather than to poor black people and, furthermore, to black people who are poorer than whites, could lead to some blacks benefiting more than some whites, unless it is accepted that the black life-style (measured in more than crude economic terms) in a racist society is always qualitatively inferior to that of whites.

In Britain, as this last suggestion is usually denied, politicians seem acutely conscious that the direction of resources to black people per se could create invidious comparisons with the treatment meted out to poor whites of similar social status: vide supra, the remarks of Mellish – when blacks are thought to be receiving similar treatment. Consequently, politicians are not prepared to interfere directly in the job market in such a way as to give preference to black workers, although they might wish to ensure equality of opportunity.

As an alternative, stress is placed on blanket welfare provision aimed at, for example, all people living in a particular geographical area, with some concession being made to the apparent objective differences, which are generally attributed to migrant status, between white and black groups. For example, language difficulties, educational disadvantages, unfamiliarity with British ways, lack of facilities for worship or leisure are frequently selected as criteria for justifying supplementary funding, but then the resources are always allocated collectively to groups and not distributively to individuals.

'Positive discrimination', insofar as the expression is used in Britain, usually refers to attempts through welfare provision to create equality of opportunity for black people. Yet the expression 'positive discrimination' is shunned in political circles because it carries the connotation of preference for blacks and discrimination against whites. 'I was asked about positive discrimination', Alex Lyon remarked in the debate on the 1976 Race Relations Act. 'I dislike the term intensely. When I refer to this problem, I refer to correcting the disadvantages of our black citizens' (Hansard, 4 Mar. 1976, p. 1666). Positive discrimination is acceptable only insofar as it entails social justice through equality of treatment for both whites and blacks, and not social injustice against whites.

With regard to class law, there is a strong tendency within the Labour Party to treat black people as a whole as social underdogs along with other sectors, such as working people, labourers, the poor, and women, and with social pariahs such as homosexuals, unmarried mothers, and gypsies. Given the level of discrimination against black people, there may be good reasons for agreeing with this, but it should be recognised that there are a number of black professional workers and businessmen who would object quite strongly to this classification.

Nevertheless, the belief is widespread in the Labour movement that black people are oppressed by injustice in the enforcement, if not the enactment, of laws that favour the rich at the expense of the poor. Tom Driberg claimed that:

> A century ago the working class of this country was
> discriminated against, treated like animals by the employers. In
> the twentieth century, it is the coloured citizens of the various
> communities who are the victims of discrimination . . .
> [Legislation] can redress the balance of social justice which is
> at present heavily loaded against our coloured fellow-citizens.
>
> (LPACR, 1967, p. 316)

A measure of sympathy is generated by the identification of black people as the unfortunate victims of the capitalist state. Labour supporters, unlike those who hold British institutions sacred, are prone to believe stories about officious or callous immigration officers, police brutality, and legal bias, and to support pressure groups which seek to redress injustice towards the black community. The more active local cadres have associated themselves, for instance, with campaigns against particularly blatant examples of racial discrimination or violence, the use of the SUS law* against black youth, or the more heartless decisions to deport persons of Asian descent. But there is a danger that the very categorisation of the

---

* 'SUS' refers to Section 4 of the 1824 Vagrancy Act under which the police can arrest anybody as 'a suspected person loitering with intent to commit a felonious offence'. A campaign for the repeal of SUS was launched on 1 Feb. 1978 by BPOCAS – Black People's Organisations Campaign against SUS.

black community as underdogs and scapegoats encourages white socialists and liberals to enter these struggles paternalistically, believing always that their frequently reconciliatory methods of approaching the issue are preferable to those of ethnic minority organisations also engaged in the struggle for justice.

Labour's libertarian approach to laws and traditional practices is illustrated by Roy Jenkins's definition of integration 'not as a flattening process of assimilation, but as equal opportunity accompanied by cultural diversity in an atmosphere of mutual tolerance' (1967, p. 267). It is generally accepted that laws and regulations which bear heavily on the family life, religion, and culture of ethnic minority groups may have to be modified. The new multi-racialism demands that rules, which are not indispensable, or whose purpose is not always obvious, or has faded with time, should be changed. Thus, a turbanned Sikh is exempted from the law requiring motor cyclists to wear crash helmets, or allowed to wear a turban in regulation blue as part of his uniform. In practice, very few alterations to laws and regulations have been made to ease the existence of ethnic minority groups, and Labour tolerance is likely to extend only insofar as cultural demands are in sympathy with Labour traditions and/or are unlikely to upset to any degree the white electorate. For example, Muslim demands for Koranic schools in which boys and girls are educated separately will almost certainly be opposed because they undermine Labour plans for a comprehensive state education system in which boys and girls are taught a common syllabus together. Yet a climate of libertarianism probably enables some small changes to be made as gestures to multi-racialism, for example, in school syllabuses, in the dietary practices of institutions, and in administrative procedures.

Labour's faith in the use of the law as a means of social reform is well exemplified by the succession of Race Relations Acts aimed at achieving equality of opportunity and at stamping out discrimination. Advocacy of the use of law against racist propaganda and racial discrimination has a long history in Labour thought. Bernard Finlay, at the 1948 Labour Party Conference argued that just as the law forbade defamation, sedition, and blasphemy, it could be used to prevent fascists poisoning men's minds with pernicious ideas (LPACR, 1948, p. 180). The vigorous campaigning of Brockway, Sorenson, and others, led to the NEC statement of 1962 calling for legislation to make illegal the practice of racial discrimination in public places (LPACR, 1962, p. 197).

Left-wingers have criticised the idea that the law can be left to correct the racial problems of society (although it is not clear that anyone in the Party actually holds such a naive belief) on the grounds that legislation is often seen as an alternative to vigorous political campaigning, whereas, in fact, the two must be complementary. In addition, they remain suspicious of the mainstream Labour Party tradition of regarding state institutions, such as the civil service and the police, as impartial forces that can be used to achieve socialist objectives as easily as capitalist ones.

Nevertheless, Labour Governments and the majority of their supporters have continued to regard the police as a necessary and beneficial British institution characterised by its impartiality. And, if on occasion, the police have been heavy-handed in the treatment of black people, this is thought most exceptional, and must be set against their sincere endeavour to come to terms with the emergent multi-racial society. After all, it is argued, in the face of extremist violence and provocation, understaffing, and over-work, the police have made moves to recruit from among the racial minorities and to familiarise themselves through special educational programmes and schemes of social policing with the black community. The answer to the difficulties between the police and the black community, it is felt, must lie in developing greater confidence, friendship, and co-operation between the two parties which have, when all is said and done, a commonality of interest.

Of course, the duality in Labour policy observed by the racial minority organisations has always detracted from its pretensions to be a party of racial justice. Whilst generally accepting the good intent of race relations legislation, these organisations point to its incompatibility with Labour immigration policy – the White Paper of 1965, the 1968 Commonwealth Immigrants Act, and the failure of the Labour administration from 1974 to 1979 to repeal the Conservative 1971 Immigration Act, all of which, in their opinion, discriminated against black immigrants.

Laissez-faire versus social ownership

The Conservative Party, its rejection of state interference in economic and social life, and its commitment to laissez-faire politics and private ownership

Conservatives have always been committed to the principle of private ownership of the means of production and have been wary of state interference in the economic life of the nation. Liberty had been endangered, W. E. H. Lecky thought, by the inevitable tendency of democracy to extend government authority into the fields of social and economic regulation, impairing freedom of contract and freedom of enterprise (1899, Vol. 1, p. 258). One of the main tenets of Churchill's Conservatism was to 'support, as a general rule, free enterprise and initiative against state trading and nationalisation of industries' (Blackpool, 5 Oct. 1946). But, though Conservatives remain deeply suspicious of government interference in industry and social life, they have not elevated laissez-faire to an unassailable article of faith. Macmillan, in *The Middle Way* (1938), wrote that Conservatism admits the truth of the powerful arguments of orthodox economists of the laissez-faire school, but then went on to claim that the arguments in favour of private enterprise, and the free play of competitive forces, 'no longer apply to the whole range of economic effort' (p. 238).

Enoch Powell (1960) believed the Conservative to be committed 'practically and theoretically . . . to the interplay of individual choice' because he rejected 'the effects upon society and upon individuals of transferring all economic decision and initiative from them to the government' (in Beattie, 1970, p. 492). As it is far more likely that, by allowing the free play of market forces, society will realise growing economic opportunities and adapt itself automatically to changing circumstances, government competence in discerning and defining economic ends is to be distrusted. 'If then the Conservative embraces, as embrace he must, laissez-faire in the economic field, he must repudiate in principle and minimize in practice, government intervention on economic grounds' (in Beattie, 1970, p. 492). But, in response to the value of nationalism, in common with most Conservatives, Powell tempered his belief in laissez-faire by making clear that the national interest must come first. 'Laissez-faire does not logically necessitate free trade any more than it excludes armaments or a health service or the Factory Acts' (in Beattie, 1970, p. 494). The principle of restriction on government intervention in the economic field is paralleled by a belief that government should be reluctant to involve itself any more than is absolutely necessary in the 'non-economic' areas of life. According to Lord Hugh Cecil (1912): 'character is strengthened by the effort to find a way out of difficulties and hardships' and will be weakened 'by the habit of looking to state help' (p. 189).

These long-standing commitments to the values of privately owned industry and the non-interference of government are reflected in the Manifestos of the Party. The 1970 programme, *A Better Tomorrow*, stated that 'under Labour, there has been too much government interference in the day-to-day workings of industry and local government. There has been too much government: there will be less' (p. 10). In the 1979 Conservative Manifesto, the Labour Party are accused of crippling enterprise and effort by enlarging the role of the state and diminishing the role of the individual (p. 6).

The Conservative position on race relations is affected in a number of ways by these stances towards government and industry. Before other values such as traditionalism and nationalism took precedence, Conservatives were likely to welcome industry's right to recruit labour on the international market and at the cheapest rates, a situation that obtained in the 1950s. But, at the same time, in accordance with Powell's thesis that laissez-faire did not necessitate free trade (either in commodities or *labour*) allowances could always be made for supra-national laissez-faire to be overridden by the Conservative concept of the national interest, the passing of the 1962 Commonwealth Immigrants Bill serving as an example of this.

Conservative stances towards the Race Relations Bills are also more easily understood in the light of the principle of minimum government interference in civic life. From the point of view of a Conservative, government interference in business and industrial relations in the matter of who was to be hired, fired, or promoted, or in housing in deciding on the letting of property, was an unwarranted attack on the employers' or landlords' traditional freedoms of choice and action and, what was even more upsetting, a denial of the effectiveness of the free market mechanism. Any attempt to legislate on social mixing in clubs and public houses was an abnegation of the right of free association: people should be able to decide for themselves on the company they kept and the friends they made. Nobody, not even the government, could – or should – make a man like his neighbours.

The Conservative criticism was not only that the government should not meddle in affairs that did not concern it, but that such meddling would, as a matter of course, be abortive. Voluntary, non-governmental measures, or peaceful persuasion, could be relied on to solve any problem that arose. Yet, in true Macmillan style, a loophole for government intervention was left. If the market mechanism was seen not to be working, with a resultant social disruption that offended against other Conservative values, then government intervention, though regrettable, could, after all, be justified. A growing awareness of the 'problem of the inner city', originally conceived of in the American context, provided the opportunity needed. In Britain, social problems, in the form of decaying terraced houses, Victorian buildings, inadequate social services, etc., testified to the breakdown of the economic system. Economic incentives were needed to 'breathe life' back into the inner areas of the cities where it so happened that most of the black immigrants had decided to live.

Civic pride in the Joseph Chamberlain tradition led many Conservative councillors, normally reticent to spend local rate-payers' money, into pressurising national government to put more resources at the disposal of the councils. Councillor P. R. Wood, for example, asserted that 'the social problems of the old, central areas of the towns in which the coloured population is concentrated must be dealt with urgently. To hold the immigrants responsible for poor education, housing, and social service facilities in these areas would be wrong – social services tend to be poor in the old central areas of many towns' (CACR, 1973, p. 37). But, of course, the Conservatives continued to argue that the only long-term answer was not a redistribution of wealth to the inner cities, but the creation of more wealth.

Only an expanding capitalism, therefore, offers the rags to riches promise of success to the enterprising black person:

> upward progression is open to immigrants of all nationalities and countries and colour in Britain provided only that they believe with us in a free Britain, a fair Britain, above all in a Britain with those essential creative economic freedoms . . . those economic freedoms which Conservatives cherish, which we believe in the end are going to be the instrument and means by which the immigrant communities of any or ethnic origin in these islands can in the end share in the prosperity and the potential of Britain. (CACR, 1977, p. 47)

Much of the hostility expressed towards the Race Relations Bills is explained by Conservative wariness of government interference in the private affairs of the individual, particularly his right to conduct his business as he sees fit. The Conservative reasoned amendment to the 1965 Race Relations Bill declined to give it a second reading on the grounds that it introduced 'criminal sanctions into a field more appropriate to conciliation and the encouragement of fair employment practices, while also importing a new principle into the law affecting freedom of speech'. Enoch Powell criticised the 1968 Bill for denying the citizen 'his right to discriminate in the management of his own affairs between one fellow-citizen and another', for subjecting him 'to inquisition as to his reasons and motives for behaving in one lawful manner rather than another', and for pillorying him for his 'private actions' (Birmingham, 20 Apr. 1968). Ronald Bell thought the Bill made 'very deep and damaging encroachments into the proper sphere of personal decision' (Hansard, 23 Mar. 1968, p. 102).

Granted that the government should not intervene in affairs that lie outside of its sphere of competence, is the Conservative able to offer any suggestions for the improvement of race relations? In common with Conservative belief in the efficacy of non-governmental agencies, William Deedes made the suggestion that the help of voluntary organisations, including the Trade Union Congress and Confederation of British Industry, might be enlisted (Hansard, 23 Apr. 1968, p. 89). For all but the most Leftward-inclining Conservatives, race relations legislation is an improper extension of state power.

The Labour Party and government intervention in economic and social relations: social ownership

Both wings of the Labour Party accept the necessity of government intervention in industry. For the social democrat, the ravages inflicted on workers by the too ruthless pursuit of profit must be alleviated by the imposition of government controls upon private industry: in this way, capitalism may be modified so that all groups can benefit. For the socialist, industry must be nationalised and socialised in order, first, that the workers' surplus product, at present expropriated, can be returned for their use, and second, that production can be planned rationally for social need, and not for profit. The two positions are disguised and reconciled behind loosely formulated rhetoric, for, according to its aims, the Labour Party has long been committed to a programme of public ownership.

In 1928, *Labour and the Nation* stated that the choice before the country was 'not between private enterprise and public control, but between the conduct of industry as a public service, democratically owned and responsibly administered, and the private economic sovereignty of the combine, the syndicate and the trust . . . in short, between public ownership or control and one form or another of industrial feudalism'. It pledged the Labour Party 'without haste, but without rest, with careful preparation, with the use of the best technical knowledge and managerial skill and with due compensation to the persons affected . . . to vest its ownership in the nation and its administration in authorities acting on the nation's behalf' (pp. 22–3).

After the war, the Labour Party nationalised a number of the basic industries such as coal-mining, power, and the railways which were failing in their work of servicing the privately owned sectors of the economy. But, by the 1960s, it appeared that 'planning' had replaced socialist nationalisation as the panacea for the nation's failure to expand economically.

The perceived need, mentioned in the 1964 Labour Manifesto, to modernise the economy by developing new science-based industries was elaborated into *The National Plan*, which committed the government to action on 'all aspects of the country's economic development for the next five years'. However, the policies devised for encouraging industry to modernise and re-equip in order to increase profitability were found to be expensive and were soon abandoned in the light of the worsening balance of payments problem.

The 1970 Election Manifesto contained hardly any hint of commitment to nationalisation, but by 1974 a new policy reconciling social democracy's support for planning and the mixed economy, and socialism's belief in nationalisation had been evolved. A form of partnership between the public sector and the privately owned companies was advocated in conjunction with the setting up of a National Enterprise Board to administer and extend publicly owned share-holdings in private industry.

On an operative dimension, the Labour Party sought to develop the efficiency of the 'mixed economy' by trying to halt the falling rate of profit. The Left were placated with cautious moves to invest more public money in the economy without incurring the displeasure of the international business world. In other words, insofar as it was possible, the Labour Party pursued with a socialist intent the goal of an efficient capitalist economy. Unlike the Conservatives, therefore, the Labour Party had no scruples about interfering in the working of the capitalist economy. In addition, it enthusiastically advocated planning – including the planning of industry's labour requirements.

Immigration controls can be seen as part of the planning process, the size of the quota varying according to the current and future needs of the economy. If it is felt the quota is too large and that a labour surplus will result, greater restrictions will be imposed. If, on the other hand, the planned expansion of the economy is endangered by a shortage of labour power, a justification exists for further immigration. Although use may be made of the value of economic planning in justifying immigration restrictions, the actual ability of governments to control economic expansion and contraction under capitalism is sufficiently limited to call into question the suggested economic motives for their actions. Nevertheless, the Labour member is likely to uphold the right of governments to control the factors of production, including labour, and to accept that immigration control – though not racist immigration control – could form part of this process.

Similarly, race relations legislation, like the factory acts, can be seen as an attempt by the Government to limit the power of industrialists to act autocratically against the public good and in the ruthless pursuit of profit. The requirement to treat black and white workers equally in recruitment, employment, and promotion constrains, for the benefit of the community as a whole, the industrialists' freedom of action, and, furthermore, safeguards the interests of already enlightened companies against competition from more unscrupulous operators.

The legitimacy of intervention in the economic sphere is extended quite naturally to the social. Decisions on housing, education, health, and other requirements are the responsibility of democratically elected bodies, which are forced to act decisively when capitalism fails to provide much-needed facilities. For example, Crossman in referring to urban renewal, thought that the Government had to concentrate on six or seven of the largest towns where the problem of housing was so bad that the local authorities were unable to cope: 'A Labour Minister should impose central leadership, large-scale state intervention in these blighted areas of cities, the twilight areas, which were once genteelly respectable and are now rotting away, where Commonwealth citizens settle, and where there are racial problems' (1975, Vol. 1, Nov. 1964, p. 44).

Apart from the evident susceptibility of Labour governments to small-scale economic and social interventionism, with consequences for immigration and race relations, the Party's race relations policy is also influenced by its perception of the alienation caused by the capitalist economic system. Opinions vary over how deeply racism and racialism are embedded within the economic structure, and whether they can be alleviated or eradicated without a wholesale transformation of the relations of production. For the social democrat, racial prejudice and discrimination are not concomitant with capitalism, but only with certain primitive forms of it. It is quite possible to conceive either of a Britain with a mixed economy where there is no racialism, or a socialist Britain in which racialism continues to survive. For the socialist, the extent to which racialism is a product of class relations, and therefore of capitalist society, is a moot point. A variety of different explanations have been offered, all purporting to show that racialism and its accompanying ideological configurations can be explained in terms of the economic relationships that exist under capitalism.

Cox (1970), for example, suggests that racial prejudice 'is a social attitude propagated among the public by an exploiting class for the purpose of stigmatising some group as inferior so that the exploitation of either the group itself or its resources or both may be justified'. Others have argued that capitalist exploitation and crisis create frustration among the workers which is deflected away from the real cause onto readily identifiable vulnerable groups (scapegoating). Racial antagonism is also explained in terms of the threat, real or imagined, posed by black workers to white workers' economic and status interests. Such theories are frequently attended by the belief that racism and racialism are part of the very nature of the capitalist order and that their threat will only finally be eliminated with the advent of socialism. Capitalism, then, is a necessary, if not sufficient, condition for the development and survival of racism and racialism. Although not all socialists adhere to this view or think that social ownership of the means of production by itself will eliminate racialism, capitalism's alienating conditions frequently loom large in explanation and solution alike.

At the Party Conference in 1948, in opposing the resolution seeking to make illegal racially defamatory statements and organisations propagating racial or religious hatred or discrimination, H. J. Laski argued that fascism – and by implication anti-Semitism – could succeed only in a country where there was mass unemployment and psychological frustration (most commonly caused by defeat in war) (LPACR, 1948, p. 181). In 1976, twenty-eight years later, after calling for the repeal of the 1971 Immigration Act, a massive propaganda drive against racialism, and other measures, Paul Moore pointed out that these alone would not be enough if the root causes of racialism were not dealt with. The fears of unemployment and bad housing could only be eliminated finally 'by a change of economic policy, by taking on the employers, by taking over the economy and running it in the interests of all workers, black and white' (LPACR, 1976, p. 216).

The hatred of many socialists for racialism gives them an added incentive to work for the elimination of capitalism. For them, racialism is a direct product of the alienated relationships of capitalism. The social democrat, however, though accepting that racialism is kindled by economic inse-curity, unemployment, and bad housing, etc, might feel that these factors can possibly be brought under control within the framework of a mixed economy. He is not so inclined to agree that the constant threat of racialism is a necessary accompaniment of a properly controlled mixed economy. Nevertheless, both socialist and social democrat will agree that government economic measures in the public and private sectors are likely to have an important effect on race relations. Manpower Service Schemes, providing jobs and training opportunities for the young black and white unemployed, exemplified the Labour Government's concern to temper the least acceptable and potentially most explosive aspect of capitalism in crisis.

Individualism, collectivism and welfare provision

The Conservative Party and the doctrine of self-reliant individualism

In the nineteenth century, laissez-faire economic policies were frequently accompanied by a philosophy of social Darwinism. The successful in business were thought to be society's fittest members whose individual or family vigour, hard work, and self-sacrifice had been rewarded by their current social standing. The poor, unable to cope in the rigorously competitive economic world, were seen as the least fitted to survive. The human species would be vitally weakened if there were any major attempt to intervene in the natural selection process exercised by the economic system. The individual had to prove his worth by self-reliance and had never to become a burden to others. A society which removed responsibility from the shoulders of its citizens and endeavoured to cushion them against the natural selection process would undermine individual self-reliance and, eventually, contribute to its own destruction.

This classical, nineteenth-century Liberal thinking is still present in the brand of Liberal conservatism that believes the economy should be controlled by the free market mechanism, with a minimum of political and governmental interference. It also believes that there is a need to restore to the individual a new sense of moral responsibility and initiative. There are, of course, other countervailing strands, some of them stemming from the old paternalism of the landed gentry, who recognised a responsibility towards the local poor, and some from a more recent corporatism which sees the need to stabilise a working class, alienated by harsh economic realities. But, despite a post-war acceptance of the inevitability of the welfare state, commitment to a concept of individual self-reliance is a hallmark of Conservative views on welfare provision.

The state, Lord Hugh Cecil believed, 'depends on the vigour of the character of the individuals which make it up; and that character is strengthened by the effort to find a way out of difficulties and hardships and is weakened by the habit of looking to state help' (1912, p. 189). Lord Coleraine, in criticising state socialism, claimed that the Conservative position was founded on 'the conviction that Government control of industry and the apparatus of social welfare, with the burden of taxation which accompanies it, tends to weaken the sense of responsibility of the individual citizen and stifle his initiative, and at the same time, by undermining his respect for the law and for himself, loosens the fabric of society' (1970, p. 105).

Yet, despite this antipathy towards collective welfare provision, post-war Conservatives have, until recently, accepted Keynesian economic theory with its interventionist prescriptions for the achievement of full employment. The Beveridge vision of a social minimum was assumed to be an indispensable adjunct of this programme, relying, as it did, on the condition of full employment, a 'never-had-it-so-good' post-war fact that many Conservatives had come to take for granted. Even with the acceptance of Beveridge, Conservatives were described by David Clarke (1947) as insisting 'that the collective provision of social security must be a "springboard and not a sofa". It must not detract from the self-reliance of the individual. It must encourage the virtues of thrift and family responsibility.'

As in the nineteenth century, Conservatives were prone to distinguish between those who were thought to deserve help from the public purse and those who abused the privilege by making no attempt to help themselves. The 'undeserving poor' or 'welfare scroungers' were seen as seriously damaging the social fabric by offending against the work ethic in *preferring* public benefit to work. They were also thought to undermine the morale of those still working, who would not be prepared to make an effort if they could see others getting something for nothing. Sennett and Cobb describe the hostility felt by workers towards people '"getting away with something I never got away with". If there are people who have refused to make sacrifices yet are subsidized by the state, their very existence calls into question the meaning of acts of self-abnegation' (1977, p. 137). And, in a low-wage economy, the comparatively high level of benefit paid to the deserving or undeserving alike would make it possible for them to maintain a 'reservation wage' rather than to undertake the unattractive and poorly paid jobs that would have to be filled if the market economy was to function effectively.

Whereas, previously, Conservatives had reluctantly come to accept the necessity of the welfare state, in the late 1970s, at a time of economic crisis, with falling levels of investment and low levels of profitability, a more militant brand of Conservatism came to the fore. S. M. Miller (1978) described the emergence of a new policy which 'decouples Keynes from Beveridge and severely modifies the macro-policies of Keynesianism'. It demanded that state expenditure for social purposes be cut back in order to provide a spur to private investment through lower taxation on corporations and higher income recipients, who were in a position to save. In parallel with this, a harsher attitude towards welfare recipients was required in order to force them to work at what were previously considered unacceptably lowly paid or unpleasant jobs. Individual initiative in welfare provision was to be encouraged in order to supplement or eventually to replace the comprehensive facilities provided collectively by the welfare state. In such a climate of opinion, it was likely that an earlier social Darwinist view of poverty and social inadequacy would reassert itself, and greater moral censure would be directed against the 'featherbed' welfare state and its 'comfortable' clients. The category of 'undeserving poor' would tend to be expanded to include not only the limited number of 'shirkers' and 'scroungers' but welfare recipients generally.

In 1970, the Conservative Election Programme promised 'firm action to deal with abuse of the social security system'. A Conservative Government would 'tighten up the administration' in order to prevent 'the whole system being brought into disrepute by the shirkers and scroungers'. But Conservatives would also tackle the problem of family poverty by ensuring that adequate family allowances went to the families that needed them. With a typical Conservative ambivalence, the value of self-reliance and the corrupting influence of collective welfare provision are set against commitment to Beveridge's social minimum and the sacred institution of the family.

A more doctrinaire approach to welfarism began to emerge after the election of Mrs Thatcher to leadership of the Party in February 1975. Rhodes Boyson, Opposition Spokesman on Education, was credited with saying 'I think the welfare state is quite evil' (Leigh, in the *Guardian*, 28 Mar. 1978), while Mrs Thatcher herself, in a speech at St Lawrence Jewry, London (30 Mar. 1978), expressed the view that:

> there are grave moral dangers and serious practical ones in letting people get away with the idea that they can delegate all their responsibilities to public officials and institutions . . . Once you give people the idea that all this can be done by the state . . . you will begin to deprive human beings of the essential ingredients of humanity – personal moral responsibility.

The 1979 Conservative Manifesto spelt out that no more money would be available to spend on the social services except in the event of the nation's prosperity being revived. The 'will to work' would be *restored* by cutting income tax, by reinforcing 'the rules about the unemployed accepting available jobs' and by acting 'more vigorously against fraud and abuse'. More would be done 'to help people to help themselves and families to look after their own', and encouragement would be given to movements and self-help groups working in partnership with the statutory services.

Conservative views on race relations and immigration were greatly affected by the long-standing commitment to self-reliance and the ambivalence towards state social welfare provision. First, the provision itself was felt to attract and create greater numbers of clients. Without stringent immigration controls it was thought that the world's poor would swarm to Britain's welfare 'honey pot', to make use of Cyril Osborne's imagery (Hansard, 16 Nov. 1961, p. 719). If, as Conservative nationalistic propaganda would have us believe, conditions in Britain were so much more preferable to conditions elsewhere – and especially in the 'third world' – then people would migrate here in ever-increasing numbers.

Hogg thought that 'because we have a system of social services which . . . would provide a standard of life which would be the envy of 19 out of 20 of the human beings who live on this planet, it is utterly impossible to suppose that, unless we erect a pretty stiff fence round our country, it will not act as a magnet which will attract all sorts of people, and present us with a situation we cannot control' (CACR, 1968, p. 72). Deedes asserted that 'the pressure to enter this country has not diminished, but has, if anything, increased. Our standard of living here is 30 times higher than that of the Indian subcontinent' (CACR, 1976, p. 43).

The idea that black Commonwealth immigrants came to Britain to work was offset by the recognition among the whites that the work available was not particularly attractive, and the widespread, and still-surviving, colonial belief that black people were lazy, pleasure-loving, and unaccustomed to work discipline. It was felt that, given the ready availability in Britain of national assistance, unemployment benefit, or social security – in distinct contrast to the absence of such facilities in the poor Commonwealth countries – black people would become a burden on the welfare state. As a result of these anxieties, Conservatives called for an end to immigration, or for eligibility to the social services to be made conditional on the length of residence or size of contributions made. In no way were new residents to be encouraged to get something for nothing, and constant demands for closer scrutiny and control of benefits were made to ensure that as little as possible of the taxpayers' money was handed out.

Commonwealth immigrants came to Britain to sell their labour power in the industrial towns and cities. In return, if they were to be treated in the same way as the indigenous population, they were entitled not only to their earnings, but to the social wage in the form of social, educational, housing, and health services paid for by their taxes and rates. As the social wage is provided on the grounds of need, rather than of work, and administered indirectly by various national and local governmental agencies, its source is not as apparent as that of the actual wage. As a form of distribution, the social wage can easily be seen as governmental largesse, unrelated to the production process.

Local authorities were required to extend the social, educational, housing, and health provision for the existing population to Commonwealth immigrants and their families. Because the social wage owing to immigrants was not immediately forthcoming, or because they saw a way of obtaining yet more resources for the population as a whole, the various local authorities and other agencies proceeded to articulate politically their need for extra expenditure by laying great stress on the problems caused by immigrants. More school places, maternity beds, specially trained teachers, and social and health workers were thought necessary to cope with the 'immigrant influx'.

Quite understandably, a presentation of the case in terms of the *extra* demands made by Commonwealth immigrants on selected social services, without mention of their contribution through taxes and rates, would confirm a Conservative predisposition to treat them as a drain on the social services and a burden on the economy. K. Jones (1967) showed quite the reverse – that in terms of the rates and taxes they paid and their distribution in the economically active age range, they made fewer demands and contributed more than the indigenous population if the social services as a whole were taken into account. From the manner in which the subject was politically articulated, however, the black immigrant was cast in the role of an excessive consumer of scarce social resources. The Conservative response, ambivalent as always, was to sanction additional necessary social expenditure, particularly to alleviate the possibility of social unrest, but at the same time to treat the immigrant as a somewhat greedy member of the undeserving poor and as personally responsible for his own lowly economic position.

The 1966 Conservative Manifesto offered 'special help where necessary to those areas where immigrants are concentrated', a proposal amplified in a statement of February 1968: 'The Government must recognise the special problems arising from the number of immigrants in certain areas. Racial tension is aggravated by poverty and overcrowding. The Central Government must coordinate and be prepared to support financially special housing, welfare, and educational programmes administered by local authorities in areas where immigrants are concentrated.'

Despite unease at the greater demands on the state, for many Conservatives, as with Labour, the solution to racial difficulties lay in comprehensive welfare provision. Robert Apps stated that 'Only by a massive capital injection for more schools, better health and welfare services, improved housing [etc.] will we even begin to get on top of our task' (CACR, 1969, p. 94). Conservatives frequently committed themselves to plans for the renewal of the towns and cities and supported urban-aid and inner-city programmes. John Pritchard claimed that 'responsible people . . . both blacks and whites, deplore violence, but demand positive action to deal with the prevalence of poverty, decay, bad housing conditions, and poor education – a vicious circle, which, combined with despair about job prospects, inevitably sows the seeds of prejudice and ethnic friction' (CACR, 1977, p. 42).

Although higher unemployment figures and poorer accommodation among black people might be explained by racial disadvantage and discrimination, blacks were still likely to be held in some way responsible for their situation. The Conservative was less likely to blame the ailing economy than an individual's lack of fitness in the struggle for survival. And, paradoxically, the very channelling of aid to the urban poor or disadvantaged black people tended to confirm the view of their being inadequate and unable to cope: why else would they be receiving aid in a society widely held to function justly and efficiently, in accordance with free market principles and with the minimum of governmental interference? The more resources that were devoted to black people, the more confirmed a Conservative might become in his belief that they were inherently unable to cope with the demands of industrial society and that they constituted a new class of 'undeserving poor'. For the average Conservative, the black was equated with the archetypal welfare recipient, a character for whom, traditionally, he spared little sympathy.

The Labour Party and the doctrine of welfare collectivism

One of the most important doctrines of the Labour Party, C. A. R. Crosland (1956) believed, was 'the rejection of the laissez faire doctrine that the state has no obligation to its citizens (save for the protection of property) and indeed a positive obligation to remain inactive' (p. 85). Instead, it affirmed the opposite view that 'the state must accept responsibility for preventing poverty and distress and for providing at least a subsistence minimum of aid to such citizens as need it' (p. 85). Crediting the Fabians with first giving overt expression to this value, Crosland claimed that in 'the shape of demands for social security and a guaranteed national minimum', it had become 'the most deeply-felt item in Labour policy' (p. 86).

My remarks under this head will be brief as discussion of welfare provision has crept into a number of previous sections. Nevertheless, I think it important to emphasise, and indeed it is difficult to avoid, the conclusion that welfare is seen as Labour's panacea for nearly all social problems, including those of hostile race relations.

The basis of the welfare state had already been laid between 1906 and 1914 by the Liberal Government of Asquith and Lloyd George, and these early foundations were slowly built on in the years that followed. But the welfare state's solid and co-ordinated development followed the publication of the 1942 Beveridge Report, which recommended the extension and integration of already existing schemes. The Report advocated insurance against loss of earning power, resulting from sickness, unemployment and old age, and a guaranteed income at subsistence level, providing the bare necessities of life such as food, clothing, housing, etc. Apart from 'want', the Report referred also to the other 'giant' social problems of disease, ignorance, squalor, and idleness. The White Paper on Employment Policy produced during the war by the coalition parties, and Beveridge's subsequent *Full Employment in a Free Society*, saw the necessity of viewing these policy recommendations in the context of full employment.

Whereas all major political parties recognised the importance of the Beveridge Report, the Labour Party embraced its proposals wholeheartedly and set out to implement them. Sydney Silverman, MP, claimed that Beveridge represented the basic programme of his party, but while still working within the framework of capitalism, in the aftermath of the war, and with massive inflation, the Labour leadership's initiatives were perforce limited. The reluctance of the Labour Party to intervene in the economy resulted in an alternative, 'soft', humanistic movement for social collectivism, rather than in a 'tough' drive towards economic collectivism.

The key principles on which Beveridge's welfare proposals were based were *compulsion* – all would contribute, and *universality* – the entitlement would be for all regardless of income. It was intended that there would be no test of means, or stigma attached to receipt of benefit. But, by insisting on the necessity of personal insurance before subsistence was guaranteed, the Beveridge Report showed signs of its Liberal origin. The principle of universality, involving compulsion, could not properly be based on the contractual insurance relationship, and it was never made clear whether entitlement according to economic requirement was to be justified on the grounds of a contractual obligation, or solely on the basis of one's being a member of society. Both the Liberal predilection for the 'individualism' of the former, and the socialist dedication to the 'collectivism' of the latter, have survived in Labour approaches to a welfare policy, in which the relative values of desert or need as criteria for benefit have still not fully been resolved. This becomes particularly obvious in the field of immigration and race relations.

The question of how and when a person qualifies to receive benefit or to become a member of the welfare collective seems to have been posed starkly by the arrival of the black colonial immigrant. One answer in the Labour movement was to view welfare entitlement as conditional on an individual's (long-term) payment in the form of taxation and rates into government funds. The new arrival – being new – was seen as not belonging, as an extra mouth to support, and as a drain on hard-earned resources.

But, in general, Labour belief in welfare collectivism necessitated the treatment of the black immigrant as part of society in which universality remained unmodified, and support was made available on grounds of subsistence needs. At local level, however, the liberal, social contractual concept of welfare provision meant that councillors often denied facilities to newcomers. Yet, the local outcry over the cost of black immigrant welfare encouraged national government to consider making further provision to local authorities. The 1965 White Paper (Cmnd 2739) pointed out that local health, education, and housing services were assisted through the General Grant or by specific subsidies. However, in the case of some local authorities who needed to undertake 'exceptional commitment by engaging extra staff in order to ease those pressures on the social services which arise from differences in language and cultural background and to deal with problems of transition and adjustment', the Government proposed to offer special financial help. At the same time, while maintaining the principle of universality in entitlement to benefit, the Labour

Government responded to popular feeling by severely restricting the number of new immigrants who threatened to inspire a Right-wing backlash against comprehensive, welfare provision.

Because from the outset the Labour Party saw prejudice and discrimination as basically emanating from the alienation caused by economic need, ignorance, squalor, and idleness, its response to racial problems closely resembled that of the Beveridge blueprint. The alleviation of prejudice and discrimination among the white population required an improved social environment in which competition on racial lines for work or for the civic amenities of housing, health, and education was reduced. With better conditions, the psychological need for scapegoating weaker groups would also disappear. But, as the more thoughtful socialists had already recognised in the implementation of Beveridge, the Labour Government's reluctance to control the economy meant that it was only capable of dealing with the superficiality of social insecurity and not with the economic insecurity fundamental to the capitalist cycle.

Where there were irregular fluctuations in the demand for labour, immigration control was the only answer to the threat perceived – however mistakenly – by white workers. The triad of immigration control, race relations legislation, and the welfare response were seen as the prime means of diffusing racial tension. Miss A. Bacon, in 1965, spoke of the concentration of immigrants in those very areas where the supply of houses, schools, and teachers was already inadequate. 'Of course we know that the immigrants did not create the shortage', she said. 'Of course we know that the immigrants are just making more apparent a shortage which already existed, but, until the Labour Government can make good these shortages, to put more on already overburdened services could lead to a very serious situation' (LPACR, 1965, p. 218). Demands for increased provision and special legislation followed.

The 1966 Local Government Act (Section II) provided for the payment of grants in respect of staff to local authorities with substantial numbers of Commonwealth immigrants. In 1967, a Conference resolution declared that race relations legislation was only a partial remedy to difficulties caused by immigration: 'there should be more positive aid for education and housing in areas with large immigrant populations' (LPACR, 1967, p. 312). In replying to the debate for the National Executive Committee in 1968, Joan Lestor referred to the Urban Development Plan aimed at relieving areas of social deprivation. But she added

> do not let us fall into the trap of talking of this as a grant for immigrants. This is a grant for help to areas that have certain difficulties. Some of them will include immigrants, some of

them will not include immigrants, and we have to avoid getting ourselves caught up in an atmosphere where immigrants can be used as a scapegoat for failure by any of us or the previous Government for dealing with socially inadequate services.

(LPACR, 1968, p. 287)

In the heady, Powellite days of 1968, this was a timely reminder of Beveridge's principle of universality. The fear that blacks were benefiting more than whites had to be allayed.

One snag, long recognised in the Beveridge principle of extending welfare benefit to all, was its tendency to dilute provision and make it difficult to pinpoint those in real need. One solution already mentioned above, was to select out for special help particular geographical areas on the basis of a catalogue of statistics of social problems, including 'immigrant' numbers. In this way, although special moneys could be directed to some degree at the black population, the target was thought sufficiently diffuse as to avoid the accusation of reversed discrimination, or black privilege, so widely believed among the white population. Unfortunately, the suspicion could not be entirely alleviated, and neither could the general stigma attached to welfare.

Parker (1970, p. 41) describes British attitudes to the social services as 'complex, inconsistent and often hypocritical'. On the one hand, they have 'elaborate ideas of social justice, of everybody's "right" to health and well-being and the State's duty to provide these', while on the other, Britain is still 'a competitive laissez-faire society which expects everybody to make his own arrangements'. 'Our pity for those who fail', Parker thinks, 'is tinged with a great deal of contempt – we are prepared to see them assisted, but still expect them to feel grateful and a bit guilty about accepting public help.'

The Labour concern to alleviate racial prejudice and discrimination by the use of welfare provision may have had paradoxical results. In a society in which socialist ideas have failed to penetrate a working-class Liberal and Conservative ideological matrix, the constant emphasis on the need to provide welfare for immigrants can only confirm the view of them as socially inadequate and economically dependant. The association of black people with slum housing, overcrowded conditions, large ill-cared-for families, persistent unemployment, welfare scrounging, and crime, is at least, in part, a product of a Labour welfare response that explains poor race relations in terms of inadequate social facilities.

Concepts of man

The Conservative Party's concept of man
It is not possible to deal adequately, within the scope of this study,

with the many facets of the Conservative concept of man, but the image the Conservative has of man will affect his approach to the relationships between different races of men.

First, man is conceived of as imperfect and imperfectible. He is neither corrupted by society as it exists, nor capable of being perfected by a new order of society. As society has developed organically to meet his needs, he is prior to society, and it faithfully reflects his character. He may alter it in a piece-meal manner to suit his changing circumstances, but a changed society will never offer the means to human perfection. Such a concept of man has much in common with the doctrine of original sin. Man is naturally flawed and his artifices, social or otherwise, far from enabling him to rise above his weaknesses, are made in his own image and likeness. R. J. White (1950) explains that, 'it is not that the Conservative is more religious than other men, but that he is less confident than some other men about man's self-dependence, more inclined to mistrust the finality of man-made remedies for human ills more prone to look for the sources of these ills, rather in a defective human nature than in defective laws and institutions' (quoted in Buck, 1975, p. 175).

It also follows that the individual rather than any dictator or man-made institution, such as the state, is best able to decide what is to his personal advantage. Rules can never be successfully superimposed by a philosopher king who possesses the intention of improving the human condition: they can only be evolved organically in a lengthy process of human interaction. Lord Coleraine (1970) tells us that the Conservative 'holds that human nature is essentially imperfect, but that men and women are most likely to make the best of it in a free society, not one which is minutely regulated from above by some agency external to themselves. He believes that his past is part of man's nature' (p. 184).

This last remark draws attention to the second characteristic – the 'natural conservatism' of man. Lord Hugh Cecil describes man's distrust of the unknown and his desire for the familiar rather than the unfamiliar. Human beings adapt to their social environment in such a way that they come to want those things to which they are accustomed: change of any sort is difficult and vexatious and 'only very slowly and gradually made' (1912, p. 15). Although natural conservatism operates with most force where personal habits are concerned, it also helps to maintain and strengthen political institutions. The Conservative concept of man notes his preference for the familiar and accepts that political change must be slow to be effective. Man has only limited malleability.

Third, the Conservative is inclined to a 'carrot and stick' concept of man in which human beings are felt to be motivated by reward or punishment. Human beings do not work without incentives, they do not behave sociably without the law to keep them in order. They have no natural love of their neighbour, and stand in need of a social policeman who administers correction through the mechanisms of the market or legal system.

These three facets of the Conservative concept of man are reflected in policies on immigration and race relations. If man is imperfect, then to describe him as prejudiced is only to mention one of his natural imperfections. The Conservative is likely to think that social reform in the shape of race relations legislation will always founder on the reef of original sin. In any case, the imposition of a noble humanitarian sentiment of inter-racial love as law from above, smacks of utopianism: race relations will only be improved if human beings voluntarily choose to move in that direction. If legislation does not emerge organically from the people, it will only ever be a misguided and inadequate anti-democratic imposition, failing to change hearts and minds, and causing resentment. Because man is imperfect, the Conservative is not surprised when an individual fails to show brotherly love towards his fellow men: surely that is a counsel of perfection rarely to be achieved.

In addition, the phenomenon of natural conservatism forearms the Conservative with a knowledge that a sudden immigration of peoples of strange appearance, customs, and habits, is likely to be unacceptable to the natives of Britain. There is little chance that change of this magnitude could ever have come about without fear and resentment. If human beings prefer the familiar, as they do, they will dislike the unfamiliar ways of the immigrants, a state of affairs that would be taken for granted by any natural conservative. In other words, the Conservative concepts of imperfection and natural conservatism provide a political context in which tolerance and acceptance, rather than intolerance and rejection, stand in need of explanation.

This is also true of the 'carrot and stick' concept of man. Without social regulation, man is unlikely to behave responsibly towards others. If immigrants are exempt from market forces or laws, they will take advantage of the indigenous population. The answer must be for the laws to be stringently enforced on all occasions, and for no well-meaning, but misguided, allowances to be made for black – or for white – people. Of course, none of these characteristics rules out assimilation, but it is likely to be a slow and painful business.

A gradual process of education offers the best possibility of change: but the extent of the change is clearly limited by the available human material. As Robert Carr put it,

> There is prejudice and it is no good pretending there is not. There always has been prejudice in this world and in this country; between Jew and Gentile, between Catholic and Protestant, between one race and another. These prejudices

have never been easy or quick to resolve . . . Colour,
unfortunately, adds a new, sharp, and strong dimension to this
human feeling of prejudice.   (CACR, 1973, p. 43)

In this analysis, his views were shared by Enoch Powell who claimed that
'in private life, people just do distinguish between their own kind and
aliens, Jews and Christians. All mankind does this.' Violent and criminal
impulses 'are common to humanity; and there is nothing strange in this'
(*New Statesman*, 13 Oct. 1978, p. 461). Races themselves are presented in
Conservative manner as permanent and unchanging. For the Conservative, the likelihood is that the separate races and the relations they engender
will continue to exist indefinitely.

The Labour Party's concept of man

For the socialist, man is ensnared in an economic and social
environment over which he must come to exercise mastery if he is to liberate
himself. In the right circumstances, which may be created by the exercise of
reason, the young human being can be brought up in harmony with nature
and his fellows. Conversely, all destruction of the physical world and
antagonism between human beings is best explained in terms of existing
social relations, particularly exploitative class relations, which have come
into being haphazardly as a result of scarcity, hardship, and the pursuit of
interest at others' expense. The vital human resources provided by nature
have been squandered in the past as a result of the failure to nurture them
properly. The socialist believes that the physical and social fabric of society
must be changed if the potential of mankind is ever to be fully realised. In
more specific terms, an attack must be made on the economic relations of
capitalism which spawn conflict between and within social classes, between
nations, and between races. Once the structural obstacles to co-operation
have been removed, an attempt may be made to rebuild the moral culture of
the people and to produce the 'new moral man'.

The social democrat, while influenced by this Marxist-orientated
account of man's future moral possibilities, may consider it somewhat
utopian in tone. The socialist claim that man can be morally improved is
likely to be described dismissively as 'a utopian doctrine of human
perfectability'. The social democrat will assert that he is no utopian
dreamer, but a hard-headed, practical politician, who promises nothing
that cannot be delivered. Although it is difficult to pin down the many
humanistic themes in Labour and social democratic thought, deriving from
such disparate sources as, for example, the philosophy of natural law,
Christian socialism, Morris's anti-commercialism, welfarism, etc. (all cited
by Crosland), it is probable that, in general, the social democrat holds that
man is basically neutral in character, but corrupted by social institutions.

Crosland (1956) mentions an ethical source of inspiration in Labour Party thought which believes in replacing first, the competitive social relations by fellowship and social solidarity, and second, the motive of personal profit by a more altruistic and other-regarding motive. By improving the social environment, by removing the sources of social conflict, it is possible to produce 'reasonable' human beings – human beings that have not been 'twisted' by the unpleasantness of their upbringing.

The reluctance of the social democrat to interfere with the economic relations of capitalism, however, and his belief in gradualism, lead to the channelling of his reformist zeal into the field of social welfare, and into education in particular. The importance of education is recognised by all who hold that the human stuff is essentially plastic and capable of many forms, but the social democrat sees it as a means of achieving equality of opportunity, social justice, and greater democratic participation in society, without his having to interfere unduly with the more formidable capitalist economic mechanisms. Education becomes the peaceful and gradual means of social engineering for socialism.

The British Labour movement has a long tradition of faith in the powers of education. Robert Owen, in 1816, wrote that: 'No human nature save the minute differences which are ever found in all the compounds of the creation is one and the same in all; it is without exception universally plastic, and by judicious training, the infants of any one class in the world may be readily formed into men of any other class' (p. 146). Leaving aside considerations of wealth, a common education could act as the great leveller, reducing differences of culture and opportunity between classes, and offering the possibility of equality of opportunity. One hundred and forty years later, the role of education in creating inequality, and the part it might play in abolishing it, were still being debated. 'A major cause of inequality in British Society', the Labour Party pamphlet *Towards Equality* (1956) informs us 'is our educational system . . . our schools not only reflect the existing class structure, but also help to perpetuate it.'

The Labour concept of man and the corresponding emphasis on education have considerable significance for approaches to race relations. If human nature can be changed for the better, it is quite clearly the Labour Party's duty to undertake such changes in the shape of race relations legislation and educational programmes. In the parliamentary debate of 7 December 1959, the Labour Party moved that the House declare its strong disapproval of racial intolerance. The Conservative Government was criticised for not doing enough to deal with intolerance in Britain. An educational campaign was necessary and there had to be legislation to prohibit, and make illegal, discrimination in any public place.

The importance of education in the Labour Party approach to race relations is reflected in a constant stream of suggestions for public education, eventually incorporated in the 1968 Race Relations Act setting up the Community Relations Commission. The Commission aimed 'to break down prejudice and intolerance through public education and information'. Arising from the heavy emphasis on the importance of education as a means of enlightenment, the racial hostility of the white population was attributed to its ignorance and lack of understanding, rather than to its economic interests. The composite resolution moved by R. Burns at the 1968 Labour Conference called for 'a massive programme of education to counteract racial prejudice in all its aspects'. In particular, it urged 'the Department of Education and Science to undertake a campaign to guide teachers in counteracting racial prejudice' (LPACR, 1968, p. 283). The 1968 Conference was acutely conscious of the need to combat the effects of Enoch Powell's speeches on Labour supporters. S. S. Gill suggested Powellism signified 'lack of education in the working class movement in this country' (LPACR, 1968, p. 285), while Frank Cousins thought that 'we have to do more educating amongst our people' (LPACR, 1968, p. 286).

Of course, the answer to inequality of opportunity experienced by black people might also be thought to lie in education. If blacks were not as well qualified as whites, then their inequality could not be attributed solely to racial discrimination. Instead, their lack of education, or ignorance of British culture, was held responsible, but, once again, these could be remedied by the provision of the proper facilities. David Pitt asked the Party to 'start first with education . . . to make sure the proper educational facilities' were available so that black people might play their full part in society (LPACR, 1970, p. 207). Black people, as well as white people, might be moulded through education to achieve racial harmony and racial equality of opportunity.

The importance of the Labour concept of man stems essentially from the firm belief that there is nothing innate or natural in the existing strained relations between the races. Rather, through carefully controlling nurture, these relations may be changed in favour of brotherhood and understanding. A danger, however, arises from the social democratic tendency to view racism as a superficial ideological phenomenon divorced from perceptions of economic interest. Racism is reduced to ignorance, and measures to combat it to a well-intentioned, but somewhat idealistic, appeal to love and understanding (reflected in some of the early activities of Councils for Racial Harmony).

Party bogies

Conservative Party bogies

Party bogies are made up of the antitheses of the values that party members hold dear. Individuals or groups come to be identified, often without good cause, with the contrary values that offend good party members to the core. The party bogy may threaten in a real sense the party's actual existence or its ideological coherence. To the Conservative, the arch-bogy is communism, represented by individual communists, the Communist Party and its 'card-carrying' members, Reds in the trade unions, Trotskyite agitators, Marxists, or the founding fathers themselves: Marx, Engels, Lenin, Stalin, or Mao. These are seen as offending almost every value the Conservative possesses, as the very essence of political iconoclasm.

Because communism is regarded as having been invented by a German Jew, and has become the political creed of the Soviet Union, it is treated as a foreign import and its adherents as somehow alien. There is always a danger that this foreign ideology may infect the nations of the Commonwealth or accidentally enter into Britain like the 'plague bacillus' mentioned in Churchill's notorious reference to Lenin. Immigrants, in particular, might be susceptible to communist beliefs because they are, after all, foreign.

In the party debate on the colonies in 1960, Anthony Grant claimed that if Britain did not help the people of the colonies 'someone else – namely the communists – will' (CACR, 1960, p. 18). A majority of the people were 'far more interested in full employment and full stomachs than in the niceties of constitutional democracy and parliamentary government', a fact 'that the communists are very quick to perceive'.

If black people become involved in Left-wing politics, there is a likelihood that they will be closely identified with the 'communist menace'. During the debate on the 1968 Commonwealth Immigrants Bill, Quintin Hogg made the curious remark: 'We may want some immigrants to go away. If I were allowed to select some of the demonstrators in Grosvenor Square recently, I should not be sorry to see their departure' (Hansard, 23 Apr. 1968, p. 71). Powell, in referring to Indian immigrants, also raises the spectre of 'subversive elements, who have had their training' in England (*New Statesman*, 13 Oct. 1978).

Conservative fears are frequently extended to all who disturb the consensual ballot-box and committee-room politics of the main parties. Taking politics on to the streets, or belonging to non-parliamentary parties of both Left and Right, are classed as 'extremism' and vociferously denounced. The 1977 Party Conference deplored 'the threat to good race and social relations posed by the extreme parties from both the "Left" and the "Right"'. In moving the motion, John Pritchard talked of Britain's proud heritage of reason and tolerance, and condemned the street violence in three major cities brought about by people who sought to stir up political enmity. The fascist Right whose 'philosophy is totally alien to the British tradition of fairness' is singled out for abusing the national flag. 'Neither fascist nor Marxist cares one jot for the liberty of the individual' he asserted (CACR, 1977, p. 42).

Because of the Conservative's felt need for political quietude, little or no distinction is made between campaigners of Right and Left, racists and anti-racists. Those anxious to change the institutionalised discrimination and disadvantage of the status quo have little hope of avoiding the ire of Conservatives content with God's handiwork in the form of the existing British constitution. It is also interesting to note that the Conservatives rarely denounce the fascist Right without balancing their attack with a reference to the Left, in keeping with the idea of fairness and impartiality – alleged characteristics of the British character.

The Conservatives have acquired one further bogy in the shape of Enoch Powell, who is seen as a traitor seeking to undermine the unity of the Party by challenging party discipline and questioning party values with his overemphasis on one strand of Conservative thinking: nationalism.

Labour Party bogies

For the last fifty years, the hatred of the Left and working class has been directed against fascism. This has arisen both as a result of the antithesis between socialist and fascist social theories, and as a consequence of the bitter rivalry between socialist and fascist organisations in the political arena, in the streets, and on the battle fields of Europe. Socialists lay stress on the ending of capitalism and the triumph of the working class, on peace and brotherhood, internationalism, democracy, and equality. While fascists likewise have at times expressed anti-capitalist sentiments, in fact they have strengthened the power of capital by destroying the organised working class and pursuing corporatist policies. They despise rational persuasion and favour appeals to the emotion. The fascist values of militarism, racial domination, strident nationalism, the cult of leader- ship, and authoritarianism are in fundamental contradiction to those of socialism. Millions of socialists have been killed by fascists: the democratic fabric has been threatened and at times demolished by victorious fascist forces. The socialist movement possesses a deep and passionate loathing for all fascist persons, ideas, institutions, and symbols. The strength of this feeling has, in the late 1970s, been tapped for renewed campaigning against the revival of British fascist parties such as the National Front and the

National Party, and against racism which has been, and still is, an integral element of fascist ideology in Britain.

Yet, although the Labour Party has accepted fascism as its arch-enemy, the bogy has never been pursued with much vigour by the Labour leadership. On a fundamental dimension, fascism has certainly been denounced dismissively, but on the operative dimension, the Labour Party policy-makers have been cautious in committing themselves wholeheartedly to popular campaigns against British fascist organisations. Fascism has been abhorred for its unconstitutional means, its provocative tactics, and its political extremism, rather than for its central ideological tenets and their effects on the working class and racial minorities. Committed to a constitutional road to the exclusion of street politics, and determined to maintain at all costs its image of law-abiding and placatory respectability, the Labour Party leadership has tended to condemn equally the extremism of both Right and Left, and to guide the Party away from mobilising the people against the fascists at home or abroad.

It has been argued that fascist organisations are best handled by denying them publicity and turning a blind eye to the provocative acts of their very small membership. Street demonstrations and protests at meetings against fascists at which there is a chance that violence might break out have been condemned for mimicking the tactics of the enemy. Instead, the Party has preferred to use its influence over the state machinery, or to pass legislation in defence of any group suffering from fascist harassment.

But, in the face of fascist activity and its destructive effects, the Party leadership has found its placatory line most difficult to maintain. Mention of the British Union of Fascists, Olympia, the Battle of Cable Street, the defeat of Republican Spain, and most importantly, the war against Hitler's Germany, rouses fierce sentiments in the breasts of the socialist rank and file that cannot easily be diffused by stressing the importance of maintaining free speech and the right to organise – even for fascists.

The fact that the traditional bogy of fascism – Nazi style – placed great emphasis on a racial conspiracy theory strengthened the hostility towards racism among socialists. The connection between anti-Semitism and colour prejudice and discrimination was clearly perceived by Labour Conference delegates in the 1940s when they called for legislation against fascist activities. In the 1970s, the power of traditional anti-fascist feeling was still capable of mobilising large numbers of people against the National Front and, therefore, indirectly against the racial policies central to the Front's political programme. The Anti-Nazi League seems to have successfully tested the tactic of approaching anti-racist campaigning by making use of the traditional fifty-year-old anti-fascist bogy, although it is likely that other motivating factors are present, such as a readily identifiable, self-professed fascist group. Racists and racialist practice are rarely as easily identifiable.

Nevertheless, the Labour Party Conference of the 1970s revealed the developing association in Labour thinking between capitalist crisis, the growth of fascism, and the possibility of using black people as scapegoats as an alternative, or in addition, to the traditional Jewish victim. The National Front's attack on black people was treated by Labour delegates as the first step in a sustained attack on working-class organisations and on socialism. In this way, socialists might be encouraged to recognise their own interests in the struggle for black people's rights.

The bogy of fascism, therefore, has had the effect of concentrating the Labour mind on a conglomeration of values antithetical to socialism. Racism is seen as an important part of fascism's ideological snare, and as a potential threat not only to the Jewish or black population, but to socialists, trade unionists, and radicals, and to everything they hold dear. Opinions differ over how the fascist threat is to be met – the rank-and-file favouring more direct action, the leadership always seeking, almost to the point of acquiescence, to exercise restraint. The fact that, in its opposition to fascism, the Labour Party is forced to mobilise against racism and to understand racial propaganda's potential for political damage in a much broader economic and class context, has not been lost on those campaigning on behalf of the black community in Britain, although the danger might arise of displacing the pursuit of specific anti-racialist goals with more diffuse anti-fascist activity, for which popular, traditional support has appeared to be more readily available.

6

The nature of discoursive deracialisation

In previous chapters, various characteristics of ideology have been discussed. In this chapter, an attempt is made to describe one of the most noticeable features of British ideology dealing with matters recognised as 'racial' by the social observer – namely, the reluctance to acknowledge the existence of a racial dimension to social relations.

People make sense of their social environment by describing (explaining) and evaluating it, and deciding on how they, and others, should behave within it. Certain features may be selected for good reason or, from the point of view of the social observer, almost randomly as having significance for understanding social processes. Among many others, family or tribal groupings, nationality, social class, and race, at different points in history, have all been used as central, ordering, and causally efficacious principles.

'Race' is a complex concept that has accreted meaning within the different explanatory and justificatory frameworks of which it has historically been a part. The term has been applied to different social groups discernible for a wide range of reasons: skin pigmentation, physique, descent, religion, cultural practices, etc. Once identified as a 'racial' group, established networks of association provide guidelines on how that group is to be described, assessed, and reacted to. A racial ideology is one in which racial description (explanation), evaluation and prescription are given pride of place. The actual differences between groups of people acquire significance insofar as they are used as anchorage for larger and larger conceptual models of human existence. In Kantian terms, the concept of race does not arise from 'raw' experience, but from the exercise of 'understanding'. The racial object is theoretically, or more correctly, in the political context, ideologically determined. But in the nineteenth and twentieth centuries, no ideology has achieved, for any length of time, an unassailable position in the struggle to command men's minds. Nevertheless, when an ideology does manage to win widespread support, it acquires simultaneously greater power to fashion the world in its own image. As an ideology comes to be established, an endeavour will be made to impose it upon the real world by implementing its prescriptions for political practice

172

and social organisation, the perception of whose effects will subsequently strengthen its claims to represent the reality of social relations.

In Britain, the fortune of racial ideologies has varied considerably. The discussion of racialisation and deracialisation should be approached with the recognition that the models men build of the world must serve their immediate political purposes, have some foundation in reality, and be persuasive when presented in the face of alternatives. In the nineteenth and early twentieth centuries, racial ideology self-evidently served to justify white mastery of the Empire, and reflected the actual relations of domination and subordination found within it. The challenge from socialist alternatives, stressing the racial equality of human kind, was as yet not strongly articulated. In the second half of the twentieth century, black people from the Empire and New Commonwealth have come to live in Britain and have brought up their children here. As in the nineteenth century, the resultant race relations complex requires explanation and justification. Different ideologies compete for the allegiance of the electorate. The possibility of distinctly racial or racist ideologies re-establishing themselves will depend upon the emerging patterns of racial domination and subordination and the concern of pressure groups to maintain or change them, but also upon the adequacy of existing justificatory systems. What follows is an attempt to elucidate one of the key features of recent British discourse dealing with racial issues.

In this chapter, I explain what I mean by 'racialisation' and 'deracialisation', and go on to outline and expand on their various forms and the difficulties of recognising their empirical manifestations. Distinctions are made between practical and ideological deracialisation, between synchronic and asynchronic deracialisation, and between systemic ideological deracialisation and strategic deracialisation. Strategic deracialisation and the intentions and motives of those who make use of it are then examined in greater detail. Mention is also made of the 'racism of the heart' and the 'racism of the head' and their bearing on deracialised discourse, as well as of the particular form of strategic deracialisation referred to here as 'sanitary coding'. Following this, three techniques of sanitary coding are described: equivocation, stress, and the use of words to facilitate mental imaging.

Racialisation

Racialisation is defined in Webster's dictionary as 'the act or process of imbuing a person with a consciousness of race distinctions or of giving a racial character to something or making it serve racist ends'. Within this definition is contained the idea of process, the act of coming to adopt 'race' in a situation in which it was previously absent. The recognition of historical racialisation is brought about by comparing time (1) without race and time (2) with it. Racialisation, in this context, is an historically comparative matter, and it is in this sense that it has come to be popularly used.

Racialisation may be used to describe changes in the real world, in conscious or non-conscious social behaviour and physical and cultural characteristics, or, alternatively, it may refer to changes in the symbolic world, in the way human beings choose to account for what they perceive, and how they act.

In the former case 'racialisation' could be used to describe the formation of racial groups. Such a process need not be recognised by the human actors themselves and is attributed in hindsight by the social observer. Alternatively, human beings may consciously and purposely pursue the goal of establishing what they regard as a race, or, in the case of Right-wing parties, such as the National Front in Britain, of preserving 'blood purity' and 'racial integrity' by preventing the 'death wish' of miscegenation and 'half-breed degeneracy' (Farr, 1978). I shall call this 'racialisation of practice' or 'practical racialisation'.

The adoption of a particular ideology as a result of a group finding itself in need of an explanation for its apparent success in dominating large areas of the globe might result in the pursuit of policies facilitating practical racialisation and the preservation of group exclusiveness, e.g. the prevention of miscegenation, control of immigration, repatriation, genocide, and wide-scale colonisation. Alternatively, the de facto pursuit of such policies might stand in need of justification best served by the adoption of a racial analysis of the situation. In either case, it might be hypothesised that the actors' ideology and observed practice are inclined to enter into correspondence.

Although practical racialisation is of great interest, the main concern of this study is with the symbolic world of discourse. With regard to discourse, historical racialisation refers to the increasing use of racial elements in a verbal context where they were previously far fewer in number, or absent altogether. Racialisation of discourse occurs when increasing use is made of some or all of the following: racial categorisations, racial explanations, racial evaluations, and racial prescriptions. Racial categories may, of course, be used without, for example, advancing racial prescriptions, but racial prescriptions necessarily entail the use of racial categories, and will frequently be accompanied by racial evaluation.

The racialisation of discourse does not require the evaluation of the relationship between racially differentiated groups to be one of morally superior to inferior. As it is used here, 'racialisation' may be said to occur whenever there is an increased descriptive mention of race. But in turning to the prime example of the racialisation of discourse in the nineteenth century, it is clear that the ideology of scientific racism did establish a moral order of the races, and constituted a racially inegalitarian justificatory system. The racial evaluations, and accompanying descriptive and explanatory matrix, supported prescriptions that when implemented would permanently disadvantage certain racial groups. While there is no logical reason why racial categorisation and explanation should in themselves be associated with racially inegalitarian evaluation and prescription, this has nevertheless been the historically recurrent pattern, leading to the suspicion in some liberal circles that the very descriptive mention of race is a harbinger of racist justification and racialism.

But it is also possible that discourse might have to be increasingly 'racialised' if certain racially discriminatory practices are to be recognised and eradicated. The stubborn refusal to see the way a social system operates on racial lines may support and maintain racially discriminatory practices. Unless political actors become more aware of the appropriateness of racial categories for describing their society, and begin to object to the fact that it is organised on racial lines, there might be little scope for eliminating racial practices. Black 'conscientisation' and white radical political development (in which a white person sees for the first time that blacks are different in the sense that they are discriminated against) could be regarded as examples of this kind of racialisation.

'Racialisation', in this sense, then, has to do not with groups increasingly subscribing to racism in a negative inegalitarian sense but to their growing awareness of, and indignation at, racial injustice. Racial evaluation and prescription is directed at refuting racism and eliminating racialist practice. Racial explanation in this context is still important as a matrix supporting evaluation and prescription, but becomes transformed as theories are adopted to explain racial differences, not as immutable natural forms whose effects account for many facets of existing social phenomena, but as superficial epiphenomena mistakenly presented as explanations by those seeking practical advantage. Race acquires importance only because of its considerable historical and contemporary success as a reified category with starkly obvious social effects. 'Racialisation', here, involves the recognition of race as a means to non-racial moral ends. To avoid confusion, it might be useful to introduce the expression 'anti-racialisation' to describe the process of altering the matrix of racial explanation and of attacking values and policies that produce racially inegalitarian ends.

Ideological or discursive racialisation refers, then, to the introduction into discourse of racial categorisation, racial explanation, racial evaluation, or racial prescription. The historian identifies ideological racialisation by comparing at least two expressions recorded on different occasions and noticing the appearance for the first time, or the increasing number of racial elements in, the temporally subsequent expression.

As the classic example of historical, ideological racialisation, Curtin (1964) mentions the 'new flowering' of pseudo-scientific racism beginning in the pre-Darwinian era of the 1830s: 'the groundwork was laid for the racial doctrines which were to dominate Western thought about non-Western peoples for a half century or more' (p. 363). The change, Curtin asserts, 'was merely one of degree: where earlier writers had held that race was *an* important influence on human culture, the new generation saw race as *the* crucial determinant, not only of culture but of human character and of all history' (p. 364). Bolt (1971) also gives a detailed account of the nineteenth-century racialisation of British thought and its pseudo-scientific basis.

Racial ideology's justificatory function for human actors is hinted at by writers such as Kiernan (1972) who mentions the use that white settlers made of the emerging 'regular body of doctrine' that 'drew on both science and divinity, pseudo-Darwin and pseudo-Bible harnessed together. It was flattering to the white man to think that inalienable higher qualities, not merely better weapons, had brought him to the top' (p. 230).

Ideological racialisation's practical consequences are described by writers such as L. P. Curtis (1968), who, in dealing with the relationships between the English and Irish during the Victorian period, claims that the stark contrast between 'English and Irish character and culture in the nineteenth century derived a good deal of force from theories about race and national character which were steadily gaining in popularity during the Victorian period' (p. 5). He hypothesises that the racialised ideas of the Victorian governing classes about the Irish people and character help to explain why 'English policy in Ireland failed to treat the causes rather than the symptoms of Irish national aspirations' (p. 3).

In summary, two main categories of racialisation in history may be distinguished, of which the latter is of more interest in the context of this study. First, there is practical, biological, or actual racialisation, dealing with the formation of racial groups, and second, there is ideological or discursive racialisation (and its antithesis anti-racialisation) constituting part of the account human beings give of their social world.

Ideological or discoursive deracialisation

This chapter is centrally concerned with the various forms of ideological or discursive deracialisation and the means by which their presence might be identified in British political discourse. Just as discourse may be racialised by introducing or increasing the number of racial elements within it, the opposite process of eliminating or reducing racial elements may also occur. The counter-process to ideological racialisation, then, is ideological deracialisation. Ideological deracialisation consists in the attenuation of, elimination of, or substitution for racial categories in discourse, the omission or de-emphasis of racial explanation, and the avoidance of racial evaluation or prescription (drawing on the definition in Webster's dictionary).

Deracialisation, involving the elimination of racial elements from discourse, should not be confused with anti-racialisation, in which racial elements are included for the purpose of achieving racial justice. Ideological deracialisation involves reduction in both egalitarian and in-egalitarian references to race. Such reduction need not occur in partnership with practical deracialisation (e.g. desegregation of schools, abolition of discrimination in public places, increasing inter-racial friendships), which is just as likely to be accompanied by strident anti-racialisation campaigns as by the attenuation of racial discourse. If, in the observer's view, deracialisation occurs because a particular society is no longer faced with any practical racial problems and therefore has no need to deploy racial categories, the situation may be described as one of 'synchronic deracialisation'. If, on the other hand, it occurs in a context in which there is plenty of evidence of actual or racial domination, oppression, and conflict, while there is obvious avoidance of racial questions at the discursive level, then deracialisation may be referred to as 'asynchronic'. Asynchronic deracialisation has often been noted as a marked feature of racially stratified social systems. Rose's account (1948) of black/white relations in the United States offers an excellent example.

> In the more formal life of the community, the Negro problem and the Negro himself are almost completely avoided. The subject is seldom referred to in the church. In the school, it will be avoided like sex. The press, with a few exceptions, ignores the Negroes except for their crimes . . . If the Negro is a shunned topic of formal conversation, he enters all informal life to a great extent. He is the standard joke. It is interesting to note the great pleasure white people in all classes take in these stereotyped jokes and in indulging in discussions about the Negro and what he does, says and thinks.
>
> (p. 16)

From Myrdal's point of view (1962) such conversational avoidance results from the great distance between the American creed of equality and liberty (the justificatory system) and the reality of racial inequality.

Whatever explanation in terms of creed or material interest is offered for the public avoidance of the topic, it serves as an example of asynchronic ideological deracialisation on a grand scale.

In Chapter 2, the characteristics of ideology were set out in some detail. An ideology was said to be a set of publicly expressed beliefs held in common by a group of people and having the effect of justifying a particular state of affairs or course of action, whether that state of affairs was intended by any human agent or beneficial or harmful to the system in any way. In discussing deracialisation, it is necessary to make a distinction between systemic ideological deracialisation (of the sort described by Rose, above), in which assessment of intention is irrelevant because deracialisation is judged as an effect of a massive, impersonal belief system, and individual or self-conscious deracialisation, in which individuals or groups operate strategically to hide their racist intentions in the face of nominally held public counter-values.*

In the case of systemic ideological deracialisation, it is quite possible that the mass of human actors might be unaware of the deracialisation process. Its identification must depend on the social observer comparing his assessment of the social process with the social actors' account of the same situation. If the social observer notes a wide discrepancy between his informed assessment of a situation as 'racial', and the account offered by the social actors, in which no mention is made of racial processes, then he might legitimately assume a state of asynchronism where some form of systemic ideological deracialisation is taking place. His opinion might be additionally supported if it is confirmed in the experience of racial minority groups who feel that their lives are circumscribed by unjust racial practices of which whites appear callously oblivious.

Whereas a general racialisation of practice and ideology could be said to have occurred in the nineteenth and early twentieth centuries (even though

---

* The distinction between, and respective recognition of, personal, strategic dercialisation and systemic, ideological deracialisation is closely paralleled by Mannheim's views on the essential difference between 'the unmasking of a lie and that of an ideology'. Mannheim writes that the unmasking of a lie: 'aims at the moral personality of a subject and seeks to destroy him morally by unmasking him as a liar, whereas the unmasking of an ideology in its pure form attacks, as it were, merely an impersonal socio-intellectual force. In unmasking ideologies, we seek to bring to light an unconscious process, not in order to annihilate the moral existence of persons making certain statements, but in order to destroy the social efficacy of certain ideas by unmasking the function they serve. Unmasking of lies has always been practised; the unmasking of ideologies in the sense just defined, however, seems to be an exclusively modern phenomenon' (Wolff, 1971, p. 66.) The central issue is that systemic deracialisation is an impersonal group phenomenon requiring independent assessment by the social observer, whereas strategic deracialisation is undertaken for what may be a variety of reasons by a conscious moral agent. The matter of whether the latter should be called 'lying' or not is beside the point in this context.

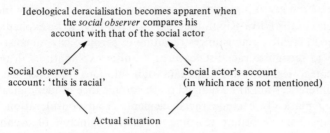

Figure 7. The identification of ideological deracialisation

when biological racism was most prevalent there were those who denied its importance), the contrary process of general deracialisation might be regarded as characteristic of the post Second-World-War era. While it is unwise to accept such unifactoral causal connections uncritically, it is tempting to associate simplistically ideological and practical racialisation with the growth of Empire and the establishment of colonies, and ideological and practical deracialisation with the end of Empire, the growth of the national liberation movements, and the defeat of fascism.

Since the Second World War, however, a new development in the form of an asynchronic ideological deracialisation seems to have occurred. A practical racialisation within Britain has come about as black migrants have been allocated to particular occupational strata and have met with widespread discrimination and rejection. At the level of general discourse, the indigenous white British have made little secret of their racial animosity, but, for a variety of reasons, that animosity has failed to find much direct expression in specialist political discourse. As a result, the deracialised feature of British ideology has become increasingly apparent. (There are, of course, many historical examples of discoursive deracialisation, see Appendix 3.)

International events and pressures, the persistence of traditional ideological formulae, the existence of ideological levels, and structural divisions between one class and another, between controllers of the media and the mass, and between politicians and populace, are some of the reasons that have so far been offered for the discrepancies between the observer's assessment of racial practice and its accompanying public justificatory forms. Whatever the observer's assessment of its causes and effects, the importance of a deracialised ideology in justifying political acts as serving the general interest of the community as a whole, including the black population, must continually be stressed.

This study is concerned with ideological configurations dealing with racial matters. Of these, ideologies with deracialised features seem to be of central importance in British politics and have consequently, in this account, been given preference of attention over the flagrantly racialised ideologies of the Ultra-Right. Ideologies do not have to be explicitly racist in order to create circumstances resulting in perniciously racialist effects. Failure to recognise racialist features, to offer explanations in terms of racial categories, or to present egalitarian solutions that take account of racial differences might be blamed on the dominance of ideological forms that systematically exclude racial elements from consideration, or re-formulate them according to some alternative principle of organisation such as social class. Ideologies of this kind may possess advantages over the classical racism of the nineteenth century. As Myrdal recognised, a popular egalitarian creed may be maintained as a justificatory form and yet serve to sanction 'subterranean' racialist practice, either by direct avoidance, or by reformulation of the practical issues.

This study, as a whole, attempts to acknowledge the importance of deracialised ideologies, which are approached from two angles. In Chapters 4 and 5 the implications of Conservative and Labour values for immigration and race relations policies are examined. The general theme running through the discussion is that Conservative and Labour ideologies deal with issues of class politics, and that racial issues are, perforce, slotted into traditionally established class-based formulae. The justification for racial practice, therefore, is invariably offered in predominantly class terms, with subsequent attenuation of, or substitution for, racial categories. Issues bearing on race can still be discussed, but the observer becomes conscious of the fact that the prevailing class milieu affects the justification offered for the policies applied to racial groups, and, more strongly, leads to inappropriate class-based policies being adopted in contexts deserving racial analyses and prescriptions. Extensive ideological deracialisation occurs as a result of the continuing use of class-orientated categories, evaluations, and prescriptions in a situation judged by the social observer to deserve at least some degree of analysis in terms of independent or semi-independent racial categories. The application of Conservative and Labour values to immigration and race relations offers a particularly central instance of the phenomenon of ideological deracialisation.

In Chapter 7 slightly more formal and general properties of political argument in the field of race relations are examined. The parliamentary debates on measures to control immigration provide an opportunity for more detailed analysis of the way racial issues are handled. Inasmuch as deracialisation occurs in this context as a result of the deployment of long-standing forms of political pleading and defensive argumentation, it may be regarded as systemic, in contradistinction to the self-consciously strategic forms outlined below.

Systemic ideological deracialisation, apparent when the social observer compares his estimate of the extent of racial practice with its lack of mention in the discourse of social actors, may be compared with what I have chosen to call 'strategic deracialisation', which constitutes a special case of the former. It is sometimes possible for the social observer to recognise a discrepancy between what a social actor intends and what he says publicly. Often it is not possible for the intentions of large groups of people to be assessed, particularly when there is advantage to be gained by disguising those intentions. In talking about deracialisation, therefore, the social scientist is more likely to be referring to the previously mentioned, systemic deracialisation than to the individual examples of strategic dercialisation which he may occasionally be in a position to recognise. Nevertheless, strategic deracialisation, and for that matter, strategic racialisation, are most interesting ideological phenomena well worthy of attention.

The social observer has two potential sources of information about the social actor's intention and purpose: the actor's discourse and his behaviour, including its performance and outcome. The observer may compare the actor's speech in private and public, or compare his claims with his purposeful behaviour.

It must, however, be allowed that although outcome might be a good guide to intention, people's intentional actions can produce unintentional outcomes. Recognition of the difficulty of proving intent in a court of law is illustrated by the 1976 Race Relations Act which, while making it an offence to use threatening, abusive, or insulting words in a public place in circumstances where race hatred is likely to result, no longer required intent on the part of the accused to be established. Of course, the sociologist need not subject his interpretation of a situation to the rigours of legal proof. Circumstantial evidence may be such as to warrant the reasonable presumption of intent in many situations in which an agent could have acted otherwise but failed to do so, with harmful or potentially harmful consequences for a member of another race. 'Intent' is used broadly in this

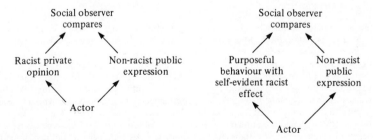

Figure 8. The identification of strategic deracialisation

context to refer to conscious design or purpose on the part of the agent, to his awareness of the meaning of his utterances and of the effect of his action. Many clues might be used by the sociologist as evidence of the agent's intent – not least, the fact that the consequences of his actions have been pointed out to him by others.

A distinction may be made between an agent's private discourse and his public discourse, particularly when the agent is a public, political figure hoping to present an honourable and persuasive face to his audience. Should the observer have access to the 'private person' – as indeed he may, if he is thoroughly investigating the many facets of a person's life* – it may be possible to contrast the agent's consciousness of race and commitment to racial values and policy with his public utterances. Both the private and public figure can then be adjudged racist or non-racist according to the estimation of the observer.

There are, in fact, four possible combinations, two involving agreement between private and public stances and between speech and behaviour, and two involving disagreement. The cases of agreement are commonplace and need only be mentioned in passing. First, there is the obvious case of the person who is racist in his private opinion and public remarks, and makes no attempt to hide his animosity towards members of other races, often vociferously expressing his opinions in order to influence others. Despite the judge's ruling, the Kingsley Read case – 'one down, one million to go' – serves as a well-publicised example. † Second, there is the non-racist in private opinion and public utterance. He may be non-racist in that racial matters neither concern him nor impinge on his social world in any way, or anti-racist in the sense that he opposes both privately, and publicly, racial explanations, racist evaluations, and racist prescriptions.

The cases of disagreement between private intent and public language have received far less attention though they are of considerable significance in the discussion of racial matters. The third case, then, is of discursive racialisation, in which a person who appears to have no racist intent makes remarks recognised by the observer to have marked racist connotations.

---

* Quite obviously, he may be given access by family, friends, or government agency to personal or private papers. Alternatively he may use all the techniques of investigatory journalism or police work.
† John Kingsley Read, leader of the Democratic National Party and formerly of the National Front, was acquitted on 6 Jan. 1978 of the offence under the 1965 Race Relations Act of using threatening, abusive, or insulting words with intent to stir up racial hatred. Read had made a speech in which he had used the words, 'niggers, wogs, and coons' and had said in reference to the murder of an Asian youth: 'One down, a million to go.' The jury made the acquittal after they had been told by the Judge, Neil McKinnon, that Read's words were not in themselves unlawful. The Judge had informed the court that his school nickname had been 'nigger'.

The same person may also unwittingly be engaged in practice that has a racialist effect. If the observer should point out to the person concerned that he (the observer) regards his discourse as racist he might be met with a number of responses, of which I shall mention two, the one signifying linguistic misunderstanding, lack of awareness, or insensitivity, the other disagreement of substance.

The actor may refuse – in good faith – to acknowledge that his utterance could carry such a meaning, or he could admit to ambiguity and immediately seek to clarify his position. These responses would indicate linguistic misunderstanding, lack of appreciation of the insulting nature of a remark, or possibly something else besides.

As examples, we may consider expressions – possibly dead similes and metaphors – that might give offence to people of another race, such as 'nigger in the woodpile', 'nigger-brown', 'working like a black', 'mean as a Jew', 'greasy as an Arab', or 'Chinese torture'. Also jokes reflecting disparagingly on the abilities of a particular racial group may be told unself-consciously, apparently without malice, and with expressed amazement at the possibility of hostile reaction – 'but I only said it in jest'. When the attention of the speaker is drawn to the wider pejorative connotations involved, or to the violent reaction he has invoked, he may be accutely embarrassed by this new self-awareness, particularly when in racially mixed company.

The case of Mr Marcus Shloimovitz's campaign to delete derogatory definitions of the word 'Jew' as 'usurer', 'extortionate money lender' and 'fraud' from British dictionaries might also serve as an example. To achieve his end Mr Shloimovitz intended to make use of the 1976 Race Relations Act which prohibits incitement to racial hatred, but the Attorney-General refused to allow his legal action against the Hamlyn group of publishers (*Guardian*, 31 Oct. 1978). Without knowing the actual reaction of the publishers we might imagine two defences. They might claim that they had neither intended nor realised the offensive nature of the entry and make an effort to delete it. Alternatively, they might argue that a dictionary definition of this kind is not evaluative but descriptive, does not imply any racist intent, and is unlikely to have a racialist effect. This is disagreement over the substance of racism. Defences of this kind are frequently offered for 'racist' jokes.*

The actor might agree with the observer's interpretation of his words, but disagree with him that a particular evaluation and prescription, implicit or explicit, constituted racism. He might stubbornly argue, for example,

* Another way of endeavouring to ensure an audience does not attribute racist intent is to get a black comedian to tell jokes about blacks, or an Irish comedian to tell jokes about the Irish.

that a particular racial difference (e.g. intelligence) did exist, and that his prescription (that schools should be segregated) did not derive from a belief in the moral inferiority of a racial group, but from a natural, psychological difference, or existing social difference, that could best be morally remedied by differential treatment (separate education). In such a case, the social observer must decide on the complexities of whether the protester is indeed racist by recourse to his own (the observer's) moral judgment of what constitutes racism. He is at least able to note the extensive reliance on racial categorisation and explanation, even though there is disagreement over application of the criteria of racism to the actor's discourse. The possibility that a person, may not be willing to recognise, or be capable of understanding, his own racism in speech (and action) must be acknowledged.

In one case, the Commission for Racial Equality investigated a complaint against Genture Restaurants Ltd, and its chairman, John Weston-Edwards, that he refused to accept a booking for a private party because there would be too many black people in it. The company first claimed it refused the booking on the grounds that the party was too large, but the booking list revealed that other parties had been accepted with larger numbers. In his statements to the press, Mr Weston-Edwards said he refused the booking because the party contained too many black people. By 'too many', he said he meant more than ten: 'We refused a party that was predominantly black because it would create an imbalance among our guests. This isn't being racialist. The club holds 200 people and if there were 195 black people inside, this would hardly encourage a white person to come in, would it?' Mr Weston Edwards was arguing, in other words, that his prescription of racial balance should not be construed as racist. And as evidence of his good intent he let it be known that his night club employed black people: 'Our head doorman, who decides who comes in and who does not, is West Indian.' Nevertheless, the effect of the policy was to deprive a private party of black people of a facility because they belonged to a general category of blacks, and this act was intended.

The fourth case, and the one with which this chapter is most concerned, is of the person whose intent is racist but who expresses himself in a non-racist manner. I have previously referred to this situation as self-conscious 'strategic deracialisation'.

The actual motives of the person who verbally camouflages his racism may be many and varied, but two categories have frequently been recognised: an affective and a cognitive, or, to describe it more idiomatically, a 'racism of the heart' and a 'racism of the head'.

With regard to the 'racism of the heart', a person may have feelings of racial animosity, fear, or uncertainty, but, for a variety of reasons, have no

desire to publicise them. For example, he may recognise that racist remarks
lack respectability, and under certain circumstances might cost him his job
or promotion. He thus strenuously seeks to eschew all public signs of his
hostile disposition towards people of another race. His public discourse is
thus 'strategically deracialised', in contrast to his private world. Jenkins
(1971), in criticising the work of Deakin, offers some indication of the
reasons that might lead to this occurring in Britain: 'if there is an ethic of
fairness embedded in our culture and system of law, one would expect a
tendency for those who practise racial discrimination *not* to mention, nor to
admit to it, in interview situations' (p. 14).

The publicly disguised, but strongly felt, racism of the heart, might most
aptly be referred to as the 'Iago syndrome', in recollection of the
treacherous villain who conspired to destroy Shakespeare's Othello. Thus,
Iago confides his secret thoughts:

> Though I do hate him as I do hell pains,
> Yet, for necessity of present life,
> I must show out a flag and sign of love
> Which is indeed but sign.   (*Othello*, Act I, Scene I.)

The disguised 'racism of the heart' can be revealed in many ways: for
example, in 'off-stage performance', in 'body language', in slips and
inconsistencies in speech, in avoidance of racial matters, in failure to
express an unambiguous view on the race issue, in a tendency to reclassify in
a non-racial manner issues recognised as racial by the observer, in the use of
euphemism, and in the discriminatory consequences of the agent's inter-
racial transactions. Sometimes an Iago can be tricked or provoked into
revealing his deep-seated animosities; sometimes he is discovered as a result
of inference from a chance remark or joke, or of an unexpected outburst at
someone who happens to be of another race; sometimes his discomfort in
the presence of black people, or their discomfort in his, gives rise to
suspicion.

In a more speculative vein, the kind of repressed racist feeling described
here is likely to be found in a group which has experienced a high degree of
alienation (interpreted racially) and which is relatively politically power-
less. The group's racism is manifest in the general discourse of everyday life,
but is not allowed to intrude into the hegemonic specialised discourse of the
political arena, where it is deemed unacceptable. Occasionally, as in the
case of Powell 'mania', these politically subterranean expressions are given
the opportunity to surface, with frightening consequences. But the Iago is
usually kept in check by his knowledge of the organisational sanctions that
can be used against all those who express or act out deviant values. His

deracialised public discourse is a product of the fear of the consequences of making known his inner anger.

'Racism of the heart' can be contrasted with 'racism of the head', although the two are by no means exclusive. In dealing with specialised political discourse, it is the racism of the head that deserves attention. Politically expedient ideological deracialisation of accounts of actions privately acknowledged to have racialist effects falls under this heading. The politician, in weighing up the overall political situation, may decide that a racialist policy is necessary to placate his electorate, or for other reasons that further his ends.

While recognising the racialism inherent in the implementation of his policy, he does not draw attention to it, but seeks rather to ignore or hide its effect. When challenged, he may deny such consequences exist, or, in admitting the consequences, argue that they are not racialist, or that they are negated on balance by the overall benefit to the community as a whole and even to the unfortunate victims of his racialism. The politician's justification is typified by its acceptance that racist belief and racialist practice are evil and should – ceteris paribus – be avoided. But in his weighing of aims and objectives, anti-racism is afforded low priority, as it may hinder the achievement of objectives of far more importance to him. Racialist effects are not 'intended' in the sense that the pursuance of them is an important end in itself as apparently was the case in the Nazi extermination of the Jews. Rather they are 'intended' inasmuch as they are acknowledged to be a necessary means to other political ends, such as placating an electorate that has expressed its dislike of black people.

For example, Crossman in his diaries admitted that in 1965 the Labour Party had 'become illiberal and lowered the quotas [of immigrants] at a time when we [had] an acute shortage of labour'. 'Nevertheless', he continued, 'I am convinced that if we hadn't done all this we would have been faced with certain electoral defeat in the West Midlands and the South-East. Politically, fear of immigration is the most powerful undertow today' (1975, Vol. 1, p. 299).

Even though a racialist policy might be followed by a politician seeking to remain in power with popular support, the policy is likely to be justified by appeal to non-racist criteria: a process of ideological deracialisation.

There are many reasons why a person might not wish to adopt a classical racism for justifying discrimination. It may be inimical to the predominant general ideological climate and to the particular ideological stream of socialism or conservatism on which he draws. Also, overt acceptance of racism may be untenable in the face of the fact that Britain waged war against the Nazis, the consequences of whose anti-Semitic policies were later revealed in all their horror. In addition, there are well-established national and international standards and conventions, such as those enshrined in the United Nations Declaration of Human Rights, deploring racism and discrimination on the grounds of colour, race, or creed. In the late twentieth century racialism is internationally condemned and those, as in apartheid South Africa, who publicly pursue racialist policies suffer strong admonition.

There are also sound economic and political reasons for avoiding overtly racialist policies. Britain has important economic interests and trade relations with countries which are likely to respond in a hostile manner if ever they learn that their Nationals or even members of their racial group are being abused. In a world divided between socialist and capitalist camps, and with the New Commonwealth having gained political independence, the importance of maintaining formally correct postures towards other racial groups has increased. For example, Rose (1969, p. 209), recognising the effect of foreign policy on attitudes to immigrants at home, mentions as considerations for delaying the introduction of immigration control in the 1950s, the general acceptance of the changed composition of the Commonwealth and the increasing stress on the importance of its multi-racial nature. The 1961 Commonwealth Immigrants Bill was later to be strongly criticised by the Commonwealth Prime Ministers of Jamaica, the West Indies Federation, Pakistan, and the Irish Republic, and the Indian Deputy Minister for External Affairs.

Internally, too, politicians, however unscrupulous, may be in two minds about exploiting the race issue. Encouragement of race conflict might create a Pandora's box, the lid of which once lifted might be impossible to close. Mindful of a Northern Ireland situation, politicians already in positions of power might be reluctant to initiate policies that could disrupt economic activity and result in large-scale disorder. Above all, those in power will never wish to run the risk of losing control of the situation. For example, Rose (1969, p. 215) describes how the disturbances which took place in Nottingham and Notting Dale in August and September 1958, and Oswald Moseley's attempt to capitalise on the latter with his political campaign in North Kensington in 1959, increased both the will to legislate and the need to reassert anti-racist sentiment. In 1968, the Commonwealth Immigrants Act was rushed through parliament in an effort to curb both the rate of Kenyan Asian immigration and the clamour from the press, pressure groups within the population, and various Right-wing politicians. In seeking to reduce racism by introducing this racialist measure, the Government could scarcely justify its action in racist terms. The danger of the consequences to law and order of overt racist rhetoric, the behaviour it results in, and the political reaction it engenders, have been recently illustrated in the riotous street demonstrations in South-East London.

Attention has also been drawn to the decisive factor of the black vote in a number of marginal constituencies (Layton–Henry, 1978). The self-conscious politician of liberal persuasion will not wish to jeopardise this possible source of support. (Nevertheless, the part played in national elections by Enoch Powell reveals the potential power of an alternative racist and nationalist ticket (Seymour–Ure, 1974; Phillips, 1977).)

Such reasons partly explain politicians' attempts to purge their discourse of racism. Less cynically, the harsh demands of the political world, the need to placate and win the support of various social groups by making doubtful concessions, set against the politicians' earnestly held moral standards, might create a dissonance that can only be resolved at a verbal level. In his person, a Member of Parliament reflects a conflict of two views of how a public figure should behave. He is an individual morally responsible in his own right, committed to his own particular conception of the 'good', but he is also a representative of the people's will – reflecting their collective goals. When the moral and the popular do not coincide, he must find ways of reconciling them.

Politics is, as Gouldner (1976, p. 29) so neatly puts it, 'a kind of selfless work' in which the ideologue 'claims to be altruistic never seeking his private interest but speaking only on behalf of "the World"'. The politician seeks always to present his policies as serving the collective good of the nation and of mankind. If he cannot actually serve both the racist interest and his vision of the collective good, he may be able to disguise his partiality behind a facade of words. This is not to say that he disingenuously conspires to fool the public all of the time: more often he uncritically – but conveniently – accepts his own public presentation of self, and cannot understand the carping criticism of those who accuse him of hypocrisy. He thinks of himself as being realistic and as making the best of a situation in which he has little choice.

If he does not directly set out to harm people of another race, can the politician be accused of deliberate racism? Is his discourse self-consciously deracialised if he cannot be shown to have privately embraced a prescription acknowledged by him to have racialist effects? In these cases, the social observer must decide by reference to all the evidence available to him: to the politician's public and private statements and to his defence of policy, the consequences of which have been pointed out to him, to the persistence and regularity of the actions that adversely affect other racial groups, and to the refusal to follow other available policies. The politician exists in the context of a political eristic that forces him to defend his position and, in that defence, makes it obvious that he is conscious of alternative interpretation of and counter-justifications for his deeds – both ends and means. In a phrase, the observer must judge the politician 'against a context'.

But the social observer's act of highlighting the phenomenon of strategic deracialisation must always be a hazardous business in which he runs the danger of losing his value-free stance and of being drawn into the political arena. To label an action 'racialist' and to impugn the motives and values of a politician are not only controversial acts in themselves, but are made doubly so when the express purpose of the politician's discourse is to justify his racialist actions non-racially. He is most unlikely ever to agree in public with the social observer's assessment of the situation. This is why strategic deracialisation is such a difficult phenomenon to pin down, and why the observer must usually content himself with a study of systemic deracialisation, recognised by noting an asynchronism between actors' and observer's accounts of the social system, and involving no insight into the actors' motives and intentions.

If the social observer has difficulty in identifying 'strategic deracialisation', then another question in posed. If, in order to placate an electorate, a politician self-consciously seeks to pursue policies with racialist effect behind an ideological edifice in which racist sentiment plays no part, how is he to lay claim to satisfying their demands? How, after deracialising his discourse, does the politician convince the audience that he is continuing to pursue racialist ends? If the social observer has difficulty in interpreting the politician's intentions, is it not likely that an audience clamouring for racialist measures will likewise be misled? This question reveals a whole new facet of the phenomenon of deracialisation – but one which is of great importance to understanding many of the features of British racial discourse.

Sanitary coding

So far I have concentrated on the actor's attempt to present his actions in a favourable light by justifying them non-racially. But the question has arisen of how, if the politician is seeking to gain political advantage from a public deracialisation of popular racialist acts, members of his electorate are to be reassured that he is acting to allay their fears. In other words, how can he communicate his intentions to the audience?

Most obviously, the deeds of the politician belie his words. His audience recognises that he has taken action as a result of public pressure in a context where no secret is made of widespread animosity towards black people. That legislation makes some provision for popular demand is easily recognised, and the presumption is augmented, paradoxically, by the accusations of racism levelled by the political opposition. Thus, despite the denial that the 1968 Immigration Act was racially discriminatory, it was clear from the timing and from television pictures of Kenyan Asian arrivals seeking to 'beat the ban' that the legislation was aimed at black people. The statement by the Archbishop of Canterbury to the effect that the legislation was discriminatory only confirmed what was popular knowledge. In whatever terms Members of Parliament described their action, the electorate understood their intentions. With the clear-cut example of the 1968 Act, there is no real difficulty of political communication, but what of the many other circumstances, particularly those preceding legislation, in which the politician seeks to gain popular support for racialist ends?

The politician's language must serve two functions: to guarantee immunity from ideological attack (nobody wishes to be labelled 'racist') and at the same time to reassure audiences – possibly no more inclined to admit to their racism than he – that he understands that their problems arise from an 'alien' presence and that he intends, or has taken action, to alleviate their anxieties.

This dual demand may be dealt with verbally in a number of ways, the popularly parodied expression 'I am not a racist, *but* . . .' being a public attempt to conjoin a respectable declaration of anti-racism with a racist prescription. Fortunately, the self-contradiction of this technique is often so obviously transparent that it proves grimly amusing to those who self-consciously oppose racism. I have also mentioned the phenomenon of politically balancing racism against non-racism and anti-racism. But there is a further, much more widespread and insidious technique available. The politician who is at odds with the dominant non-racial justificatory systems can make use of a phenomenon that I have chosen, for obvious reasons, to call 'sanitary coding'. Below, I outline three common techniques of sanitary coding: the use of equivocation, stress, and the use of words to facilitate mental imaging. By 'sanitary coding', I mean the ability to communicate privately racist ideas with a discourse publicly defensible as non-racist.

First, there is the technique of equivocation. A distinction has long been made between the denotation of a term – the class of object to which it applies – and the connotation of a term – the properties possessed by all of the objects denoted by the term. In Logic, 'connotation' refers to a term's total informative significance rather than to its emotive significance, alone. We may distinguish three different kinds of 'connotation': the objective, the subjective, and the conventional.

A term's objective connotation is the total set of characteristics common to all the objects that make up its denotation. The objective connotation of a term does not vary according to the perception of the individual: it is conceived as existing independently of those who perceive the common characteristics of the objects in question. The difficulty arising from the concept of objective connotation is that even when all items denoted by a term are known, the list of *all* the characteristics that those items have in common would be massive and virtually impossible to compile. The public meaning of a term cannot consist of the objective connotation.

The subjective connotation of a term, on the other hand, is the set of all the properties that an individual *believes* are possessed by the items denoted by the term. The subjective connotation varies from one individual to another. For example, for any individual, the term 'curry' may be understood to refer to Indian food as a whole, to Indian food of a particular consistency and taste (excluding, for example, Tandoori chicken), to food that contains a certain amount of curry powder (garam masala), turmeric (haldi), chilli (laal mirch), cumin (jeera), etc., to a method of cooking, or something else besides. The subjective connotation varies according to experience of eating and cooking, cultural contact, knowledge of spices, etc. Subjective connotation changes from individual to individual, and for the same individual through time, as he acquires new beliefs through experience.

Logicians and lexicographers consider the subjective connotation of a term inappropriate for purposes of definition because of its interpersonal variation through time. Instead, they concentrate on conventional connotation which emerges from the need to communicate with as little misunderstanding as possible. A group's members attach the same meaning to a term when they agree to use the same criterion for deciding on whether any item belongs to a term's denotation. These agreements over usage, existing in the memory, or vocalised in instructions to children, or systematically laid out in the lexicon, are normative as well as descriptive. A term is governed by public rules of correct usage: there is a way in which a term has been used in the past and ought to be used in the future. Humpty Dumpty was wrong in telling Alice that when he used a word it meant just what he chose it to mean: in order to be understood by others, he had to rely on conventional, as opposed to subjective, connotation.

But the relationship between subjective and conventional connotation is complex. By coming to share their subjective meanings, individuals can eventually establish a new conventional meaning. A term with an old, established conventional connotation can begin first to carry a subjective and then a new conventional connotation. Furthermore, both old and new conventional connotations – with different denotations – may exist side by side, giving rise to equivocation in many situations in which the context does not make the meaning obvious.

In Logic, equivocation has always been dismissed as an informal fallacy of ambiguity, but in political rhetoric it has valuable uses. The lexicographically formalised, conventional connotation of a term can always be appealed to as the 'real' meaning of a word, and the new inter-subjectively established connotation dismissed as a mere colloquialism or as an unintended and accidental accretion.

How words come to gain a respectable and formalised connotation, or to lose one, why there is a constant generation of new connotations, and whether some words are more prone to change than others are interesting questions which cannot be extensively explored here. However, it is clear that many words denote (more or less obvious) items in the physical and social world and that there are important differences in the part these items play in the life of the community. Social institutions vary in their exercise of power and public influence, and their susceptibility to change. The significance of what a term denotes, and which person, institution, or grouping denotes it, determines its formal connotation and the likelihood of it maintaining its original meaning. A legal term used in a stable legal institution may maintain its meaning for many hundreds of years; in politics a term may change its connotation significantly in the space of a few decades, while a term used in youth culture may change as suddenly as fashion.

The political aspects of changing meaning patterns can be glimpsed in a number of ways. Expressed fear of slang and neologism can be seen as an attempt to maintain secure patterns of publicly established meaning against the covert connotations of various social strata, sub-groups, roles and statuses, movements and cults. Without shared public meaning, it is always difficult to be sure what other groups are discussing, and subversion of the established order may always be possible. Neither should the symbolic value of language difference be neglected: because patterns of speech are difficult to acquire, they serve to identify people's class position and to perpetuate ideas of class exclusivity. Domination, particularly ideological domination, requires the ruling group not only to be identified and understood when it seeks to be identified and understood, but to understand those it must control. Sub-groups can advantageously use their patois, dialect, jargon, idiom, etc., to thwart outsiders and officialdom, just as officials may use officialese, technical terms, and legal expressions to intimidate, impress, or deceive the public.

A useful distinction may be made between, on the one hand, the publicly expressed and publicly permissible connotations sanctioned by the norms of major public institutions and regarded as traditional and, on the other hand, the widely shared, privately expressed, but publicly inadmissible connotations sanctioned within primary and other groups, and often rapidly changing. In the light of the many contexts in which language can be used appropriately or inappropriately, such a simple dichotomy must be treated as a very crude tool of analysis. It serves, however, to reveal a common political technique known to all students of the 'double entendre' since time immemorial.

By relying on the public and private connotations of a term acting in tandem, a variety of effects can be achieved. Two statements may be made simultaneously, one relying on the public, the other on the private, connotations of the single expression used. A vulgar or unwholesome matter can be described politely: the euphemism. Or an expression referring superficially to a non-tabooed act may have a further contextually detectable tabooed referrant: the sexual pun. The coexistence of public and private connotations, one announcing what ought to be mentioned, the other announcing what ought not to be mentioned, can be regarded as a form of code or cipher. The underlying private message, however, is not secret in the sense that it is known to only a select few: most or all of the audience might recognise its presence and be able to decipher it with ease. It is secret in the sense that the speaker is in a position to refute it.

When challenged to account for his remarks, the speaker may defend himself by denying the presence of the underlying message, and asserting that the public meaning should be taken at its face value. What he *really* said is there in public for all to see, and the private connotation is a product of his audience's minds, of their subjective connotations. And how can he be held responsible for others' subjective interpretations? Anyone who challenges him to justify his use of the private code runs the risk of being asked to provide evidence that it has been used at all. In addition, to admit to knowledge of the existence of such a code implicates the challenger in a connotative conspiracy. The motives of someone who is forever reading unwholesome meanings into a wholesome discourse or imagining insult when none is intended must be extremely suspect. The speaker indignantly protests his innocence and points at the guilty challenger. The speaker cannot be held responsible for meanings supplied by his audience.

To the politician, coding of this kind has many advantages. He is able to make use of a publicly justifiable discourse to make private assertions that would be indefensible if expressed at an overt public level. He is able to be publicly non-racist and privately racist. Sanitary coding reconciles the need to justify morally a statement with the need to make known a dubious attitude and policy.

The one commonplace example of sanitary coding is provided by politicians' use of the ubiquitous terms 'immigrant' and 'immigration'. Dummett has concisely identified and exemplified the syndrome in the following manner:

> At all times the propaganda in favour of 'controlling
> immigration' has been understood on every side to mean
> 'cutting down on coloured immigration', yet as with the
> wording of the law itself the defender of control can exclaim
> indignantly that he never mentioned colour but only the

number of people coming into the country: while if he is
attacked from the right, he can point out that everyone
understood his remarks to refer to coloured immigration.

(1973, p. 185)

Dummett went on to provide examples in which the contextual usage of
the term contrasted absurdly with the traditional connotation (thus
offering evidence of the presence of another private connotation).

> *The Times* had a headline in 1970 stating 'Immigrant births on
> the increase', a nonsensical statement if we are to suppose that
> an immigrant is a person who has travelled from another
> country to this one; if you are born here your only migration
> has been from your mother's womb to the outside world. The
> text below the headline, moreover, made it clear that the births
> referred to were of non-white children, and not of the children
> of Italian, Cypriot, Hungarian, Irish, Australian, or other
> white immigrants to this country. Politicians and journalists
> refer quite often to 'second and third generation immigrants',
> a meaningless description, again, of people born here to
> ancestors who were not born here.   (pp. 237–238)

Dummett suggested that:

> The way the word 'immigrant' has come to be used is
> particularly striking when we look at the fact that migration
> has been so mixed. Had all, or even almost all, the new
> arrivals in this country been non-white over the last twenty-five
> years it would be a very natural thing for the word
> 'immigrant' to have become synonymous with 'non-white'.
> But this has not been the case.   (p. 239)

She went on to ask why the term 'immigrant' occurred instead of
'coloured' which could also have been used as shorthand in newspaper
headlines for West Indians, Indians, Pakistanis, etc. This term, however,
would have had the disadvantage that, had it been used consistently, 'a
number of news items would have looked as racist in presentation as they
actually were' (p. 240). Although 'coloured' has been used particularly in
crime reporting, 'immigrant' has been more popular in the quality press.
Dummett mentioned the example of a *Times* headline, 'Immigrant Visitor
Excluded', placed over a Law Report:

> Under the law in question, the Immigration Act 1962,
> immigrants and visitors were two separate categories the
> former entering the country with a view of taking employment.

The headline, therefore, made no sense at all in relation to the report, but it would have been most unlike *The Times* to put 'Coloured Visitor Excluded'. It might also have given the unfortunate impression that colour was the reason for the exclusion of the man in the case (which of course it was). But *The Times* readers would have no difficulty in understanding that an immigrant visitor was a non-white person trying to enter the country temporarily.   (p. 240)

As a further instance we may take Enoch Powell's speech delivered in Birmingham on 20 April 1968 (Powell, 1969, pp. 281–90). Excluding the passages in parentheses, Powell referred throughout to 'Commonwealth immigrants', 'immigrants' and 'immigrant-descended population'. However, the audience was left in no doubt as to the racial connotation of these terms. The tone was set in the second paragraph by the quote from the 'middle-aged, quite ordinary working man' who claimed that 'in 15 or 20 years' time the black man will have the whip hand over the white man', and by the letter that Powell read from a woman in Northumberland who was woken and abused by two 'negroes' and followed by 'wide-grinning piccaninnies'. In this particular passage, it was obvious that, with the help of the attribution mode, (see p. 213) 'immigrant' and 'black' were being used synonymously. With these apparently very tenuous indicators, set against an already well-established usage, 'immigrant' meant black *and* alien. Dummett was quite right in pointing out that the word also suggests a person strange to this society, alien and different: 'it is then very easy for white people to make the transition to believing dark-coloured people, however many generations from now, to be "aliens in our midst"' (1973, p. 238).

Of course, frequently used terms may begin to lose their sanitary nature. What then happens when a government is forced to take in more immigrants against the wishes of many party supporters as in the case of the Ugandan Asians? Here, there is a very real need to escape from the by now well-established private connotation and to find a more neutral or positively evaluated term: One speaker at the 1972 Conservative Party Conference, in attempting to justify the Government's decision to admit the Ugandans, claimed they were 'refugees and not immigrants' (CACR, 12 Oct. 1972, p. 74). Further examples of coding are offered in Appendix 4.

Of course, sanitary coding is not confined to equivocation in the use of terms. Ambiguity can be assured, and an underlying racial meaning imparted, by the use of emphasis or stress: a technique better known in Logic as the informal fallacy of accent.

The effect of accent can be achieved in a number of ways. It is most likely to be made use of in newspaper reporting, where certain points can be stressed or unstressed by being mentioned or omitted in a particular context. A newspaper may emphasise or de-emphasise an item of news by situating it on different pages, by devoting more or less space to it, by giving it headlines, by placing certain words in bold or italicised case, or by accompanying the story with a picture. In speech, the effect of accent can be achieved by stressing different words or phrases.

When challenged to justify a particular pattern of emphasis conveying an unwholesome meaning, a defendant will readily admit to what he has said, but deny the existence, or, instead, the significance, of his accenting of the item. This cannot so readily be shown to have been intended. Because the meaning of stress is not so apparent, so clear cut, or so unambiguous, there is always a route of escape from the implications of the original message. The challenger is accused of reading in unintended elements for which the person who spoke or wrote cannot be held responsible, and who now claims he is being cruelly misunderstood. The challenger can often only justify his position by insisting that the discourse in question be considered in context and accompanied by its 'accents'.

The Press Council's condemnation of John Junor, the editor of the *Sunday Express*, for identifying a doctor in a manner likely to stir up race hatred serves as an example of racist stressing and its defence in terms of another stress intended. The editor had described how when an old vagrant had been taken to hospital by the police, the doctor who examined him had 'sent him packing'. Later the vagrant had been found dead in a car park. In the next edition, Junor gave the doctor's Arabic name, pointing out that he had omitted to mention it previously. He added that he did not know his nationality but suspected he did not wear a kilt or come from Auchtermuchty. The Press Council upheld readers' complaints that the way the doctor's name was published with distinctly racial connotations was totally unjustifiable. In defending his action, Junor claimed that studiously avoiding mentioning a man's colour or origin was a kind of inverted racism and that printing a name did not contain innuendo unless one believed a doctor making a fatal error should be shielded from public criticism (Aug. 1978).

The manner in which the press operates by selective coverage and in an already existing cultural context has been adequately described by Halloran (1974), Hartmann and Husband (1974), Hall *et al.* (1978) and others. The Community Relations Commission Memorandum (1977) recommended the Press Council to draw up a code of conduct on the reporting of race relations using the following headings: accuracy and objectivity, moderation and balance, interpretation and context, avoidance of stereotypes and of reporting race or colour unnecessarily, the widening of sources of information. Among questions journalists were recommended to ask themselves were: is the story given a front-page lead? How much space is it given? Is the story treated sensationally, or is it placed in the context of a background of facts or overall policy? Has the other point of view been expressed? Is the story only newsworthy because a black person is involved? Is the story joining a 'bandwagon' of crime or immigration stories? Nearly all of these questions are related to methods of stress.

Use of words to facilitate mental imaging

Hall *et al.*'s repeated references to 'images' in discussing the reportage of racial issues (1978) are not accidental, and it is only in an examination of 'imaging' that a fuller account of the process of sanitary coding can be offered. Like Berkeley, we must distinguish between the ideas imprinted on the senses ('ideas of sense' – objects perceived) and ideas 'formed by the help of memory and imagination' which he calls 'images'. Referring to images, Berkeley wrote 'I find I can excite ideas in my mind at pleasure . . . It is no more than willing, and straightaway this or that idea arises in my fancy' (Berkeley, 1910, par. 28.)

For psychologists, imaging refers to the 'sensory-like experiencing which occurs in the absence of appropriate sensory stimulation' (Hunter, 1957, p. 184), or, as it is usually metaphorically put, to 'seeing in the mind's eye'. Hunter points out that much remembering occurs in the form of imaging, or reliving an experience in a sensory manner: this is 'memory imaging' (as opposed to 'after imaging'). The use of 'imaging' is not limited to the realm of the visual, e.g. imaging of a black or white face, but can be extended to include auditory imaging, e.g. the howl of the lynch mob, the sound of reggae music; tactile imaging, e.g. the feel of smooth skin, or of clammy hands; gustatory imaging, e.g. the taste of hot pepper sauce, salt fish, or rum; olfactory imaging, e.g. perfumes and smoke; and organic imaging e.g. feelings of fear, nausea, cold, stomach ache, repletion after a large meal. Neither must imaging always be of the real: it is also possible to image – or imagine – mythical creatures, e.g. women with the tails of fish or men with the bodies of horses, and mythical events. An image is not necessarily static or single but may convert into another, or unfold as a series.

In the nineteenth century, Francis Galton investigated the imaging of a hundred men of whom at least half were distinguished in an intellectual discipline. Questions were asked about the clarity and detail with which they could image various experiences such as that of their breakfast tables. Galton's research indicated considerable differences between individuals in their ability to produce images. Some reported no images at all although they could describe their breakfast tables in verbal terms, while others reported images of the finest detail.

Subsequently, other research has confirmed the wide range of individual differences in imaging and also differences between the various sensory modes: visual, auditory, etc., and within any one mode, e.g. visual imaging need not be coloured. Nevertheless, certain generalisations are possible. Visual imaging is the one which occurs most commonly, followed in declining order by auditory, and then with similar frequency gustatory and organic, and then olfactory. Individuals who are good at imaging in any one mode tend to be good in others. And, most interestingly for our purpose, ability to image in any one individual varies according to what he is trying to recall. Hunter (1957, p. 192) states:

> If it is a concrete unique object such as a face or voice, imaging tends to occur more frequently than if it is an abstract argument, a decision or logical deduction. Even although these latter items were originally experienced in concrete terms, such as a seen or heard communication, their recalling is accomplished with a lesser accompaniment of imaging.

Another important aspect of imaging is that:

> people who deal chiefly with abstract lines of thinking report a less than average ability to 'summon up' images. This fact was first noted by Galton who found his hundred men of intellectual distinction lower in imaging ability than children and adults selected from non-professional walks of life. Confirmation came in 1909 from an American psychologist, G. H. Betts, when he asked both college students and professors about their imaging. The students most frequently reported their imaging as slightly better than 'moderately clear and vivid' while the professors most frequently reported it as slightly better than 'vague and dim'. The relation between skill in abstract thinking and lack of imaging ability seems well established . . . the reason for it seems to be that the more efficient and successful the thinking, at least of a logical nature, the less it is accompanied for most people by imaging. It would appear that images are too concrete and specific to be of great service in reaching solutions by high-level thinking. And as an individual's skill in abstract thinking develops, it increasingly interferes with and weakens his somewhat outmoded skill in imaging, until he may not be able to image even when specifically asked to do so.
>
> (Hunter, 1957, pp. 192–3)

Berkeley argued against the possibility of abstract general images (or ideas), and in favour of seeing the image as a particular. By this he meant that insofar as the aspects of an image are specifiable, then it must be possible to specify them consistently. Luria's case notes on Shereshevskii, the mnemonist, also confirmed that imaging was closely related to the specific and sensorily experienced and not to the abstract and generalisable, for which words and logical mathematical symbols were more suited.

In comparison with generalised terms, images retain the status of 'examplars'. They may hinder the understanding of the more complex physical and social relations which words and word formulae enable us to grasp. Nevertheless, it is apparent from Luria's account of Shereshevskii's phenomenal memory that he relied for recall on his conversion of elements into visual imagery: 'the visual quality of his recall was fundamental to his capacity for remembering words. For when he heard or read a word it was at once converted into a visual image corresponding with the object the word signified for him' (1975, pp. 29–30). Images, then, may act as powerful memory enhancers, while at the same time, as exemplars maintaining the link with the specific, they may weaken the capacity of the individual to form higher level generalisations.

The link between mental images and terms is a complex one, possibly because of the ambiguity of the word 'idea', which from the time of Locke has been used to refer to a variety of entities: the immediate objects of sensory awareness (sense data), memory images, concepts, and others besides. In this context, I must simplistically distinguish between images, whether internal or external, and the terms or sentences of language. As Taylor (1970) explains:

> sentences differ enormously from pictures, even conventional pictures like maps and geometric representations. The latter at least preserve some of the characteristics of what they represent, in particular spatial relationships: their mode of representation is not wholly conventional. Language, on the other hand, is wholly conventional in its relationship to the world. (p. 133)

Mental images, when described in words or drawn publicly on paper, can often be seen to have much in common: but whatever their external manifestations and culturally inspired origins, they are experienced privately and must be converted into public 'symbols' in order to be communicated. Despite the complexity of the relationship between language and imaging, we may suppose it to be two-way: language may give rise to images and images may give rise to language.

First, it seems clear that the language of a speaker may vary in its propensity for inducing images in a listener. Poetry, for example, frequently presents word combinations that succeed in providing the individual with particularly rich, exciting and unusual images. But this effect is scarcely a feature of scientific prose or of legal documents: in fact, such effect would appear to be deliberately avoided in these contexts. The general and the abstract are not prone to presentation in the specific form required of the image. And, in addition, as I argue below, memory imaging is likely to have an effect on the listener's response. The advantage of prose or poetry, containing expressions that lead to prolific imaging, might lie in the pleasure they give to the listener in their immediacy and motivating power, and in the ease with which they may be remembered at a later date.

Second, the sentence giving rise to the image, the image itself, and the later interpretation of the image must be distinguished. Most importantly, an image is not, and cannot be, represented by a sentence. Rather, by holding in mind a particular image, an individual may compose a number of different sentences to describe its aspects.

From a moving visual or auditory image, of, for example, a ghetto, a number of descriptive sentences may be derived. The housing is multi-storey, grey, drab and illkept, and the streets are dirty and full of garbage. Whole families, crowded immodestly together, live in single rooms. People dressed in shabby clothing stand shiftless and idle on the street corners. The siren of a police car wails; a black youth runs past; a white policeman orders him to stop; he runs on; there is a loud crack of gunfire; the youth falls wounded in the back; red blood soaks into the gutter. And these are not all: the imager may be able to describe other details: the dress, age and appearance of the people in the street, what was said, the number of policemen, the size of the pool of blood. These are properties of an individual's image, or series of images, of the ghetto, not of the term 'ghetto' and its conventional connotations. The image of the ghetto does not make any single sentence about ghettos, but can be used as an inspiration for the development of many sentences. Individuals can produce a wide range of sentences from their images. The image can be compared with a model in science: from the model, a number of hypotheses may be arrived at.

Although images may derive from the idiosyncratic, personal experiences of an individual, popular images often come to be shared by large numbers of people. People not only lead a common social life in worker and consumer roles, but they are also exposed from an early age to the visual and auditory matter comprising (non-linguistic) culture. The pictures of Little Red Riding Hood and the wolf, or of Hugh Lofting's King Koko of Dr Dolittle fame (see Suhl, 1975), of witches, and of cannibals and cooking pots help to create the child's visual images. Pictures and cartoons, illustrations of all kinds, in newspapers, films and on television, provide an immense library of folk imagery on which large numbers of people must draw in their mental reproduction or composition (through combination) of images.

Hartmann and Husband (1971, p. 5) point out that:

> The prevalence of images and stereotypes deriving mainly from the colonial experience and at least implicitly derogatory to coloured people may be gauged from the existence of a number of traditions of cartoon jokes. These include the missionary in the pot, the fakir on his bed of nails, the snake charmer, and the polygamous Eastern potentate with his harem.

With the advent of television, in particular, the scope for imaging large areas of the unknown in a standard manner, rather than with idiosyncratic fantasy images drawn from vividly descriptive prose passages, has probably increased considerably. It is worth noting the powerful visual and auditory impact of many advertisements. Where personal contact with black people is not available as a direct referent as in an all-white context, even more reliance is likely to be placed on media images.

This is not, however, the place to discuss with exactitude the changing substance of the mental image: of significance here is the likely existence in many individuals' minds of images that have some, if not a great proportion, of features in common. And because of the similarity of much human experience, certain images will be regarded by their imagers as pleasant and enjoyable, while others will be seen as frightening, unwholesome, or nightmarish. Possibly, this is to state the obvious, but it acquires considerable significance in the discoursive context.

The politician may use sentences that are particularly effective in producing mental images in his audience. From his familiarity with the cultural milieu, he may intuitively or consciously select and describe images which the audience can be relied on to capture in a predictable way. If he is particularly skilful he need not provide a detailed verbalisation, rather he can depend on his listeners' interpretation of a mediating image to enable them to arrive at the conclusion he intends for them. As with the other forms of sanitary coding dependent on equivocation and accent, the provision of images has a number of advantages.

The politician need not state his message in full but can rely on his audience to construct bogy men and demons, holy innocents and heroes, from their prevailing cultural or folk images. In this way, if they are to make an accusation of evil intent, his ideological opponents must accuse the population of possessing sacrilegous images and at the same time acknowledge that they themselves have cognisance of them. The politician denies all responsibility for the meaning his audience has derived: images, as with dreams, may be interpreted in a number of ways. The technique, like others, does not exist in a cultural vacuum. It depends on already existing, prevailing and well-established folk images of which there is no shortage in the long history of British and colonial race relations. Hartmann and Husband (1971) stress that race communication exists within 'the framework of meanings that serve to define the situation within any social group'. However, the range of available images is immense and new ones can be invented and established if sufficient social commitment is forthcoming.

The other advantages of 'image provision' have already been mentioned: an image may act as a mnemonic and, perhaps, at the same time, serve as a barrier to abstracted general thinking, the latter proving a positive advantage to an anti-rationalist politician. Most famous examples of oratorical discourse, of speaking to the people, are replete with image-building terms. We need only think of Churchill's post-Dunkirk 'We shall fight in France' speech, in which the images created become increasingly definite as the scenario of the fighting shifts from seas and oceans to fields, streets, and hills.

Where racial discourse is concerned, it is instructive, if commonplace, to examine Powell's speech of 20 April 1968 for its plentiful supply of expressions that are apparently successful in inducing vivid images, particularly those of conflict between black and white. Of course, the fact that others' conversation is reported within the speech (the mode of atrribution, see below) in no way lessens impact, and the commonplace nature of the simile and metaphor probably increases it:

> the black man will have the whip hand over the white man.
>
> a decent, ordinary fellow-Englishman, who in broad daylight in my own town . . .
>
> It is like watching a nation busily engaged in heaping up its own funeral pyre.
>
> to enact legislation of the kind before Parliament at this moment is to risk throwing a match on gunpowder.
>
> they found themselves made strangers in their own country. They found their wives unable to obtain hospital beds in childbirth, their children unable to obtain school places, their homes and neighbourhoods changed beyond recognition . . .
>
> she saw one house after another taken over. The quiet streets became a place of noise and confusion . . . Windows are broken. She finds excreta pushed through her letterbox. When

she goes to the shops, she is followed by children, charming, wide-grinning piccaninnies. They cannot speak English, but one word they know. 'Racialist', they chant . . .

This description of one white old-age pensioner living in a 'respectable street' may provide the listener with a homely Anglicised image of the formation of the black ghetto, augmented in its topicality and strength by the presentation on the television screens at that time of the rioting, looting, and arson of the 1968 American race riots. The American experience was associated directly with English developments as is illustrated by the section of the speech that followed: 'As I look ahead, I am filled with foreboding. Like the Roman, I seem to see "the River Tiber foaming with much blood". That tragic and intractable phenomenon which we watch with horror on the other side of the Atlantic . . . is coming upon us here by our own volition and our own neglect' (Powell, 1969, pp. 281–90).

7

Deracialised justifications: a case study (an analysis of the parliamentary debates on immigration)

Many features of British deracialisation are well illustrated by the speeches made in favour of the 1962, 1968, and 1971 Immigration Bills. In the previous chapter, I indicated some of the methodological difficulties of establishing that deracialisation had purposely been practised in any given discourse. Nevertheless, in the examples that follow, the tendency for immigration controls to operate in a racially selective manner is most marked, while the justification offered for the Bills rarely makes use of specifically racial description, evaluation, and prescription. The observer is entitled to remark on the discrepancy between the actual racial context and the politicians' account of it.

But, apart from the systematic nature of the deracialisation, there appears to be plenty of evidence that the politicians were fully conscious of the racially charged atmosphere in which they were operating. The effect of the Bills, of which all were either fully conscious – or were made aware in the context of the accompanying ideological eristic – was to reduce the number of black migrants. While the real intentions of the legislators cannot be unquestionably established, there is ample evidence that their purpose was the placation of a racially hostile electorate. Needless to say, the tactical 'racism of the head' was seldom admitted in the debating chamber. And the claim that all those who supported the measure were self-consciously employing techniques of strategic deracialisation is impossible to vindicate.

This chapter is confined, therefore, to an examination of the actual texts of parliamentary speeches on immigration policy made in the decade 1961 to 1971. Although I hint at the likelihood that self-conscious strategic deracialisation is being practised, I concentrate on the actual argument forms used in support of immigration control. The formal and recurring nature of many of these forms in debates on a wide variety of topics provides yet more evidence that established ideological structures circumscribe public utterances about racial issues.

In the context of political eristic, the specific formulae (mentioned previously) are arranged into persuasive argument forms and used as rhetorical devices. While political values may differ markedly between the parties, argument forms are likely to be shared in common – although the frequency of their use will depend to a large extent on their suitability for the task in hand. Of course, one reason why argument forms appear to be so ubiquitous is that, as socially observed features of discourse, they are formulated at a higher level of abstraction than party values. Nevertheless, their consideration reveals substantially more of the underlying structure of British political discourse, its techniques of persuasion, and its effective deracialising properties.

I offer a brief account of the provision of the three Bills under examination, their stated objectives, the grounds on which they were contested, and of the remarks of their chief supporters and critics. I then go on to examine, in detail, the argument forms and rhetorical modes used in the speeches made in the main parliamentary debates over the Bills.

General outline

The object of the 1962 Commonwealth Immigrants Act was 'to control the immigration into the United Kingdom of Commonwealth citizens from other parts of the Commonwealth and to ensure the deportation of such citizens on the recommendation of the criminal courts'. In moving the second reading of the Bill on 16 November 1961, Mr Butler indicated that the control was to be exercised through an employment voucher system, the vouchers being issued by the Ministry of Labour. There would be three categories: A, people with a specific job to come to; B, those who had recognised training, skills, or qualifications which were useful to the country; and C, those who did not fall into either of the above categories, who would be issued with vouchers on a first come, first served basis. Wives, and children under sixteen, of voucher holders were also allowed to enter. (Distribution of Category C vouchers was reduced, and finally abolished by the 1965 White Paper *Immigration from the Commonwealth*.)

The Bill was strongly contested in its passage through parliament by the Opposition Labour Party and a number of Conservative members. After the Conservative Home Secretary, Mr Butler, moved the second reading, Gordon Walker replied in favour of the Labour Opposition amendment declining to approve a Bill which:

> without adequate inquiry and without full discussion at a
> meeting of Commonwealth Prime Ministers removes from
> Commonwealth citizens the long-standing right of free entry to
> Britain and is thus calculated to undermine the unity and

strength of the Commonwealth; gives excessive discretionary
power to the executive without any provision for appeals; will
be widely regarded as introducing a colour bar into our
legislation; and through providing for health checks and for
the deportation of those convicted of certain criminal offences,
fails to deal with the deplorable social and housing conditions
under which recent Commonwealth immigrants and other
subjects of Her Majesty are living.

(Hansard, 16 Nov. 1961, p. 705)

In the course of the debate, Hugh Gaitskell, Leader of the Opposition,
claimed that the Government wished to exclude Commonwealth citizens
because they were coloured and because of the fear of racial disorder. The
exemption of the Irish from the Bill revealed it to be 'a plain anti-
Commonwealth measure in theory and a plain anti-colour measure in
practice'.

In summing up for the Conservatives, Mr Hare, the Minister of Labour,
denied that the Bill had been based on racial discrimination and promised
that the Government would deal with the Irish anomaly if a way could be
found of making control measures work in practice.

The Bill was strongly criticised by Commonwealth governments and the
government of Eire. Norman Manley, Prime Minister of Jamaica, issued a
statement declaring that the Commonwealth would never again be the
same: 'England has failed the first time it has had to cope with the problem
of assimilating a fairly substantial number of persons of different races and
colour. There is no question of economic necessity.'

Despite the strength of the Opposition, which clearly demonstrates the
universal awareness of the racialist effects of the measures, the Bill received
the Royal Assent on 18 April 1962.

The decision to introduce the Commonwealth Immigrants Bill of 1968
was first announced by Mr Callaghan on 22 February 1968 in the House of
Commons. As a consequence of Kenyan legislation designed to implement
a Kenyanisation programme, approximately 7,000 Asians holding British
passports had arrived in Britain in the previous three months. Mr
Callaghan feared that if no action were taken the numbers of immigrants
entering would increase and create strain on the social services in areas of
settlement. A Parliamentary debate on 15 November 1967 had already
raised the fears of the Asian community in Kenya that, despite their British
passports, they might at any time be deprived of their right of entry, and
this also had had the effect of increasing the rate of immigration.

In early February, leading Conservatives began to demand legislation to
reduce the number of immigrants, despite the fact that many of the Asians
of East Africa were citizens of the United Kingdom and colonies. On 23

February, the Labour Government published the Bill which was enacted one week later on 1 March 1968. The bill provided for the application of immigration control to citizens of the United Kingdom and colonies, holding UK passports, who had 'no substantial connection' with Britain. All citizens of the United Kingdom and colonies would be subject to immigration controls except those who had been born, adopted, or naturalised in Britain, or who had obtained citizenship by registration under the British Nationality Acts of 1948 and 1964. A British passport holder whose father or paternal grandfather fulfilled any of these conditions would also be exempted from control. Other provisions of the Bill made it an offence for a Commonwealth citizen to land in Britain unless he had been seen by an immigration officer and for anyone who helped an immigrant to land without authorisation. Immigration officers could also require an immigrant as a condition of admission to report to a medical officer. The existing right of a dependent child under the age of sixteen to be admitted where only one parent was living in Britain was also removed.

After the Bill was published, a protest march of 2,000 demonstrators delivered a petition to 10 Downing Street. The Archbishop of Canterbury, Dr Michael Ramsey, in his capacity of Chairman of the National Committee for Commonwealth Immigrants, declared that four features of the Bill were 'thoroughly wrong'. Racial classification would for the first time be embodied into the Law, the Bill failed to include the recommendation of the Wilson Committee for an appeals system, the number of Asian immigrants to be allowed to enter was 'unreasonably timid' and unjust for people classed as United Kingdom citizens, and a class of virtually stateless people would be created.

The Home Secretary, Mr Callaghan, moved the second reading of the Bill on 27 February 1968, claiming that the main political parties were committed to the development of a multi-racial society and that the Bill had to be considered in conjunction with the Government proposal to introduce a Race Relations Bill, to establish equality of treatment in the sensitive areas of housing and jobs: 'Both Bills are essential parts of a fair and balanced policy on race relations.' Mr Callaghan regretted the need for the Bill, yet emphatically repudiated the suggestion that it was racialist in origin or conception.

For the Conservatives, Mr Hogg stated that he viewed with abhorrence the idea of devaluing a British passport but felt the Government had a right to legislate. The Bill was not a racialist measure in any offensive sense of the word, because, in addition to the Asians, it affected many people in Kenya of white origin, and control would still have been needed if Britain had been faced with the prospect of the same numbers of immigrants from Scandinavia, Italy, or France.

It seems clear from these defensive remarks denying racialism, that those principally involved in the legislation were fully aware that it would mainly affect a racially identifiable group of British passport holders.

The Conservatives put down an amendment to establish a right of appeal against the Act's provisions. The Bill was given a second reading by 372 votes (209 Labour, 162 Conservative, 1 Independent Conservative) to 62 (35 Labour, 15 Conservatives, 10 Liberals, 1 Welsh Nationalist and 1 Scottish Nationalist).

The 1971 Immigration Bill repealed the 1914 Aliens Restriction Act, much of the 1962 Commonwealth Immigrants Act, and the whole of the 1968 Commonwealth Immigrants Act and the 1969 Immigration Appeals Act, replacing them with a single system of immigration control for Commonwealth citizens and aliens. It specified the categories of people – known as patrials – who would have the 'right of abode' in the United Kingdom and who would be free from immigration control. Patrials were people born in Britain or who were citizens by adoption, registration, naturalisation, or who had a parent or grandparent who was born in Britain or who had acquired citizenship by adoption, registration, or naturalisation. It also included citizens of the United Kingdom and colonies who had come from overseas and had at any time been settled in the UK for a continuous period of five years and Commonwealth citizens who had a parent or grandparent born in the United Kingdom. All people, including Commonwealth citizens, coming to Britain for employment would require a work permit issued for a specific job, place, and period, and only wives and children would be allowed to accompany the permit holder.

The Bill received its second reading on 8 March 1971 by 295 votes to 265. In moving the Bill, the Home Secretary, Reginald Maudling, said that 'patriality' had been attacked as a racial concept, an argument he wholly rejected. There was no reason why a country should not accord those who had a family connection with it a particular and special status: 'It is said that most of the people with patrial status will be white. Most of us are white, and it is completely turning racial discrimination on its head to say that it is wrong for any country to accord those with a family relationship to it a special position in the law of that country' (Hansard, 8 Mar. 71, p. 46*).

In replying for the Labour Opposition, Mr Callaghan claimed that the Bill adversely affected the legal status of Commonwealth citizens resident in Britain, without altering the numbers of immigrants. The Bill was 'sailing under false colours' and was 'a sop to prejudice'. It was a thin attempt to make those who had not studied it believe that it would reduce immigration (8 Mar. 71, p. 59). He went on to say, however, that he did not consider the provisions of the Bill were racialist in conception because they could apply to a white Australian but not to a black Jamaican. 'In regard to

* Subsequent dated references of this kind are to Hansard.

a black Jamaican who is born here and leaves to go to Jamaica, if his son or grandson decides in due course to come back he will be free to do so . . . But a white Australian who originated in Italy will not . . . be able to come here' (8 Mar. 71, p. 66). Enoch Powell said that the only part of the Bill relevant to reducing immigration was the provision for repatriation.

What then are the criteria used in the Bills for distinguishing between categories of people and reducing the numbers entitled to enter Britain? Most obviously, despite their discriminatory effect against various racial groups, the Bills never make use of overt racial categories. The 1962 Act purported only to 'control' immigration, and to relate it to work opportunity; the 1968 Act to control citizens of the United Kingdom and colonies who had 'no substantial connection with Britain', and the 1971 Act 'to accord those with a family relationship . . . a special position in law'. By taking some other non-racial feature of black people, the fact that many were unskilled or found it difficult to obtain jobs at a distance, that their parents or grandparents were not born in Britain, superficially non-racial reasons could be offered for exclusion.

Quite clearly, a racialist practice was being publicly justified by politicians with non-racist discourse. This phenomenon becomes more interesting when set against the views of a section of the electorate that made no secret of its hostility towards black people. The news media reflected the electorate's preoccupation by focusing on specific and frequently negative features of black immigrants and sensationalising them, with the overall effect of increasing and spreading already existing alarm and anxiety.

Argument forms and rhetorical modes

An analysis of the twenty-seven parliamentary speeches made in favour of the 1962, 1968, and 1971 Immigration Bills on the occasion of their second readings provides a further opportunity for understanding the techniques of British deracialisation. If racism is defined in Banton's words as the doctrine that 'a man's behaviour is determined by stable inherited characters deriving from separate racial stocks having distinctive attributes and usually considered to stand to one another in relations of superiority and inferiority' (1970, p. 18), then no overt acknowledgement of belief in racism is to be detected anywhere in those speeches. Banton is absolutely right when he says that 'as a biological doctrine, racism is dead' (p. 28). But, as I have repeatedly argued, it is not sufficient to claim that the old definition of racism does not apply, and to abandon the study there. What is said in favour of the proposed legislation with its recognised racial effects must be described with the aid of more refined tools.

Table 4. *List of argument forms and rhetorical modes*

Argument forms

1. *Personalised, dispositional, and agential*
     (i) blacks inferior to whites
    (ii) blacks different from whites
   (iii) blacks a threat to whites
    (iv) blacks privileged in comparison with whites
     (v) other/general/vague

2. *Abstracted social process*
     (i) black focused
    (ii) white focused
   (iii) government focused
    (iv) other/general/vague

3. *Populist*

4. *Economic*

5. *Pro bono publico*
     (i) to advantage of all (general population, both black and white)
    (ii) to advantage of whites
   (iii) to advantage of blacks

6. *Reciprocity*
     (i) they do it – why not us (agential)
    (ii) they are affected, we are affected (effective)
   (iii) debit balanced against credit (cancelling)
    (iv) other symmetry

7. *Means-orientated*
     (i) descriptive of means
    (ii) procedural – correct procedure followed
   (iii) effective – has intended effect
    (iv) consistency – is internally consistent

   Rhetorical modes
    (a) Techniques of quantification
    (b) Analogical transformation
    (c) Ambiguity
    (d) Attribution

The deracialised arguments put forward during the course of the three parliamentary debates are analysed below with the aid of a seven-fold classification and a scheme of rhetorical modes. I mention all of them briefly before going on to deal with each in detail. Examples are drawn from the speeches as set out in Hansard in *favour* of immigration control.

1. Personalised, dispositional, and agential arguments are those that single out the personality, behaviour, or other personal and group characteristics of (black) immigrants, in order to justify the actions, policies, or attitudes (in this context, legislation) directed at black people.

2. Abstracted social process arguments. Accounts of the social processes that occur as a result of blacks migrating to Britain are used to justify legislation.

These two categories rely largely on their substantive content of negative attributes for their persuasive effect and are more subject-specific and less formally constituted than the other arguments mentioned below. In this respect they resemble the ideological formulae described in the chapters on party values.

3. Populist arguments. Mention of the fact that a measure is popular, or a belief or attitude widely shared, is used as a reason for taking action.

4. Economic arguments. The assertion that there is a shortage or maldistribution of resources in a variety of social services, etc., is offered as a justification for limiting immigration. It is regarded as axiomatic that the citizens of a country should have first claim to its resources, irrespective of their abundance.

5. Pro bono publico arguments. The politician tries to establish that the action under consideration will benefit all or most members of the community. The argument consists in describing how the benefit accrues.

6. Reciprocity arguments justify legislation in terms of balance or exchange. They may consist in making a comparison of the behaviour of two agents ('if they do it, why shouldn't we?'), in giving an account of the effects of an action on different parties ('both black and white are affected'), or in matching a positively against a negatively evaluated action (cancelling technique).

7. Means-orientated arguments concentrate not on deciding whether a goal should be pursued, but on the ways of achieving a goal that has already been taken for granted.

In addition to the seven major forms of argument, four rhetorical 'modes', which have the effect of helping to deracialise the discourse still further, are extensively employed in debating the Bills. They are:

(a) Techniques of quantification. These refer to the variety of ways in which the politician quantifies the people, actions, or social processes which he is describing. In the case of opposition to migration, the rhetorical device will be used to stress the magnitude of the immigration, and possibly to imply that the group as a whole possesses adverse qualities. Often quantification involves fallacies of division and composition, the confusion of distributed and undistributed characteristics, the use of vagueness and indeterminacy (e.g. 'many', 'a large proportion'), the misuse of mean, mode, and median, faulty correlation and its confusion with causation, and analogical transformation (see below). As a common species of the quantification technique we must also mention argument by example. Some politicians depend heavily on anecdotal material, relying on their listeners to convert the individual case to a general law. The reverse strategy that the general law applies to each individual without exception is also a common presumption that has even come to be seen as part of the psychological definition of a prejudiced attitude.

(b) Analogical transformation. Analogy involves the comparison of a phenomenon existing in one sphere with that in another, with the effect that a structure is recognised or suggested in the first phenomenon by the structure in the second. Two of the most popular analogies in the debate on immigration are the comparisons of migration with 'flooding' and 'invasion':

> Black immigrants (A) are to Britain (B)
> in the same way as
> flood water (C) is to land (D)
> (or invasion (C) is to a country (D)).

The terms A and B, together, are generally known as 'the theme' while the terms C and D are known as 'the phoros'. The precise qualities of the phoros need not be spelt out. With the help of accompanying imagery, it is easy for audiences themselves to supply to the theme the known qualities of the phoros, e.g. that floods and invasions are dangerous and destructive. Metaphor can be seen as a condensed form of analogy combining an element of the theme with an element of the phoros, e.g. 'immigrants are flooding into Britain'.

The 'trope', or analogical transformation of a term or phrase possessing a direct referent to the real world into one possessing metaphorical connections, is widely used in political discourse. Its advantage is that while the phoros can be read harmlessly ('flood' need only have the implication of rapid movement), an additional effect can be achieved indirectly from its many other (unstated) properties (the destructiveness of floods). As the properties of the phoros are not normally spelt out in this way, analogical transformation may be used as an obscurantist, defensive strategy that shields the politician from an accusation of racism. And yet analogy, when used in argument and for didactic purposes (e.g. Aesop's fables), can have immense persuasive power.

(c) The mode of ambiguity is related to the techniques of quantification and analogical transformation. Put simply, this consists in creating difficulty in deciding on the full connotation of a word or phrase, as, for example, when talking about 'the problem' in a particular context without specifying the precise nature and cause of the problem, its circumstances, consequences, agents and their motivation (if any).

(d) Another commonly occurring defensive mode is that of *attribution*. Instead of making an assertion outright, a politician may quote the assertion of another with which he agrees. In this way, quotation marks can morally insulate him from the accusation that he himself is responsible for that assertion. At the same time the remarks retain their rhetorical effectiveness. In addition, if his evaluation or prescription can be attributed to another person or persons, it may be presented as a matter of fact. That it has been said is a fact, even though the truth of what has been said remains in dispute. Thus, to replace 'I say', 'I think', with 'you say', 'he says', 'they say', 'they think' acts as a useful mode of absolution from the accusation of racism.

(1) Personalised, dispositional, and agential arguments

The arguments that people are most disposed to regard as 'racist' are those that focus on the unfavourable characteristics of members of another race. When these characteristics are regarded as generally distributed, virtually unchangeable over long periods of time, and indicating an inferiority in the performance of the essential human functions – particularly in the sphere of the moral – then it is most likely to be claimed that the discourse is racist in a classical sense. In the past, nature, inheritance, or birth, rather than nurture, culture, or upbringing, have been used to explain the discrepancy between one group's behaviour and another's, and, therefore, if skin colour is taken as the example to go by, nothing can be done in later life to change it. It should, of course, be borne in mind that other hereditary characteristics may be subject to cultural modification, but to those who think along racist lines, culture may also be something determined, perpetual in its fundamentals, linked closely to biological characteristics, and in most respects immutable. As I have observed elsewhere, the genetic/cultural distinction is probably irrelevant to the vulgar racist.

In justifying various actions directed at members of another race, it is plainly not necessary to use a definitive form of racism in terms of belief in genetic inferiority. Other possibilities exist. There is, of course, no requirement to employ arguments that mention a racial group's characteristics at all, but even when they are mentioned, there are a number of ways of avoiding the accusation of racism.

First, for example, the claim that blacks are inferior to whites may be defended by reference to non-moral criteria: technological, educational, medical, economic, hygienic, etc. It is not, of course, the blacks' *fault* that they are inferior in these respects, but then again, it remains a fact of life that must be taken into account in policy-making. Even when the difference is seen as cultural and 'adjustable', emphasis may be placed on cultural evolution with thousands of years being deemed necessary for adaptation to modern civilisation.

Second, it does not have to be stated that blacks are inferior to whites: a mere suggestion that they are different will suffice. The audience is usually in a position to judge for itself the merits of those differences, and rank racial groups accordingly. Poorer conditions among blacks have only to be mentioned for both the conditions and those bearing them to be seen as undesirable. The point here, however, is that the politician does not have to go as far as to evaluate overtly the differences. And even if differences are regarded as being between equals, they may still be seen as an obstacle to relations between the groups, indeed as a good reason why they should remain separate in their own 'zones of influence'.

Third, blacks may be seen neither as inferior nor as personally different from whites, but as a group whose loyalties lie to itself, and whose interests if pursued would be harmful to, or irreconcilable with, those of the whites. Blacks are seen as a threat, then, not necessarily because they have different needs, but because they are competing with whites to satisfy similar needs. The view that black aims are politically malignant might easily be grafted on to this stem if the stance of economic competition is reinterpreted in terms of a black personal moral agency directed at overcoming entrenched white interests. Sometimes this line of thought is extended further in the claim that, in relation to whites, blacks have been given unfair advantages and are privileged citizens. How else, we might infer as the suppressed premise, can the inferior ever be in a position to threaten the superior?

A number of axes of emphasis can be identified in the arguments concentrating on the characteristics of a racial group. First, the group may be treated either as an abstract collectivity whose properties, of whatever kind, belong to the whole, or as numerous, separate, but identical individuals, each performing in like manner. Second, the group may be regarded much in the same way as a natural, but not necessarily physical, phenomenon, having no morality, rather like, for example, a plague of rats, or, alternatively, it may be imbued with moral, probably evil, purpose. Third, it can be either passive or active, dispositional or agential.

As a rule, in any situation of race conflict the (black) minority group will be seen as the initiator, and moral blame will be attributed to it rather than to the (white) majority group. Thus, the responsibility for expressions of white animosity towards black people is likely to be placed on the shoulders of the black victim. It is the black immigrant who is seen as disturbing a perfectly satisfactory status quo. Change itself comes to be treated as undesirable and the black immigrant has only to be present in a situation in which before he was absent, to be held responsible for the reactions to any change.

For the reasons outlined in the preceding two paragraphs, it is frequently difficult to preserve the distinction between assertions of inferiority, difference, and threat. In addition, treatment of the group as an abstract collectivity possessing the characteristics of a natural phenomenon some-times makes it hard to decide whether an argument should be classified as 'personalised, dispositional, and agential' or as 'abstracted social process'. This is particularly so where analogical transformation is extensive. The merit of any consequential indeterminacy lies in its extension of the possibilities for deracialised discourse.

With regard to other techniques of discursive deracialisation, the two model characteristics of faulty or ambiguous quantification and analogical transformation can obscure the actual dispositional and agential assertions being made about the category. Put simply, it is not always clear what proportion of the category possesses the characteristic in question, and whether the word used to refer to the category is metaphorical or factually descriptive. Analogical transformation must always raise the question of the respects in which the analogy holds good. The politician's defence against racism lies in denying that an assertion of difference or inferiority refers to all members of the group in question or that an analogy holds good in the respect considered by others to be racist. It also lies in drawing attention to characteristics that have some empirical basis even though (from my point of view) the empirical basis can scarcely serve to justify the immense significance with which the characteristics have become embued.

In the speeches examined here there was considerable variation between individual politicians in the emphasis they placed on personalised dis-positional and agential argument. Some Conservatives, like Cyril Osborne and Harold Gurden, used them extensively, whereas others, such as R. A. Butler and John Hare, rarely mentioned them. Neither were they the prerogative of the Conservatives: a good sprinkling could be found in the speeches of Labour members, such as Charles Pannell and Roland Moyle. Of the seventeen examples of dispositional and agential arguments in the three Bills, only three could be interpreted as implying the inferiority of black people, and then not without complication. As a whole, personalised dispositional and agential arguments accounted for approximately 12%*

---

* These figures were arrived at by taking all speeches in favour of the Bills and examining each for the seven kinds of argument. A speech was credited with an argument form if that form were found one or more times within it. Theoretically, up to seven different argument forms might be found within any one speech, but in practice only two or three would occur. However many times a single argument form appeared in a speech it was only counted once. Each argument form is expressed as a percentage of the total occurrence of all seven argument forms found in the twenty-seven speeches made in favour of the three Bills at their second readings.

of the total justification in favour of the three Immigration Bills as debated in second readings in the Commons.

Personalised, dispositional, and agential arguments as pure forms without numerous protective modal shields were not often to be found, and, in providing examples, it is probably more useful not to strip them of these deracialising defences but to present them, shrimp-like, in all their complexity.

Black inferiority

Of immigrants, Osborne (C) said: 'Either we have got to bring their standards nearer to our standards or we have got to let them drag our standards down to theirs, or we have got to have control of immigration' (16 Nov. 1962, p. 721). It is clear from this that immigrants were considered inferior because their standards were lower, but indeterminacy serves to obscure the nature of the standards in question. They could be moral or technical, or something else besides. The accusation of classical genetic racism is at first made improbable by the suggestion that their standards might be raised, but then the strong agential reference to them dragging 'our standards down', and seeming to want to, implies a deep-seated disposition on the part of the immigrant to favour low standards. Quantification is of the universal rather than the particular kind: *all* coloured immigrants have these standards. It is worth comparing the above example with the remark of the Labour MP, Charles Pannell: 'It is usually when the immigrant impinges on working class standards that there is so much intolerance in the working class' (27 Feb. 1968, p. 1283). It is never made clear where, when, and in what way the immigrant impinged on working-class standards.

Black difference

Assertion of black difference cannot easily be distinguished from assertion of black inferiority. There was wide agreement that certain differences, e.g. poverty, overcrowding, ignorance, lack of skill, and slum-dwelling were most undesirable: the audience did not need to be told this, and the degree to which the black person was seen to be an agent of his own dismal condition was hinted at, but rarely spelt out. Charles Pannell (L) said 'we must consider the ethnic groups which come within these islands and the fact that their whole way of life is entirely different from ours' (27 Feb. 1968, p. 1281). Roland Moyle (L) claimed that immigrants 'inhabit their houses more thickly than we do because that is the way of life to which they have become accustomed in warmer climates' (27 Feb. 1968, p. 1308). Is this just another way of asserting, with moral overtones, that blacks prefer overcrowded conditions and given the choice would select them, or is it a genuine, if misinformed, attempt to provide sociological information? The interpreter has to decide. Reginald Maudling (C) argued that 'The problem arises quite simply from the arrival in this country of many people of wholly alien cultures, habits and outlook . . . who tend to concentrate in their own communities' (27 Feb. 1968, p. 1345). But we are not treated to details of alien ways and why a problem arose, and the question of the desirability of and responsibility for 'concentration' remains vague.

The theme of difference itself, repetitively emphasised, but still left at a conveniently ambiguous, abstracted level, is exemplified by John Hall's claim that 'We cannot overwhelm ourselves with the large number of people who, however worthy, are alien, have alien cultures, different temperaments, totally different backgrounds and habits and different ways of life' (27 Feb. 1968, p. 1320). That they were innocent victims of fate and morally blameless seems to be the defensive function of 'however worthy', but this cannot counterbalance the sheer fact of being alien, with all its unpleasant connotations of externality, of not belonging, of not possessing a functional place in the social order, and hence, inferentially, of being a 'foreign body' and a hazard to that scheme.

Cyril Osborne provided a number of fascinating arguments which centred on the characteristics, quite obviously undesirable, of immigrants. In one example he used attribution – a Sunday Times quote – to the effect that 'a certified job is no guarantee that the immigrant will not worsen the slum problem' (16 Nov. 1961, p. 723). In the same speech, he made reference to immigrant poverty and numbers, accompanying it with the classical colour-is-not-my-criterion defence: 'In my opinion, had they faces as white as snow, their great numbers and their great poverty would have made control of their coming into this country inevitable' (16 Nov. 1961, p. 721). Also of great interest, is the typically ambiguous quantification of 'great numbers' and 'great poverty'.

Black threat
The more virulent strains of justification in terms of black difference merge imperceptibly with those of black threat. Harold Gurden (C), for example, concerned himself with the crimes of coloured immigrants. The police had to settle 'little brawls which take place, not only among coloured immigrants but certainly among immigrants' (16 Nov. 1961, p. 738). 'Crimes are not committed only by coloured immigrants, but those that are are out of all proportion to the number of immigrants and are of the worst kind – murder, rape, bloodshed, theft, dope peddling, sex crimes and so on' (16 Nov. 1961, p. 739). Gurden's faulty crime statistics might be sneered at in the House, but his use of qualification and quantification illustrate a common and effective rhetorical device.

Crime rates in two different populations are compared and it is freely admitted that crime in itself is not only a hallmark of immigrants, but that theirs is more frequent and of a worse kind. The assertion of greater frequency of criminal acts as a property of the class of immigrants is then distributed among members of the class, each individual being thought of as criminal. The argument from the general to the particular, and from the undistributed property of a crime rate to a distributed property of a criminal propensity in all blacks is fortified by the simultaneous use of the contrary technique of arguing from the particular to the general. This is achieved by the inclusion of anecdotal material – the individual who inflicted grievous bodily harm on a fifty-three-year-old woman, and the man inspired by witchcraft to wield a chopper. By a process of simple enumeration of crimes, the conclusion is reached that the whole class is criminal. And, of course, if all immigrants are considered criminal, their presence, collectively or singly, is a threat to the indigenous population.

In a vicious piece of attribution, Gurden also used a letter purportedly written by a West Indian to the editor of the *Trinidad Guardian*. This mode obviously works well if a black person himself is credited with the expression of his own exploitative intent. Of the numerous calumnies quoted, these serve as examples: 'We extract millions of dollars from Britain and America and we don't even have to show appreciation . . . We breed like flies and don't have to bother with marriage and responsibility for the kids' (16 Nov. 1961, p. 740). The disparaging simile of 'breeding like flies' (rather than like human beings) reveals how easily inferiority, difference, and threat can be combined. The letter as a whole also draws attention to the undeserving nature of black people – to their profligacy. The suggestion seems to be that they should be seen and treated in the same way as the British undeserving poor of the last two centuries. If such a comparison is made by the audience, it provides a powerful traditional guide to attitude and action.

Gurden's speech is very near to what many informed people would consider to be racism, but its interest lies in the modalities of quantification, analogy, ambiguity, and attribution, which provide it with some degree of protection, although perhaps not as much as was expected in parliament in 1961. It is worth pointing out that both Osborne's and Gurden's speeches were repeatedly interrupted in the Commons (as recorded, Osborne thirty-nine times, Gurden fourteen times), probably not only because they carried heavy responsibility for the Bill under discussion, but because what they were saying was so thinly disguised and repulsive to other members.

(2) Abstracted social process arguments

Not all social process arguments are abstracted, and sometimes it is difficult to distinguish them from personalised arguments. Gurden, for

example, gave a description of slum development in which the characteristics
and complicity of the immigrants appeared to play an important part, but
personal blame was not clearly attributed:

> Opponents of the Bill say that the housing problem was with
> us before the immigrants arrived but the Birmingham problem
> has been aggravated to an extent never before known. Slums
> now exist in hundreds or perhaps even thousands where
> previously they could be measured in dozens. Never was there
> such filth and obscenity. The humiliation and degradation of
> these people are dreadful.   (16 Nov. 1961, p. 742)

The social process argument differs from personalised argument in that
emphasis is placed on the specific process of interaction between two or
more parties, rather than on the characters that they manifest when they
exist separately. Nevertheless, although interaction involves at least two
parties, the initiation of, or blame for, the outcome of the process can be
ascribed. Where the process of immigration is concerned there are a
number of possibilities: the agents might be seen as the black immigrants,
or as the indigenous white population, or, possibly, as the government of
the day that permitted, or omitted to stop, the migration. But, just as in the
case of strikes, where the immediate cause of disruption to production – the
workers' withdrawal of their labour power – is held responsible for the
situation, and where the role of government or management is played
down, we might expect the black migrant to be seen as the main culprit in
any outcome arising from migration.

However unjust the existing state of affairs, disruption to it is generally
defined as undesirable, and those who disrupt it are thought of as
undesirables. What is noticeable in the arguments about the effects of
migration is the widespread absolution from responsibility and blame of
the white population and the techniques employed for achieving this. The
chief ones mentioned here are those of depersonalisation, abstraction, and
ambiguity in the ascription of causality, accompanied by analogical
transformation on a massive scale. Mention of the 'dangers of racial
tension' reveals little or nothing about the agent or his motives. Indeed, the
social process arguments tend to convert the immigration issue into a
scientist's laboratory report in which various chemicals come to be mixed
by some mysterious third hand. The statistical analogies ('rate of growth
figures') and natural disaster analogies ('flood', 'avalanche', and 'explosion') provide the backcloth for a reign of chaos without the need for moral
agency. It is not the immigrant, but immigration, and not the white racist,
but poor race relations, that cause the havoc. Here we see the displacement
and dissolution of the moral issue through the deliberately clumsy mesh of

abstracted social relations. The role of analogy and the construction of social models play an important part in both deracialising the justification and yet nevertheless justifying the discriminatory legislation.

In attempting to classify the social process arguments, I distinguish those whose primary focus is on black immigration, those whose focus is on the state of the indigenous white community, and those which appear to be unfocused. Arguments in favour of immigration control nearly all centre on black immigration. The massive extent of the accompanying analogical transformation might also permit of a typology of analogies to be devised. Approximately 22% of the argument forms used in the second readings of the three Bills, and in support of them, fell under the heading 'social process' and there was almost no difference in frequency of use between Conservative and Labour members.

In the context of the Bills, the social processes that need to be described are first, immigration and, second, the resultant pattern of settlement and contact. Both issues require analysis in terms of cause and effect, but where immigration control is the main issue, the effect is of greater concern, for this is offered as reason for control.

It is difficult to find many examples of social process arguments that are not abstractly indeterminate or analogical in some sense or another. Obligingly, Reginald Maudling (C) argued that control of immigration became necessary 'because of the scale of immigration which took place, and because of the speed at which it took place, and because of the way in which it was concentrated in certain areas where whole districts changed their character very rapidly' (8 Mar. 1971, p. 43). With regard to settlement and contact, Roland Moyle (L) asserted that 'where people of different cultures and races meet, there are bound to be tensions' (27 Feb. 1968, p. 1306), while Patricia Hornsby-Smith (C) talked of 'the concentration of too many in too few areas' (8 Mar. 1971, p. 117). The use of words such as 'tensions' and 'urgent social problems' encourages an audience to believe measures should be taken to alleviate the 'problem', but avoids spelling out, in detail and without ambiguity, its nature. As Nigel Fisher (C) so clearly recognised, the phrase 'social strains and stresses', 'in simple and rather cruder language . . . really means colour prejudice' (10 Nov. 1961, p. 780), an unpleasant accusation better left unstated by electorally conscious politicians.

The use of numbers

Reference to an individual or group in terms of a number is often looked upon as the epitome of an abstracted and depersonalised relationship. It is no accident that those seeking to deracialise a situation should discover the 'problem of numbers', and make extensive use of analogies borrowed from the world of statistics. The sheer 'void' of the categories presented enables the listener to paint them in with his own mental image of swarms, hordes, and flows. R. A. Butler talked of 'the sheer weight of numbers' and 'unlimited numbers', Cyril Osborne of the 'ugly facts of these figures' and the numbers 'growing and growing', John Hare of the 'rate of growth of the figures' and the 'steeply rising curve', and Duncan Sandys of 'astronomical figures'. In all these cases, the indeterminacy of the quantification and the emphasis on size and immensity play a part in convincing the listener that action has to be taken. And, in addition, copious statistics and accompanying jargon decorate the discourse with the status of science.

Flux analogies

Perhaps the most popular treatment of black immigration is to compare it to the flow of water, which, in sufficiently large quantities, is likely to overwhelm and destroy life and property. The use of the analogy is probably encouraged by reference to 'population flows' in demography, but its benefit also lies in its suggestibility of the need for orderly control of an impersonal force. The measure taken can then be projected as a worthy piece of civil engineering comparable to building a barrage or river embankment. In dealing analogically only with inanimate matter, it raises no moral question about the effect of confinement on real immigrants. 'Influx', 'inflow', 'great flood', 'upsurge', 'wave', 'pouring in', 'danger of being swamped and overwhelmed' encapsulate the very essence of the parliamentary language of immigration control. The popular solution lies in the social process of 'absorption', a slow and limited business if we retain in mind the image of blotting paper. Only a few can be 'absorbed', and then but slowly and with care. Such is the nature of an analogically transformed social process.

Volcano analogies

Once immigration has taken place, the local storage tank of the ghetto comes to the fore. Roland Moyle (L) claimed that 'the immigrant problem builds up into the ghettos in our cities' (27 Feb. 1968, p. 1309). Here the immigrant fluid exerts such pressure on housing and education that the services run the risk of 'collapse'. Patricia Hornsby-Smith (C) mentioned the 'truly enormous problems stored up and waiting to be solved in about twelve of our great cities and conurbations' (8 Mar. 1971, p. 117).

'Pressure' on resources is easily metamorphosed – no doubt with the aid of the 1968 'conflagrations' in American cities – into volcanic and explosive form. Quintin Hogg (C) talked of immigration as 'a difficult and explosive matter', Reginald Maudling of the serious consequences if the rate of immigration went ahead too rapidly: 'There is bound to be a flashpoint somewhere and if the flash occurs everyone will be burned and probably seriously burned' (27 Feb. 1968, p. 1345). Sir Frederick Bennett warned that 'we have an enormous responsibility to do our best to ensure that the safety valve is not invoked at too high a rate and does not build up undue pressure' (27 Feb. 1968, p. 1339). With a change to a white focus, John Hall claimed that there was 'bound to be an explosion among the indigenous population' (27 Feb. 1968, p. 1319).

Proliferation analogies

Although the Immigration debate did not employ the immigrant birth rate and family size as a central theme, it should be noted that alleged rapid rates of immigrant reproduction – or to use a term with animalistic imputation employed in common parlance: 'breeding' – provide ample opportunity for developing analogies with insects and animals, e.g. locusts, flies, and rats, that have the reputation of speedily reproducing in large numbers.

Martial analogies

Another popular grouping of analogies are those that compare immigration to invasion, and treat the meeting of two peoples as a battle ground for space and other resources. Through this transformation, social process arguments begin to resemble economic arguments. But in that the soldiers of an invading army are human beings, frequently malevolent in intent and action, the analogy has a resemblance to the first category of personalised argument, and provides opportunity for the attribution of more virulent qualities to immigrants. As examples, James Callaghan (L), in reference to the Kenyan Asians, warned of 'the prospect of an invasion' (27 Feb. 1968, p. 1247), and Charles Pannell (L) referred to 'hordes of Asians coming into this country at an alarming rate' (27 Feb. 1968, p. 1280).

Other possibilities for pejorative metaphor and trope lie in comparisons with the spread of disease: plague, viruses, bacteria, infections of the body politic. The list of possibilities is extensive.

Apart from the commonly recurring analogies used to convince the population of the need for immigration control, some other slightly more original comparisons provide bases for cognitive ordering and explanation of a more complex kind of the processes of migration. In the passage of the Bills under consideration, Cyril Osborne's 'honey pot' and Quintin Hogg's 'run on the bank' spring readily to mind.

In attempting to answer the question of why immigrants come to Britain, Osborne pointed out that the standard of living here was much higher than in their own countries. 'In Pakistan and India, they work harder for a week's wage which is less than they can get here on the dole for doing nothing.' Britain was 'the honey pot to which they will come, so long as there is any honey in the pot' (16 Nov. 1961, pp. 719–20). The analogy manages to draw together an explanation of migration in terms of attraction to the good life (pull factors), the presentation of an image of immigrant numbers (swarms of perhaps dangerous insects) and a view of the immigrant as a welfare scrounger whose excesses in consuming hard-earned social benefits would exhaust the supply for the indigenous population. More imaginative unpacking of the metaphor might provide images of indolent wasps stealing the winter stores of deserving worker bees, together with the moral that is usually drawn from such fables.

In examining the relationships of Britain to the Commonwealth countries, Lucas Tooth (C) likened them to those of parent and child. 'The obligations of the parents to their child are quite different from the obligation of the child to the parents' and, therefore, Britain had to have a higher standard of behaviour with regard to immigration than the countries of the Commonwealth. 'The child should be free to go to its parents' house . . to share the food, though possibly making a contribution . . But the child is not entitled to come in and turn the parents out of the house' (16 Nov. 1961, p. 768). Limitation of the child's behaviour in the interests of the family as a whole was considered necessary because of the child's unreasonable demands. For this reason the Commonwealth Immigrants Bill had to be placed on the statute book.

Quintin Hogg (C), quoting from an official report, used the analogy of the bank to justify the limitation of Kenyan Asian entry to Britain:

> They have an absolute right of entry because they have, for historical reasons of one sort or another, a British passport. Quite obviously, like the customers of a bank, if they all entered and asked the bank for payment of their outstanding balance at the same time, they would cause a run on the bank.
> (27 Feb. 1968, p. 1260)

Just as an honest man would take control in an emergency and relax control when things improved, the Government had to introduce controls to limit migration from East Africa.

Where analogy is concerned, it is always important to question whether the phoros has any bearing on the theme: did the migration resemble a flight to a honey pot, a child's mistreatment of his parents, or the sudden withdrawal of large quantities of money from a bank? The first describes the entomic world where morals do not obtain, the second a domestic tiff where, if the fifth commandment is to be observed, the child is clearly in the wrong, while the third refers to a dilemma of the commercial world in which the very existence of business morality – as opposed to legality – can be questioned.

Although the Race Relations Bills provide better examples of the intellectual strategies devised for absolving whites from the blame for racial prejudice and discrimination, the Immigration Bills also contain their share. Basically, they follow, in rudimentary form, the technique Sharf (1964, p. 170) noticed in relation to the treatment by the British press of Jewish refugees:

> If more Jewish refugees meant or might eventually mean, more anti-Semitism in host countries, then the cause of anti-Semitism was the Jew. And since anti-Semitism, at least in its more virulent form was clearly wrong and barbarous, the only course was to prevent any notable increase in one's own Jewish population.

Hartmann and Husband (1974) point out that 'the same argument has been resurrected in defence of Britain's reluctance to accept Ugandan Asians . . . Over 30 years later, the old double think is being employed without embarrassment or question' (p. 186).

An example of precisely this thinking is provided by Quintin Hogg at the second reading of the 1968 Commonwealth Immigrants Bill, when he argued along the lines that black immigration led to insecurity among the whites which created prejudice, which in turn resulted in the need to 'control' black immigration:

> the honourable Gentleman must never forget that at its worst – and it can be very vile indeed – racial prejudice is often based on insecurity and insecurity is largely the result of want of control, and want of control is precisely the thing which the Government are trying to get rid of by what admittedly is a measure which none of us like.   (27 Feb. 1968, p. 1267)

(3) Populist arguments

To argue that because a measure is universally subscribed to, or is popular with the electorate and, therefore, that it is correct and proper to implement it, has been recognised as an informal fallacy from the time of the Greek philosophers. Yet although the argumentum ad populum ('band-wagon' version) is always susceptible to the criticism that what is popular is not necessarily right, its occurrence in a representative democracy, in the context of political debate, has special significance.

The axiomatic belief that democracy is based upon the will of the people, and that the people's representatives should serve their electorate, seems to give extra force to those who claim that, in the framing of legislation, consideration should be given to the popular voice. If democracy is based upon belief in the popular will, those who oppose the popular will are surely undemocratic. However, an elaborate 'rule' as opposed to 'act' utilitarian justification for democratic decision-making has been developed to protect the vulnerable parliamentarian from the volatile Jacobin mob. What is democratic is what follows democratic procedure. The politician is only directly accountable at intervals to the electorate and recognition is given to the fact that, unlike a delegate, he is entitled to represent his constituents according to the dictates of his conscience. And yet the ambiguity remains. Institutionally, through the electoral system, and, ideologically, through his commitment to democracy, he is susceptible to public pressure.

Not surprisingly, then, the politician is likely to turn to expressions of the popular will for justification of his stance on particular legislation. But not only will he do this when he is seeking to advocate a measure in which he believes strongly, but also when he is doubtful about its acceptability to others and his role in its implementation. If legislation can be construed as racist, the ad populum allows him, like Pontius Pilate, to wash his hands of responsibility for the injustice about to be perpetrated. The will of the people takes precedence over his qualms of conscience: it is they, not he, who wished it. In the face of black immigration, whether white 'feeling' is right or wrong is seen to matter very little – of importance is the fact that it exists as a potent force that politically must be taken into account. Immigration control is regarded as a simple, understandable method of satisfying the people. It may be personally repugnant to the politician (and it is surprising how many supporters of control claim to be disturbed by it) but the people and circumstances so require it. If absolution is achieved, it occurs inasmuch as the blood of the immigrant is felt to rest on the populace and not on its representatives. In that the measures are undoubtedly inspired to a great extent by popular feeling among sections of the population, the ad populum can also be regarded as a truthful admission of the actual social pressures at work on the politicians.

Approximately 6% of the arguments used in the three Bills' second readings may be classed as populist. Because populist arguments are somewhat predictable I offer only the following examples:

> I have received thousands of letters from people who live in these areas and are affected by this problem . . . The right hon. Member for Smethwick gave not nearly enough attention to

the English people in the great cities who are affected by this
problem.   (Osborne, 16 Nov. 1961, p. 717)

the public obviously wants a Bill of this type. From the Gallup
poll of last week, there is no doubt about where the public
stands on this issue. I believe that the public is wrong, but I do
not think that hon. Members should utterly disregard a strong
expression of opinion by 90.3 per cent of our own electors.
                                            (Fisher, 16 Nov. 1961, p. 782)

We sometimes debate matters as if we lived in a hot house
isolated from the rest of the country. We must take into
consideration every time that we debate a measure of this vital
importance the feelings of the people whom we represent
throughout Britain . . . The [local inhabitants] will be
overwhelmed by [immigrants]. Wrongly or rightly, these views
are held and we must be aware of them.
                                        (Hall, 27 Feb. 1968, pp. 1316–18)

The basis of control for foreign and Commonwealth citizens
and aliens is what was stated at the election and what the
people voted for.   (Maudling, 8 Mar. 1971, p. 43)

The moralist counter-claim that it is what is right and not what is popular
that should be pursued is represented by Denis Howell: 'In a Christian
country . . . it is not the job of political leadership to decide its first priority
on the basis of electoral advantage. The only decent basis for decisions by
the Government is that of ethics and morality' (16 Nov. 1961, p. 765).

In turn, a populist reply can be juxtaposed that recognises the moralist
position:

First, while we should obviously have concern for moral
obligation for Commonwealth ideals, for non-racialism and the
rest, as MPs in a genuine democracy we have a duty as elected
representatives not deliberately, because of our own particular
feelings, to create a society contrary to the wishes of the
majority of the people who live in this country. It is not our
job to over-rule people simply because we may wish to pursue
ideals of our own, paying no regard to the sort of society in
which the majority of our people wish to live.
                                        (Bennett, 27 Feb. 1968, p. 1338)

(4) Economic arguments

Modern politics might be regarded as a debate about how goods
are to be produced and distributed, about the best way to organise the

factors of production and to share the products. Some might argue, for example, that at a personal level goods ought to be distributed according to need, others that risk to capital or wealth should be rewarded, and others that ability, skill, or hard work should be taken into account. The weight of emphasis given to these and other values will vary, but within any political system a practice will develop that reflects the power relations between particular interest groups. If the practice remains comparatively stable over long periods of time, persons who seek to defend existing production and distribution relations will present many aspects of economic choice as if they were unchanging natural phenomena.

Descriptive economics will provide a web of propositions not only about very general economic phenomena, to be found in almost every social context, but also about the particular society or societies for which it seeks to account. Its predictive success will depend on the adequacy of its theoretical concepts, the accuracy of its methods of measurement, and upon the stability of the economy with which it is dealing.

As a general rule, where power relations between countries and classes remain stable, governments will seek to maintain the existing patterns of production and distribution. In order to achieve this, they will apply policies based upon the descriptive and explanatory theories of economics. Subsequently, the 'laws' of economics will be used to justify their policies.

In order to achieve particular economic goals certain technical means must be applied. The 'must', of course, is dependent upon the goals desired and the economic theory which purports to show how the means and the achievement of the goals are related. But, in time, 'must' acquires a politically and morally prescriptive significance. The political values of the mode of production and distribution are first taken for granted, and then the means of achieving them by economic engineering become codified in fairly elaborate economic prescriptions, e.g. 'In order to bring down inflation we ought to reduce public expenditure, impose a wage freeze.' A subsidiary economic value system emerges which has only tenuous relationships with more fundamental questions of social justice, equality, and welfare. The need for reduction of inflation, industrial efficiency, higher levels of investment, higher wage incentives for managers, more exports, fewer strikes, a safeguarding of the expenditure of public moneys become the values of the moment, replacing other primary values.

The economic arguments about immigration may be seen as a debate about 'optimum population' first brought to the fore as a theoretical issue by Thomas Malthus. Economically, the optimum population is defined as the amount of labour which combined with the other factors of production yields the maximum output. If there are job vacancies, immigrant labour might be thought necessary to maintain or increase output. Alternatively, migrants might be seen as part of the 'constant tendency in all animated life to increase beyond the nourishment for it', or, in other words, as a burden on resources. The division between production and consumption within the moneyed economy creates the possibility of two kinds of argument.

In 1961, the contribution of migrant labour to the economy provided a powerful Labour argument against immigration control. By 1968, immigration was seen as a recipe for achieving scarcity – a reason for control. Available resources, already thinly distributed, would be unable to satisfy adequately the needs of an increased population, and would lead to a decline in provision for the existing population. Chief areas of shortage were in the essential services of housing, health, and education. Possibly, belief in a popular version of the economic theory of marginal utility supplemented anxiety about scarce resources. The immigrants were thought to be relatively unsatiated consumers whose voracious appetites for commodities would be unlikely to be met for a long while.

Economic arguments usually take it for granted that nationals have first claim to any resources at a country's disposal. Governments are invariably expected to pursue a national economic interest perceived in this context as that of ensuring the maintenance and improvement of existing supplies of goods and services, rather than of preserving good Commonwealth relations. But what is omitted from the economic argument in favour of restriction are questions of emigration, and of whether the proposed controls limit white immigration from the Commonwealth and Common Market in the same manner.

Economic arguments, then, justify the limitation of migration in terms of the shortage of scarce resources. Some simply express popular concern about perceived or experienced shortage of houses, school places, hospital beds, and jobs. Others are couched in the jargon of the discipline of economics and accompanied by the assumption of subsidiary economic values such as the importance of productive labour, labour efficiency, the maintenance of wage rates, which tend to disguise more fundamental moral questions. The arguments make use of the distinction between production and consumption to de-emphasise the contribution of immigrant labour to the production of goods and services. They are generally used to stress the dangers of population increase due to immigration and the immigrants' part in creating shortage. In other words, the cause of shortage is the assumed growth of population in particular areas, the answer to which lies not in the provision of more goods and services but in the curtailment of demand by a halt to population growth.

Yet the relationship between immigration and scarcity must still be established. There is a tradition of counter-arguments which asserts that black immigrants are being scapegoated for government and industrial failure to supply goods, that prejudice results from misplaced blame for scarcity, that immigrants are productive, that the worst housing shortage, unemployment, and strained social services are to be found in Scotland and Northern Ireland where there are very few black people. The arguments succeed to the extent that they break the hypothesised causal link between the presence of blacks and increased scarcity for whites.

In arguing for the 1961 Bill, Butler stressed the thickly populated nature of the country and mentioned the possibility of a future recession. Osborne (C) argued 'we have neither the room nor the resources indefinitely to take all who would like to come' (16 Nov. 1961, p. 722). Fisher (C) claimed that one good reason for the Bill was the housing shortage: 'and as houses take time to build this, in itself, constitutes a good reason for, at any rate, a temporary check on immigration' (16 Nov. 1961, p. 782). But still the Labour Party stress on the contribution of migrants to production, exemplified in the Gordon-Walker speech, pervaded the 1961 debate. The subsidiary economic values of the expanding economy and the dangers of labour scarcity were unassailable.

> The fact, to which the right hon. Gentleman [R. A. Butler] and many others who support this Bill shut their eyes, is that an expanding economy creates new jobs. In the Birmingham area, between 1955 and 1960, 60,000 new jobs were created. The services in an expanding economy are continually short . . . We could not run the economy without some immigrant labour from somewhere . . .
> . . . therefore, an expanding economy, even one expanding at the rate laid down by this Government, produces labour scarcity. We have to accept this as a fact of life. There is a direct relation between labour demand and immigration. Ninety-five per cent of immigrants get jobs quickly. They do not just move about casually. They are able to take a share in the working of our economy.
> (Gordon-Walker (L), 16 Nov. 1961, pp. 709–10)

By 1968, in addition to housing shortage, the unavailability of school places and hospital beds came increasingly to the fore as issues. Pannell (L) allowed the immigrants to take the blame for economic deprivation by his use of the mode of attribution: 'The working-class people of this country see the immigrants, however ignorantly, as an increased pressure on housing, schools, and the Health service, and additions to the unemployment figure of 600,000' (Pannell, 27 Feb. 1968, p. 1283).

John Hall stressed the fact that immigrant mothers had priority for maternity beds 'because the conditions in which they live make it necessary for them to be taken into hospital for their confinement' (27 Feb. 1968, p.

1318). In other words, not only did immigrants create scarcity, but they took more than their share.

Patricia Hornsby-Smith (C) explicitly admitted (with the aid of the attribution mode) that whites should have first claim on the country's resources: 'Today the figure is 750,000 [unemployed] the majority of whom are what are now called white patrial citizens. Are these people to be called racists because they think that there should be permit job control and they should have the first claim on jobs in Britain?' (8 Mar. 1971, pp. 117–18). The conflict of the principle of need versus that of priority for a country's nationals is also illustrated by her subsequent remarks:

> Let us also spare a thought for the hard-pressed local
> authorities whose social services have been far outstripped by
> the influx of immigrants. In some areas, if the housing
> committees allocated their property exclusively on the basis of
> social need, no white family would get anywhere near an
> allocation for the next 10 or fifteen years.
>
> (8 Mar. 1971, p. 118)

Economic arguments accounted for 15% of the total of argument forms, and although there was similarity between the rates of use for both parties, Labour MPs were on the whole more prone to adopting economic justification and of relating it to their other ideological predilections. It could, for example, be easily reconciled with a concept of economic planning as Andrew Faulds (L) indicated:

> I entirely accept and with a constituency interest I should
> make it clear the need for some sort of quota system based on
> the perfectly reasonable argument that we should absorb no
> more than our resources, economic and social, can take in.
> That is an aspect of planning which I accept in an ordered
> society.   (27 Feb. 1968, p. 1295)

If the problems that immigrants are felt to create are reducible to those of economic scarcity, then the socialist might see the answer in terms of redistribution of goods to those in need. This is partly the essence of the Labour amendment of 1961 which criticised the 1961 Bill and, by implication, the Conservative Government, for failing to deal with 'deplorable social and housing conditions'. In 1968, Renee Short (L) saw the immigrant issue in very much the same light and stressed the hardships caused by the economic effects of immigration in order (successfully) to gain financial concessions for her town of Wolverhampton: 'Unless Wolverhampton receives some relief in respect of the constant numbers that are coming into the town, it may well lose hope' (27 Feb. 1968, p. 1333). It is important to recognise that the naive economic equation of immigrants = shortage has the advantage that it can apparently be solved with a simple reallocation of resources, a point that was not lost in 1968 on the clamorous MPs, local politicians, and council officials of Wolverhampton.

Unfortunately, much as the man who pays maintenance for a child is thought to acknowledge paternity, a government which contributes money to solving the 'immigrant problem' is seen to agree with the propositions that it is culpably responsible for the presence of immigrants *and* that they constitute a financial liability. Later, when the problems are not solved by payment, the economic argument can be usefully salvaged by claiming that not enough was given, that it was given too late, or that it was wrongly allocated. As a means of deracialisation, reducing the complexities of race relations to the business of resource allocation, the economic argument has served respective governments well. Responses to racial inequality have invariably taken the form of Urban Aid and Inner City programmes directed at geographical areas and serving the population as a whole – both black and white. It would seem that the somewhat feeble attempts to reallocate resources from richer to poorer areas was felt to be politically acceptable, while reallocation from white to black was not.

(5) Pro bono publico arguments

This category covers a wide range of argument based on the plea that people will benefit from the measure, that the greatest good for the greatest number will be served. The people concerned might be the indigenous white population, the black immigrants, or all people, both white and black, treated collectively. The advantages to be gained from immigration control may remain unspecified with heavy reliance being placed on the mode of ambiguity, or detailed benefits may be listed. In this latter respect there may be overlapping with economic and social process arguments, as, for example, when it is felt that the public good is served by the reduction in prejudice brought about by excluding the cause of prejudice – the immigrant himself.

In the parliamentary debates, the consciousness of race was reflected in the constant occurrence of the claim that blacks would also gain from immigration control. Blacks outside of Britain would benefit from being prevented from coming into appalling urban conditions, while those already here would benefit from diminished pressure on resources, and the advantageous effects of immigration control on white attitudes. The idea that the control would help both whites and *blacks* was used to counteract the charge that the Bills were racialist in effect. In this respect, the pro bono publico arguments have a resemblance to the reciprocity arguments described below.

The virtue of the pro bono publico argument is that it accepts that certain actions in themselves may be undesirable but that, in summation, the greatest good is done, or that there is a balance of good over evil, or that, of two undesirable actions, the less undesirable is chosen. Even if it were acknowledged that black people would suffer from the legislation, the legislators would still be justified in their action because the overall effects were the best that could be achieved. Pro bono publico arguments accounted for 20% of the total of argument forms in the debates, but this might have been due to the fact that many arguments were of such a vague and summary nature that they could only be placed in this bracket. Because of their repetitive nature, I shall only offer a limited number of pro bono publico arguments put forward by leading proponents of the three Bills:

> The Government regret having to produce these proposals but they believe that this Measure is rendered necessary by the course of events. It would have been perfectly easy just to go on watching the situation, but the Government have preferred, admittedly after hesitation, to take a course which is as distasteful to them as it is to many of their critics. We consider this course to be right. I believe this course is right and will be to the advantage of Commonwealth relations . . . I hope that we can make the Bill a good and humane instrument for doing a very necessary job.   (R. A. Butler, 16 Nov. 1961, p. 705)

> Merely to wait for difficulties to accumulate, to wait until the need for action had become apparent to all, would certainly have made the job of the Government easier. But it would have done no good to our own people, no good to relations with the Commonwealth. It would have been an abdication of responsibility.   (Hare, 16 Nov. 1961, p. 811)

> The Government, Parliament, all parties in the country, are fully committed to the development of a multi-racial society in Britain – a society which will be diverse in culture and will be equal before the law; a society in which all communities will have respect for each other; a society in which there will be unity in purpose and common allegiance. These are the aims, as I see it, of the great debate that is now overtaking the nation, as well as Parliament, on this issue.
> (Callaghan, 27 Feb. 1968, p. 1241)

> I hope they will acknowledge . . . that it is possible that the origin of this Bill lies neither in panic nor in prejudice but in a considered judgement of the best way to achieve the idea of a multi-racial society.   (Callaghan, 27 Feb. 1968, p. 1242)

I suspect it has been the objective of every hon. Member on
either side of the House, to assist in building at home a
homogeneous society of which all of us can be proud and
which will command the allegiance of everyone dwelling within
it. We desire no second-class citizens, we desire no race
discrimination, we desire no dilapidated areas, housing
different communities from the majority.

(Hogg, 27 Feb. 1968, p. 1259)

I want to stress that the main purpose of immigration policy in
the situation which this country faces is as a contribution to
the great problem of ensuring that the varied communities
which we have here can settle down progressively over the
years to live together in peace and harmony.

(Maudling, 8 Mar. 1971, p. 43)

By 1968, the reluctance of 1961 to cut off sources of labour, appeared to
have been jettisoned in favour of an eagerness to benefit the community by
immigration control. The system of justification developed into a 'full-
blown', deracialised form when it was insisted that blacks would benefit
also, or more so, from the measures.

We have to take account of the needs of Commonwealth
countries as well as our own requirements. I think the House
will agree that it would be quite wrong to try to lure away
people with skills of which those countries are in urgent need.

(Hare, 16 Nov. 1961, p. 806)

I do not think it would be right for us to sit back and allow
Commonwealth citizens to come into this country in vastly
increased numbers unless we are satisfied that reasonable living
conditions are available to them.

(Hare, 16 Nov. 1961, p. 807)

I am also concerned to avoid that these people who are
coming to our country and whom we are wishing to integrate
shall be treated not as second-class citizens.

(Lomas, 27 Feb. 1968, p. 1324)

I cannot think it profits anyone to bring families into such
conditions.   (Short, 27 Feb. 1968, p. 1332)

If immigrants already here, although they will not say so too
publicly, are actually pleading for their difficulties not to be
made greater by stepping up the rate of absorption to a point
at which they know friction will be caused, the lesson to be

drawn is that we must pay serious heed to their view if we claim to have in mind the interests of the present immigrant population.   (Bennett, 27 Feb. 1968, p. 1338)

(This combines the pro bono publico argument with the populist argument.)

serious consequences will follow for everyone including the Asians themselves [if immigration is not limited].
                              (Maudling, 27 Feb. 1968, p. 1345)

The simple fact is that some control has become necessary in the interests of society in this country, including, I must again emphasise, those immigrants already here.
                              (Maudling, 8 Mar. 1971, p. 43)

Providing the Bill is administered with sympathy and humanity it can make a contribution to better race relations by allaying the fears of white people and thereby improving the climate in which so many black people have to live and work.
                              (Hunt, 8 Mar. 1971, p. 95)

In my view the then Government were absolutely right. They pursued these policies not simply in the interests of this country, but in the interests of the community relations and the immigrants themselves.   (Deedes, 8 Mar. 1971, p. 101)

I welcome the new arrangements and controls not only in the interests of people born in this country but in the interests of a very large number of immigrants who have already been allowed to enter.   (Hornsby-Smith, 8 Mar. 1971, p. 116)

(6) Reciprocity arguments

Reciprocity arguments seem to be based on an idea of elementary justice for which it is assumed that human beings with similar characteristics, or in similar circumstances, should be treated in the same way. The argument involves picking out the relations of either symmetry, in such a manner that a measure is seen to be justified, or asymmetry, in which case it is judged unacceptable. Reciprocity arguments and the precepts they reflect can be discovered in many systems of ethics. The Judaeo-Christian ethic of 'do as you would be done by' ('Therefore all things whatsoever ye would that men should do to you, do ye even so to them' (Matthew 7: 12)) and Kant's moral maxim ('Act only on the maxim whereby thou canst at the same time will that it should become a universal law' (*Foundations of the*

Metaphysics of Morals, Section 1)) deny that any individual is entitled to a morally privileged position.

As racism has often to do with the acceptance of a moral prescription to the effect that members of other races are not entitled to equal treatment, we might expect that arguments about the enshrinement in the framework of law of unequal treatment of different groups hitherto entitled to the same provisions would involve considerations of reciprocity. In what way are the individuals involved similar or different? By arguing that another race are 'sub-human' the classical racist does not have a case to answer: sub-humans do not have to be treated equally. But what of those who formally concede that the races are equal?

Part of the strength of the principle of reciprocity derives from the quasi-logical symmetry of the argument form: it is as if actions or their effects must be balanced in a mathematical equation, or, more appropriate, on the scales of justice. Thus actions are not judged wrong in themselves but only in relation to other actions. Guilt can then be assuaged in a number of ways.

Against the accusation that whites are racist, the counter-accusation is made that blacks behave badly, too. If others have legislation that discriminates against certain groups, then why, it is reasoned, should we not have similar legislation? The requirement that groups should receive equal treatment irrespective of the colour of their skin is met if it can be shown that whites are affected in the same way as blacks. Those who argue in favour of immigration control must argue either that they are behaving in the same way as others have behaved in like circumstance (e.g. blacks also do it to whites), or that their proposals affect both black and *white*, or that there are sufficient non-racial differences (asymmetry) between the groups involved to justify their differential treatment. Another possibility is to admit to unfairness in one sphere, but to promise to compensate for it in another. In this way, debit and credit cancel one another out.

A number of important arguments in the race field are centred on the idea of reciprocity. They constituted 9% of the total of argument forms exemplified in the debates on the Bills.

First, there were a whole collection of arguments designed to show that the Bills affected, or were intended to affect, whites as well as blacks. Of these, perhaps the most notorious was that dealing with the unsuccessful attempt to include citizens of the Irish Republic under the provision of the 1961 Bill. As R. A. Butler pointed out:

> the Bill was drafted to cover the citizens of the Irish Republic and this is the effect of Clause 1 (4). The Government have always realised the very great difficulty there would be in

> operating the control against the Republic for practical reasons
> that I shall explain . . . I fully realise, of course, that our
> decision can be and may well be misunderstood . . . The Bill is
> drafted so that there is no racial discrimination.
>
> (16 Nov. 1961, p. 700)

But the Labour Opposition regarded as highly significant the reason for including the Irish under the Clause, but of admitting that controls could not be enforced. Gordon-Walker accused the Home Secretary of putting the Clause in: 'as a sort of fig leaf to preserve his reputation for liberalism. Now he stands revealed before us in his nakedness. He is an advocate now of a Bill which contains bare-faced open race discrimination' (16 Nov. 1961, p. 706).

In 1968, the Bill aimed at curtailing Kenyan Asian immigration to Britain was similarly excused by arguing that were there whites with the same characteristics as the Asians and, were it practical to do so, the measure would also apply to them: 'if we were threatened suddenly with a potential influx of 1 million Scandinavians, Italians, or French, even if we thought that the majority would not come, we should not be called racialists if we sought to control the situation' (Hogg, 27 Feb. 1968, p. 1264). And, again, a little later: 'It must be added that a number of people of unblemished white descent will be covered by its provisions' (Hogg, 27 Feb. 1968, p. 1265). Of course, the reciprocity argument may be used in reverse: if Commonwealth immigrants originally had privileges over, for example, aliens and there is no difference in kind between Commonwealth citizens and aliens, then control restores parity.

Next, there are those arguments which justify British control of certain kinds of migrant on the basis that others do the same, or have a responsibility to do the same, which they are not fulfilling. In 1961, it was the White Commonwealth with its empty spaces that was at fault in not coming to Britain's aid. And if the White Commonwealth excluded 'Commonwealth' immigrants, would not Britain be wise to follow a similar policy? By 1968, the comparison was being made with the Kenyan policy of Kenyanisation. As this was thought to be an undoubtedly racialist measure that had led to the Kenyan Asian migration, then Britain, in responding to this policy with legislation, was simply protecting her interests and could not be held responsible for initiating the chain reaction. Both policies might be undesirable, but the question of 'who began the business' becomes significant. The exchange between Hogg and Henig serves to illustrate this kind of thinking:

> *Hogg:*   I heard Mr Tom Mboya on the wireless recently
> claiming that it was lawful to disciminate between residents of

a country if they were of a different nationality from one's own. I ask myself when does discrimination become respectable? The answer appears to be when it is called Nationalism and is done by someone else against a third party's race. I ask myself what we have done wrong and why the right hon. Gentleman should be accused of being a racialist, when all that he is trying to do is to cope with the situation he did not create.

Henig: There is one point in the right hon. and learned Gentleman's argument which I have not followed. He mentioned the fact that Mr Mboya is passing legislation to discriminate against certain people and it appears from his argument that he is saying that, because they are being discriminated against in Kenya, we should keep them out. But where are these people to go? What is to become of them?

Hogg: I was not making that point. I said that we are trying honestly to deal with a situation which was not of our making and that if accusations of racialism or discrimination could be made against anyone, it was not against us.

(27 Feb. 1968, p. 1264)

Finally, the idea of legislatory compensation of a group for the way it has been maltreated on an earlier occasion is, I submit, illustrated by Callaghan's remark that:

This Bill . . . must be considered at the same time, and in accordance with, the proposal of the Government to introduce a Race Relations Bill which will establish in this country equality of treatment in the very sensitive areas of housing and jobs, which is to be introduced by the Government during the next six weeks – certainly before Easter. Both these Bills are, in my view and my judgment, essentially parts of a fair and balanced policy on this matter of race relations.

(27 Feb. 1968, p. 1242)

As early as 1965 the dual approach of combining tight immigration controls with policies for 'integrating into the community the immigrants' already in Britain was seen as the Labour Party's 'balanced' solution (Crossman, 1975, Vol. 1, p. 149).

(7) Means-orientated arguments

The previous arguments were used to justify immigration control by giving reasons for the acceptance of the prescription that people of a certain kind ought to be restricted in entering Britain. But there is another type of quasi-argument providing a pseudo-justification for control. The argument is not concerned with ends or values thought to be furthered by the Bills. Rather, the Bills are taken as given, and attention is directed towards the means by which the ends are to be achieved.

Four types of means-orientated argument may be distinguished: the descriptive, the procedural, the effective, and the consistency.

Descriptive 'arguments' consist in outlining in detail the various clauses of a bill, and are especially to be found in the speeches of those who move second readings and who reply to debates. Such arguments do not justify the Bills in the sense of providing *reasons* for the acceptance of their prescriptions, but they have a strong persuasive effect in that they project, as taken-for-granted, the Bills' values, to such an extent that the casual listener may not even consider the possibility of other lines of action. By the time a bill receives its second reading, it usually exists in such a polished legalistic form that it is a skilled task to penetrate, let alone undermine, its structure. At its second reading, a bill is almost a fait accompli and as such is capable of providing a limiting mental set for those who read it complacently.

Another pseudo-justification for a bill lies in claiming that proper procedures were followed in coming to the decision: for example, that Commonwealth Prime Ministers, or the National Committee for Commonwealth Immigrants, or various concerned pressure groups were consulted in the correct manner. Naturally, if these parties had not been consulted, this would be regarded as a weakness. Again, correct procedures are not directly related to the values and prescriptions propounded by a bill and, in practice, conveniently displace their consideration.

To describe in detail the likely effects of a bill without evaluating them, and in order to illustrate that a bill's instruments fulfil their purpose, may serve as a further strategy for detracting from more fundamental questions about any implicit racist values.

Finally, considerations of the internal consistency of the clauses of a bill, while undoubtedly important in the implementation of any legal measure, are no substitute for a debate on whether the clauses ought to be present in the first place.

Means-orientated arguments accounted for 20% of the total of argument forms.

There are numerous ways in which legislation with racialist effect (as recognised by both the sociologist and a large proportion of the politicians responsible) can be justified without recourse to classical racism. The deracialised discourse is wide-ranging, but in all cases is defensible against the accusation that it is racist. In this way, the politician is absolved from

Table 5. *Percentage distribution of argument forms in the parliamentary debates on immigration*

Argument forms	Conservative	Labour	Total
Personalised	12	13.5	12
Social process	21	24.5	22
Populist	6	8	6
Economic	10	13.5	11
Pro bono publico	24	8	20
Reciprocity	7	13.5	9
Means orientated	20	19	20
Total arguments	100 (100)	100 (37)	100 (137)

Note: The figures in brackets refer to the overall number of argument forms. For explanation, see p. 215.
Sources: Second readings of the 1962 and 1968 Commonwealth Immigrants Bills and the 1971 Immigration Bill.

guilt and allowed to maintain a functional ambivalence in the face of the conflicting pressures placed upon him.

In general, the deracialised discourse succeeds in its purpose here by providing other non-racist criteria for discriminating against a group, e.g. shortage of resources in Britain, and by obscuring the fact that the largest numbers of people to be affected by the legislation under debate are distinguishable by their colour. In the main, exclusion of blacks will be the unstated intention of politicians who, faced with a knowledge of their constituents' strongly expressed views about black people's presence in Britain, support Bills aimed at controlling and reducing black immigration.

8

Conclusion: ideology and British race relations

The purposes of my conclusion are to emphasise once more what I see to be some of the salient features of British racial discourse, to restate in a more concise way some of the main arguments presented in earlier chapters, to point out what I believe to be the weaknesses in my account, and to indicate the directions in which the subject might be developed.

'Ideology' has been chosen here as the pivotal concept on which to study discourse about race. This has the immediate effect of limiting the area under examination, for not all discourse – interpersonal communication on a given subject – need be treated as ideological. Focus on the concept of ideology has the prime effect of highlighting the social and political context in which discourse takes place and of producing questions and providing answers in terms of people's social patterns and of the interests that arise from their social positions. With an awareness of the various connotations of 'ideology', particularly of ideology as a major integrated justificatory system helping to support or undermine social practices, dialogue between audiences need not be judged solely in terms of its content, but in terms of its congruity or incongruity when assessed against a backcloth of practical relations. The comparisons of discourse with action, or of one group's discourse with another, provide a method for explaining discursive content in terms of the differing social, political, and economic circumstances of the actor.

The discourse of individuals and groups may possess random elements but, nearly always, variation occurs on a regular and discernible basis. What is said is not only a matter of individual preference but of collectively experienced social stimuli and of jointly learnt and shared responses. Theoretically, if aspects of British social structure and institutions as they relate to racial differences are adequately described in conjunction with the long-term cultural and ideological responses of the mass of the population, taking into account, of course, differing experiences and interests, then the substance of discourse on the relatively recent black Commonwealth immigration and other racial matters should be predictable to some degree. Naturally, regularities within and between passages of discourse may be apparent without the deployment of the concept of ideology, but the significance of the regularity will only emerge when set against the total social reality of race relations. The reason for emphasising this point becomes clear when considering the possibility of the existence of racially repressive social systems in which race rarely features as the subject of public discourse, and, should it do so, is discussed with the help of non-racial categories. If public discourse is studied in isolation from practical social relations, it becomes impossible to identify the deracialised subject matter.

The focus on 'ideology' as a link between discourse and discoursive context helps to avoid two traditional pitfalls that have endangered the development of the scope of social science in this area. These are: studies of the things said about race in terms of 'racism', a word frequently used in political and historical studies of race relations, and of 'prejudice', as it has come to be stipulatively defined in social psychology. Both of these popular concepts unnecessarily circumscribe the study of discourse dealing with race, but for different reasons.

'Racism', when used to refer to the particular kind of discourse dealing with race is not infrequently contrasted with racialism, the practical act of treating members of another race in an unequal and inferior manner. 'Racism' is used to describe a belief or system of belief, usually manifest in discourse, that races of human beings exist, differing from one another in significant and enduring ways, and that the differences have social consequences. This might be termed 'weak racism' but, in general, 'racism' entails more than this: namely that a moral evaluation is being made that the differences between races are of superior to inferior, or, in addition, a moral prescription, that the superior races are entitled to more favourable treatment. These possibilities I have termed respectively 'medium' and 'strong' racism.

Most studies of racism stress the congruity between racist belief and racialist practice, and seek in the same way as I to show the relationship between the racially stratified social structure and the dominant beliefs of a given society. Thus the racism of the southern States of North America might be explained as a legacy of slavery, or as an attempt to retain anachronistic white social status when the economic grounds for such relations have collapsed. And the origins of British racism might be traced to the nineteenth-century expansion of the British Empire which produced the need for a justification of the right to rule over subject peoples. But congruity theories of this kind need to be supplemented in two ways. They frequently fail to deal with counter-instances and they incline to provide monocausal explanations of the subject matter.

Both problems may arise partly as a result of applying the definitional boundaries of the term 'racism', and partly in the pursuit of commonsense explanation as an over-simplification of the complex relationship between social structures and belief systems. Some of the more interesting cases of racism are those in which incongruity exists between the publicly expressed beliefs about race relations and the common practices of the population. The possibilities of racialism unaccompanied by racism, or of racism without racialism, must also be considered. And once these scenarios are recognised, it has to be admitted that discourse purged of racial content, non-racist, or even anti-racist discourse, particularly when set against widespread racialist practice, is also a necessary subject for attention.

If 'racism' alone is adopted for study, then the existence of egalitarian (or anti-racist) ideologies, of ideologies judged non-racist in general but containing some racist elements, and of non-racist ideologies justifying racialist practice are very likely to be neglected; so also will the more complex accounts required of the origin and persistence of, and interests served by, such ideologies. Nor can it any longer be assumed, as it frequently is, that at any one time racism and racialism are brought into being by the same or similar causal mechanisms. Some histories of the growth of British racism in the second half of the nineteenth century do recognise the differing social forces at work, some in favour and some against acceptance of racist belief, but frequently their method remains one of highlighting the development of a consistent pattern of distinctly racist belief to the neglect of opposing ideologies. I feel there is a need for a detailed historical study, positively focused not on racist ideologies but on the anti-racist aspects of twentieth-century Conservative, Liberal and Socialist thought. Meanwhile, it must be concluded that it is unduly restrictive for the study of 'racism' to be substituted for a more general study of all ideologies that have a relationship with (for instance, in acting as a 'camouflage' for) those issues thought racial by an independent social observer.

A similar, if not more serious, criticism may be levelled at the scope of social psychological studies of racially prejudiced attitudes, which until recently constituted a very popular form of research into contemporary race relations. The 'prejudice discrimination' axis described by Blumer (1966) as dominating American race relations in the post-war period until 1958 was widely adopted by British policy-orientated researchers such as Richmond (1955) and Abrams (1969) with a number of important consequences for the study of race relations.

I argue elsewhere (1982) that social psychologists (by a steady process of stipulating alternative meanings) have deprived the term 'prejudice' of earlier and useful connotations. I question four commonly held assumptions about race prejudice: that prejudices are attitudes, that prejudice is primarily a negative phenomenon, that prejudices are necessarily empirically unfounded, and that prejudice can be defined in terms of certain psychological functions. All such approaches to the study of prejudice detract from the study of the totality of ideological configurations dealing with race.

The claim that a prejudice is an attitude – its treatment as a property of mind – draws attention away from its existence as a segment of public discourse. Prejudice has also been associated with, and in some cases defined in terms of, accompanying emotional states and behavioural outcomes. And yet some of the most interesting examples of prejudiced expressions are those in which people give voice to feelings they do not experience or where they justify racially discriminatory actions with racially bland remarks.

In addition, concentration on the negative attributes of prejudice has resulted in neglect of the totality of utterances about racial matters. 'Prejudice', delineated in an extremely narrow way, has been studied at the expense of the consideration of lengthier discoursive passages and interchanges. For example, positive evaluations of a racial group, uttered with malevolent intent, or in the full knowledge of likely injurious consequences, have been omitted. Instead of studying the intricacies of language used about racial matters, social psychologists have come to focus far too narrowly on racial stereotypes.

For the best of intentions, a number of positivistically inclined researchers seem also to have concluded that the cognitive element in prejudice is empirically unfounded, that prejudice is misguided because it is false and that the reasoning processes involved are irrational and unscientific. In making these claims, they appear to have neglected that there are descriptive, evaluative, and prescriptive aspects of expressions dealing with race relations and that evaluations and prescriptions are just not the kinds of expression that can be verified or falsified by the use of scientific method. Besides, much of the social science of the nineteenth century that deals with racial matters has now been categorised as 'scientific racism' and judged by most learned authorities to be unfounded when judged against more rigorous scientific standards. Nineteenth-century science has become the prejudice of today.

I have argued that greater insight can be obtained by regarding 'prejudices', whether they take descriptive, evaluative, or prescriptive forms, as part of broader justificatory systems. With this must go the realisation that commitment to racial justice and inequality are moral and political issues that are incapable of being established scientifically, at least in any limited sense of the term. Thus, the common claim that prejudice is 'irrational' can be viewed as a pseudo-scientific strategy aimed at fortifying a self-evidently liberal opinion with the status of science. One of the major problems in employing the concepts of 'prejudice' and 'racism' in the social scientific study of discourse about race relations is that they both appear to be based on a limiting metatheory of racial justice as the unchallengeable norm against which other beliefs and practices must be judged.

The functions attributed to prejudice dwell sometimes on the satisfaction of individual needs and sometimes on the needs of the group. The political question of whether prejudice might serve or fail to serve the needs of individual, ethnic group, social class, or society as a whole, has often been ignored in favour of the tacit assumption that there is no incompatibility between individual, sectional and collective goals. Such a consensual, apolitical premise has led to the idea that prejudice is easily identifiable in terms of its dysfunctions to the individual, group, or society. This naive conception of symbolic and social interaction, has, I feel, to be rejected and replaced by one in which, if 'function' is to be used to refer to purpose, rather than effect, the individual or group with 'function' must be identified vis-à-vis other individuals or groups with differing functions. The fact that one man's prejudice will be another man's reason provides a further argument for rejecting the narrowly defined, social psychological concept of prejudice in favour of a broader concept of an ideology that deals with, or manifestly fails to deal with, racial matters.

When employed in the study of race relations, the concept of ideology has both a descriptive and explanatory role. Initially, it is important not to limit such a study to '*racial* ideology'. Racial ideology is ideology that accounts for events in the social world by making extensive use of racial descriptions and explanations and assigning major causal significance to racial categories, and that also utilises racial evaluation and prescription to a substantial degree. But the ideology that makes no apparent use of racial categorisation, yet results in, or justifies, behaviour which an observer believes has an adverse effect on a racial grouping, needs also to be examined. It is important to recognise that a 'racial ideology' is a much narrower category than 'an ideology associated with a race relations structure', though for convenience of expression the former is sometimes used (by me, as well) as shorthand for the latter.

An ideology is identified in terms of its internal logical relations, the kind of substantive, cognitive elements that go to make it up, the shared nature of its constituent beliefs, its justificatory purpose, its public availability, its relatively enduring life-span, the social agents that develop, profess and make use of it, and the social arenas in which it is most commonly manifest. Ideology is a discursive system, seeking to justify a particular state of affairs or course of action. It emerges only when human beings are trying to account for their actions to others, that is when they are expressing their sectional interest as if it were in the collective interest and serving the common good.

Two central questions have to be posed in a discussion of the relationship between British race relations and 'ideology'. They are: What is the nature of the ideologies used in Britain to justify race relations practice? How have they been generated and sustained? Attempts to answer these questions have to take two forms which it is not always possible to reconcile: the general and the particular. General answers are concerned with the characteristics of ideologies everywhere that are used to justify race relations structures, and with features that are common to ideological production. Particular answers deal with the unique features of British ideologies on racial matters and with their grounding in specifically British structures and institutions. General approaches, usually derived from economic and sociological theory, are often considered unsatisfactory because they fail to explain the wide diversity in ideological form, whereas specific accounts (frequently historical in genre) rarely attempt to draw general conclusions. My attempts to reconcile the two approaches by discussing, on the one hand, the economic foundation of racial division and, on the other, the historical development of Conservative and Labour Party values inasmuch as they have a bearing on racial matters is a solution, but not an entirely satisfactory one.

In approaching the issue from the general point of view, I make a distinction between the economic structure on the one hand and the population's perception and response to that structure on the other. If the accepted, institutionalised behaviour of the population (which is both structural and 'responsive' in its effect) is borne in mind, it becomes clear that this analytical distinction is difficult to maintain in the face of reality. Furthermore, the economic structure is represented as a capitalist mode of production sustaining two main social categories or classes, a bourgeoisie and a proletariat, but, particularly in the field of race relations, this kind of simplification of the actual complexity of class structure and of interests is scarcely acceptable except as a rubble core to a more sophisticated intellectual edifice – one which could easily collapse on such rude foundations.

The claim that human beings do not live in a crude economic world of stimulus/response, but represent that world symbolically to themselves and to their fellows may sound plausible, and so also the assertion that certain responses appear to be more obviously related than others to the ideally conceived, pure, economic reflex, but I am unable to provide any simple, persuasive theory of symbolisation (who is?), or to explain very convincingly why some reflexes are more 'economic' than others. It is worth asking whether explanations of racial hostility in terms of white people's perception of the threat that increased numbers of blacks pose to limited resources, and of blacks as a threat to whites' self-attributed status, and to the meaning they have invested in individual effort can be derived, in the final analysis, from the postulated 'square of economic alienation'. Do these 'explanations' genuinely emerge as a result of considerations of deeper structure or are they merely abstracted restatements of common discourse about racial matters?

In recognition of the problems of offering explanations derived directly from idealised economic relations, I postulate a secondary response of control, institutionalised in the form of the state, and arising as a result of the threat to social stability created by economic alienation. In other words, the responses summarised in the square of alienation, are articulated within a political context presided over by the state. There is a need to persuade the population to accept the legitimacy of the existing political order. And the state's justification for its race relations policies must be located in the general context of its attempts at legitimation. The kinds of racial policies and justificatory forms that emerge are likely to be compatible with, and indeed part of, those major ideological configurations providing legitimation for the capitalist structure as a whole. At least this is likely to be the case in a situation where the socio-political structure has been comparatively stable for many years.

This general theory of race relations structures and the ideological context of discourse dealing with race has to be supplemented by a more detailed account of the specifically British situation. For this purpose, I make use of the concepts of 'ideological level', 'political versus general discourse', the 'fundamental' and 'operative' dimensions of ideology, 'ideological integration', 'themes', 'foci', 'formulae', 'eristic' and 'values' – all explored at greater length in Chapter 4 and Appendix 2. The last-mentioned category of 'values' is further developed in Chapter 5, which attempts to show how decisions about immigration and general race relations have been influenced by enduring political party values.

With the help of these conceptual and analytical tools the following arguments are advanced.

First, because sections of the population respond differently according to their position in the socio-political structure and are involved to a greater or lesser extent with state and political institutions, the justificatory and persuasive content of their discourse is likely to vary considerably, thus producing different levels of expression and justification, ranging from a straightforward declaration of racial alienation to a politically sophisticated statement of racial significance. In short, the general discourse of the population as a whole can be distinguished from the specialised political discourse of the politician, as he carefully weighs up how to achieve his objectives or to avoid losing his influence.

Second, with the aid of the typology of Right and Left values, an assessment may be made of the significance of Conservative and Labour ideological networks in relation to the justification of race relations policy. I argue that Conservative and Labour ideologies are predominantly class-derived, and usually account for racial phenomena by making use of existing formulae developed over many years in response to class demands. Traditional formulae provide the patterns against which racial issues are described, interpreted, evaluated, and acted upon. The two parties' racial policies have been justified along traditional class lines and the policies themselves are presented as conforming with the parties' established values. For example, Conservatives draw upon tradition, nationalism, the importance of stability, social order, laissez-faire, and self-reliant individualism, while Labour stresses economic rationalisation, internationalism, egalitarianism, social justice, government intervention, and welfarism. Thus, Conservatives might seek to justify a racially restrictive immigration policy by emphasising the value of nationalism expressed in terms of the defence of the British people against dangerous foreign influence.

The important point to note is the way in which an ideological matrix used primarily as a basis for interpreting existing class relationships can simultaneously act as a means of justifying policies specifically aimed at racial, as opposed to class, groupings (particularly when these categories do not coincide in the real world) and of maintaining a race relations structure.

It is quite inaccurate to describe this phenomenon as 'racism' though it frequently succeeds in justifying racialist practice. In concentrating on overtly racist ideologies peddled by extreme Right-wing groups, social scientists have somewhat neglected the most salient feature of British ideologies as they are deployed in the field of race relations. In mainstream political circles, justification of measures inimicable to blacks or the blatant omission of considerations of racial justice are simply not explainable in terms of overt belief in the inferiority of blacks, although this is not to say that politicians never hold private racist opinions.

By focusing on the specialised political discourse of two major political parties, this study has neglected a number of related areas of relevance to British race relations. For example, there is no discussion here of intermediate levels of discourse about race, to be found in specialised social institutions and organisations, such as education, the police force, or prisons. Some writers have assembled the common myths about black education and crime but the inter-institutional comparative study of discourse dealing with race relations (of quasi-ideologies) remains un-

developed. There is also room for exploring the methods of communication, and influence between levels, or, in other words, for the creation of a
dynamic model of levels to extend the relatively static model presented
here. The 'Powellmania' of the late sixties and early seventies would
provide an ideal case study of the dynamic relationship between popular
racism (*sic*) and other levels of discourse. At the same time, it might provide
a fascinating insight into the operation of 'hegemonic forces' within
ideological complexes. Why did the supporters of Powell feel so strongly
that they had been prevented by the political establishment from expressing
the 'real truth' and why did they welcome Enoch Powell as the only man
who spoke their mind for them? Perhaps what had qualified as acceptable
comment on race relations up to that point was insufficiently explicit to
satisfy certain sections of the white electorate who intuitively recognised
the way in which the specialised class-based rhetoric acted as a constraint
on their means of expression.

Another important study that remains to be done, and I am actively
pursuing this interest, is to examine, on the one hand, the discursive
strategies of black people situated in racially oppressive structures and
faced by seemingly impervious 'deracialised' white ideologies, and, on the
other, the verbal contortions of white politicians when confronted by
racially conscious black audiences. No doubt, whites' attempts at deracialising such situations lead inexorably to a black perception of white
political duplicity on a grand scale. The interplay and parallel forms
produced in the eristic (or lack of it) between white power holders and black
groups is an obvious candidate for investigation, and would also be aided
by the development of a typology of the ideologies and proto-ideologies
that exist among the black population. Identifiable 'black' ideologies such
as Garveyism, Pan-Africanism, Black Power, and Rastafarianism may
benefit from being seen as attempts to 'racialise' dominant deracialised
forms adhered to by whites and blacks alike. Vacillatory, black rhetoric, in
which black militancy melts into recognisably Right or Left discourse, may
be unwittingly stimulated by entering into dialogue with a blatantly
deracialised Conservatism or socialism. Consistency of stance might be
more easy to maintain in the face of overt racism. These remarks should not
be construed as suggesting that black ideologies are generated only as a
reaction to deracialised white ideologies.

If it were felt worthwhile to pursue the study of general discourse, the
political values explored as part of ideological networks in Chapters 4 and 5
could be modified and used as a basis for developing a typology of quasi-
ideologies, i.e. the semi-developed ideologies commonly used by the white
population for justifying their views on race in the particular situations in
which their opinions are called for. Themes are remarkably recurrent: the

black presence is seen as a threat to national security or to physical safety or to the economic well-being of workers, consumers, or other sectors of the population, or to standards (whether moral, educational, material, or aesthetic). Blacks are regarded as an onerous financial burden, or as an extra, moral responsibility for right-thinking whites to shoulder. While the themes are difficult to classify because they so readily merge into one another, the quasi-ideological popular substance out of which the more coherent values of specialised political discourse: nationalism, national security, preservation of existing traditions and standards, paternalism, etc., is refined and fairly explicit. Circumstances such as the much-televised rush to beat the immigration controls, the release of black crime statistics, or the reporting of a homeless black family living at rate or taxpayers' expense in luxurious hotel accommodation will usually ensure that one theme or another will be uppermost in the public attention at any one time.

The couching of references to racial matters in an ideological matrix, primarily distinguishable in terms of its class-based formulae, is but one aspect of the important phenomenon of ideological deracialisation. Ideological deracialisation can be defined as the attenuation of, elimination of, or substitution for racial categories in discourse, the omission or de-emphasis of racial explanation, and the avoidance of racial evaluation or prescription. Its converse is ideological racialisation in which social structures are increasingly understood and interpreted with the help of racial categories (a phenomenon clearly discernible in Britain as the nineteenth century progressed). Once it is recognised that ideological deracialisation – a characteristic of discursive structures only – does not have to occur in tandem with practical deracialisation –'a characteristic of the actual social relations existing in a society in which the significance of a specifically racial identity is in decline – then at least two interesting scenarios may be identified. The first is synchronic deracialisation in which ideological and practical deracialisation occur simultaneously. The second is asynchronic deracialisation in which ideological deracialisation is accompanied by practical racialisation. The possibility of attenuating, eliminating, or substituting for racial categories in discourse, of omitting or de-emphasising racial explanation and avoiding racial evaluation and prescription in situations which, for the social observer, continue to display signs of racial domination, oppression and conflict, closely fits one popular concept of ideology as a 'facade' of social structure.

This notion of what I have chosen to call 'asynchronic deracialisation' seems particularly appropriate for describing post-war, British race relations. A practical racialisation within Britain has emerged as black migrants have been allocated to particular strata and have met with widespread discrimination and rejection. And while, at the general level of discourse, many of the white British have done little to hide their racial animosity, specialised political discourse has failed to provide a mouthpiece for the direct expression in racial terms of these circumstances. This is not to say that it has been inadequate to its task. The massive, systemic, impersonal, discursive deracialisation, of which political actors are unaware or only partly conscious, exists side by side with practised techniques of strategic, discursive deracialisation where the skilled politician self-consciously camouflages racialist action or racist beliefs for his various political purposes. He may or may not feel hatred for members of other races: the point is that his political advantage is served by camouflaging, with deracialised discourse, actions, beliefs, or feelings which may be politically injurious to him or his cause.

One particularly potent form of self-conscious deracialisation – what I call 'sanitary coding' – may also be identified. Here the politician uses language to avoid being identified as a 'racist', but also to reassure audiences, possibly no more inclined to admit to their private racism than he, that he understands their hostility to the presence of blacks and that he intends to take action to remedy the situation. This communication involves a subtle form of coding by equivocation, stress, and the use of words to facilitate mental imaging. 'Sanitary coding' is the ability privately to communicate racist ideas with a discourse publicly defensible as non-racist.

In addition to conscious deracialisation, specialised political discourse provides the means for justifying, in non-racial terms, policies – some oppressive, some not – intended to affect British race relations. Perhaps the most interesting characteristic of the parliamentary debates on (black) immigration control and race relations legislation is the way these policies are justified non-racially. Chapter 7, on immigration legislation, provides just such a case study of the relatively complex rhetorical techniques by which this effect is achieved. For reasons of space, I have omitted another carefully worked example of deracialised discourse – that of the parliamentary debates of 1965, 1968, and 1976 on the Race Relations Bills – but I feel that it is worth mentioning the gist of the argument to support my general point about the general nature of British political discourse about race relations.

In brief, the enactments of increasingly comprehensive legislation prohibiting racial discrimination posed a number of problems for Members of Parliament. The justification for such measures could only lie in massive evidence of discrimination practised by the white population and fear of the likely consequences of this behaviour should it be allowed to continue unabated. But if the practice of discrimination was so widespread did not this call into question the degree of support for anti-discriminatory legislation and, worse, challenge prevailing self-laudatory stereotypes of the 'tolerant' and 'fair-minded' British public? Persons arguing for the legislation were confronted, on the one hand, with the need to justify anti-discriminatory measures in terms of the alleged discrimination by, and prejudice of, the British public and, on the other, with the need to assert the widespread democratic support for the legislation by all decent-minded citizens.

The tendency among politicians of both major political persuasions to underplay or excuse what were considered to be undesirable traits, completely out of keeping with the British character, was accomplished by the judicious use of various rhetorical techniques such as: the exaggeration of certain characteristics of the white electorate and black population; the manner in which discrimination or prejudice was described, the explanations provided for these phenomena, and the accompanying patterns of justification. For example, politicians invariably stressed the 'tolerance' and belief in 'fair play' of the British people and the need for equality of treatment for blacks, whose characteristics were rarely mentioned (in contrast to the way they were described in discussion of the Immigration Bills). Racial prejudice might be redefined as 'resentment', 'tension', 'friction', 'genuine anxieties', 'real worries', 'deep feeling', and the consequences of discrimination described as 'grave disadvantages' or 'handicaps'. Only a small minority (usually 10%) of the population were identified as racially prejudiced. The existence of prejudice among whites was explained in a variety of ways, as resulting from: social processes such as the rate of immigration and economic forces such as urban decay, the unusual cultural characteristics of blacks, the effect of immigration on whites' livelihood and economic interests, whites' historical predispositions towards blacks, and the diffusion of Right-wing ideas by politicians or through the media.

The issue of white prejudice and discrimination was handled in a way that avoided attributing moral responsibility to the electorate as a whole, and had the effect of assuaging the white offender's guilt to the extent that an observer unfamiliar with British race relations might have been entitled to ask whether the legislation was necessary at all when evaluated solely in terms of the justifications offered for it.

One conclusion to be drawn from case studies of the parliamentary debates on immigration and race relations is that the *explanations* for existing race relations complexes offered by politicians (and social scientists too) act also as *justification* for existing practice or proposed change. For example, the explanation for white prejudice as a response to a perceived black threat is held by many to be a reason why blacks *ought* to be excluded from the country. In dealing with 'ideology', it is worth considering all explanations as a species of 'objectified justification', the apparent factual status of the explanation supporting, in some way, the pretension of the justification.

An explanation is usually defined as a statement or set of statements which enables what has to be explained to be logically inferred and which reduces its problematic character. Acceptable explanations must appear to be relevant and true, but the criteria for accepting an explanation as true will vary considerably. Where scientific explanations are concerned, the evidence of the senses, rather than faith or divine revelation, is required as the test of truth. But the lack of rigour in the testing of explanations of the social world, the kinds of sensible evidence made available and the suitability of the uses to which it is put, and questions of explanatory scope in dealing with 'freely choosing' human beings, create difficulties in deciding on its validity and scope. Although politicians would like to believe in the scientific status of their factual assertions and frequently make use of 'watered down' versions of social scientific theory, the explanations that they use are likely to be partially selected, dogmatically asserted, and generalised beyond the context for which they were originally formulated. The politician, like the Mulla Nasrudin in our preface on 'Objectivity', will select his explanation and the frequently inadequate evidence in support of it, on the basis of his political needs of the moment, rather than with an overwhelming desire to establish the truth. In other words, his primary purpose is to justify rather than to explain the kernel of ideological discourse.

Justification refers to the reasoning aimed at inducing the audience to accept, in this case, a moral or political evaluation or prescription. A justification reassures, convinces, or persuades the self or others of the rightness of a belief or action. Analytically, it differs from an explanation of an event in terms of cause or function. The ambiguous question 'Why are the British colour prejudiced?' might be construed as a request for either a justification or an explanation.

A colour prejudiced white might claim that he hates blacks because they are taking over his country – a country which, he feels, *ought* to belong to the whites such as himself. His expression aims at convincing the audience that he is morally right in holding such an opinion and at illiciting their support for his views. Alternatively, a social scientific explanation in terms of the white man's status insecurity, in itself, does not entail a commitment to supporting or condoning prejudice, but only to providing a reason for its existence. A person who accepts an explanation of why prejudice exists is not automatically committed to accepting that prejudice ought to exist or to be condoned. Despite the fact that he can see only too clearly why some people embrace prejudice, he may still wish to reject their evaluation in favour of making no evaluation whatsoever, or of making a contrary one of his own.

The distinction between explanation and justification centres on the evaluation implicit in the latter. The way the social world is, is no reason for supposing that it is the way it ought to be. At least, this is the classical Humean position, based on a logical distinction between fact and value. The history of political thought, however, gives us little reason for believing that such a distinction has ever, in practice, been rigorously maintained. From time immemorial, political justification has been based on accounts and explanations – mythical or historical – of the existing natural world and social structure. Explanation also serves the function of justification. The justificatory systems of modern politicians are likely to prove no exception. Having explained a social phenomenon in terms of a specific causal factor or function, the politician will then use the factor or function in a normative manner to decide upon its moral standing. In the case of prejudice and discrimination, the explanations offered for their existence serve morally to condone or condemn the words and deeds involved.

For example, the advantage of explaining prejudice in terms of the social processes of immigration and urban decay is that it avoids attributing moral responsibility to identifiable social groups. Social processes are treated much in the same way as natural events such as floods, crop failure, or plague, which twentieth-century man has excluded from the moral sphere. Furthermore, attention is mainly focused on the initiating causal factor rather than on the human reaction, the link between these two remaining unspecific. A cruder technique is to explain white prejudice in terms of the adverse characteristics of black people. Moral blame is transferred from the perpetrator of the act to his victim. The victim's 'offences' may include his audacity in making his presence known, his obvious social differences, the inferiority of the standards he is said to possess, or the way in which he 'unfairly' competes with the white population. Whites, therefore, are thought to be justified in their hostility, which is regarded as an understandable response in the face of provocation.

Given this overwhelming tendency to conflate explanation and justification, the relatively simple message of this book is that mainstream British politicians have generally supported, or opposed, unequal, discriminatory, and oppressive racial practices by resorting to traditional class-based explanations and justifications for the situation in which blacks find themselves in Britain. They have *not* dealt in an overt racism in which the relative position of blacks in white society is explained and justified in terms of their specifically racial inadequacy and moral inferiority to whites. Although class-based ideological approaches to race relations may be preferable to overt racist stances, they seem to obscure recognition of the full extent of the racial dimension to British society. And, as might be expected, the implementation of effective racially egalitarian policies is adversely affected by the resilience of the existing class structure, the constraints of class politics, and the inevitable transmutation of many measures originally conceived of in relation to racial minorities into general policies for the socially disadvantaged as a whole. It is perhaps to be regretted that the policy implications of the deracialisation of British discourse have not been more fully examined here, but this was not my purpose. Nevertheless, a realisation of such ideological constraints underlying decision-making in this area may highlight the inadequacy of existing initiatives.

Appendix 1 Nomenclature

Very considerable problems of nomenclature arise in writing about British race relations. Questions of nomenclature are of even greater pertinence for a study which is specifically concerned with British discourse about race and which seeks on occasion to make points about other people's usage. Requirements which have affected the choice of terms in this context are mutual intelligibility, familiar and respectable usage, political acceptability, descriptive accuracy, suitable levels of differentiation, logical compatibility of different schema, conciseness of expression and style.

Terms used by the author must be clearly understood by the reader. But frequently, members of the academic or political community do not share or agree on particular word usages. Another difficulty in the study of race relations is the changing connotation of significant words which increases the user's chances of being misinterpreted. In a sociological text which seeks to explore the categories used by social actors, there is also a danger that the social observer will be accredited with those terms he is forced to use to communicate with, or to describe the language of the actors he has chosen to study.

The term 'black' has been selected to refer generally to those people, usually of Afro-Caribbean and Indian sub-continent geographical origin who have black or brown skin colouring. The term focuses on skin colour as the important factor in categorising people as either black or white, a distinction that is of social significance because it is used as a basis for social action. The 1967 PEP report, and all studies since, for example, have revealed 'substantial discrimination against coloured people', and that the 'differential treatment and experiences of coloured immigrants as against other minority groups (such as Cypriots and Hungarians), leave no doubt that the discrimination is largely based on colour'. 'Black' is also widely accepted among people of Afro-American and Afro-Caribbean descent as the proper way of referring to their skin colour and the term has been found increasingly appropriate by people of both Afro-Caribbean and of Asian descent as a means of signifying their similarity of experience and commonality of interest in the face of white hostility in Britain. The term 'white' is used in contrast to 'black', to refer to people usually of European geographical origin with white or light skin colouring.

In referring to black people, alternative expressions in current popular usage are 'immigrant', 'coloured', 'ethnic minority', and 'racial minority'. They are unsuitable for the following reasons.

The term 'immigrant' is inappropriate, first, because it has been, and still is, widely used as a euphemism for 'black person', immigrant or otherwise, and second, because it implies a newcomer status, whereas, in fact, many former black migrants have been resident for over a quarter of a century, and their children (now roughly half of the black population) have been born in Britain. A euphemism is a means of designating an unpleasant or offensive phenomenon by a milder expression. Black people object to their distinguishing attribute being regarded as so offensive that it cannot be referred to directly.

Politically conscious blacks also object to the euphemistic overtones of the term 'coloured'. They suggest that reference to a dark skin as 'coloured' implies that the speaker is ashamed or embarrassed by the fact of blackness, and is seeking unconsciously to alleviate its impact. 'Coloured' also has the South African connotation of 'mixed race'. Black people point out that they are perfectly content with their blackness, and do not wish to increase their status among racist whites, as might have been possible formerly in some of the colonies, by foolishly laying claim to white ancestry.

Much the same objection can be made against the expression 'ethnic minority', which in recent years has become increasingly popular. Traditionally, an 'ethnos' was regarded as a group that could be identified by ties and traits of both race and culture. In recent years it has shed its bio-racial connotations and has come to refer to a group identified by its common history and cultural attributes. Indeed, scholars have preferred the term 'ethnos' to 'race' precisely because it removes the biological criteria of group identity. In community relations circles the term 'ethnic minority group' is used stipulatively and with prescriptive addenda to refer to all minority groups whose culture is felt to differ sufficiently from that of the majority English. Thus, the Poles, Ukranians, Jews, and Irish are purposely included in the category with Afro-Caribbeans and others, though there remains considerable ambiguity over whether the Welsh and Scottish also qualify. But, whatever the prescriptive definition that informed persons have chosen to impose, the term is widely understood to mean dark-skinned ethnic minority groups. Politically conscious black people believe that white ethnic minority groups are only included as a sop to white liberal elements who wish to avoid talking about the real issue: skin colour. If, on the one hand, the category is to include white groups then, without further qualification, it is unsuitable for referring to black people. If, on the other hand, it is to be popularly used to mean 'black groups', then it acquires the characteristics of another inexcusable euphemism.

'Racial minority group' is perhaps a more exact term, referring as it does to differences of race – defined in terms of certain physiological differences. But even here, the classical bio-racial differences are of less importance than those perceivable or imagined physiological differences that have acquired social significance in the British context. Of these, skin colour is still the most significant. Thus, Indians, who have traditionally been regarded as at least partly Caucasian, have been classed separately from European Caucasian. (See form PTI used by certain Area Health Authorities.) If 'racial difference' is understood to refer to physiological group differences of socio-political, as opposed to biological, significance, then 'racial minority group' presents a possible alternative to 'black group'. As a result of its association with nineteenth-century scientific racism and the Nazi legacy of racial genocide, however, it is unlikely to be enthusiastically adopted in liberal academic circles, for fear the concept of socio-political race might acquire a new scientific legitimacy in the popular mind. It has not been easy for sociologists to draw a distinction between a social construction of a bio-scientific category and the social creation of a reality to accompany the category.

For these reasons the term 'black' has been selected in preference to other contenders. There are problems, however, in maintaining the consistency of this terminology. The first arises from the fact that the term 'black' is still not widely used by white people, possibly because of the difficulties of displacing a traditional usage affording some euphemistic shelter for a new one to which whites may be less politically sympathetic. The second arises as a result of the term 'black' coming to be identified with persons of Afro-Caribbean Negro ancestry and thus excluding the category of Caucasian people originating from the Indian sub-continent, a distinction preserved by some Indians anxious to distance themselves from Afro-Caribbeans. Those who previously interpreted the expression 'black' as applying only to persons of Afro-Caribbean descent should treat it here as shorthand for 'black and Asian'. In other words, 'black' denotes the traditional English category of 'coloured', but without its politically offensive connotations.

Although the rough distinction between black and white people is perfectly adequate for discussion of what whites perceive as a socially significant group, there are occasions when the category of black persons needs further refinement. It is possible to distinguish between groups of people by considering the following commonly used criteria: skin colouring (black/brown), racial grouping (Negro/Caucasian), geographical origin:

continental (African, Caribbean (West Indian), Asian (Indian)), national (Barbadian, Jamaican, Pakistani, Indian, Bangladeshi), constituent regional (Punjabi, Gujerati), or religion (Sikh, Hindu, Moslem). 'Indian', of course, can refer both to persons from the Indian Republic (Bharat) or from the Indian sub-continent. As a result, the even more ambiguous term 'South Asian' has recently become fashionable in race relations circles. For reasons again of popular usage, the geographical terms 'West Indian' and 'Indian' have sometimes been used to describe the two main sub-groups of black people that feature in this study, despite the fact that many of these people were born in Britain, and the term 'West Indian' is racially ambiguous. An attempt has been made not to mix categories unduly, but occasionally, for stylistic reasons, or to avoid undue repetition, some variety of terminology has crept in. Sometimes, too, the expression 'of Afro-Caribbean origin or ancestry' has been shortened to 'Afro-Caribbean'. The expression 'Afro-Caribbean' more clearly describes (from a racial angle) those people whose ancestors came from Africa via the Caribbean to Europe than the term 'West Indian', which is far more racially ambiguous. In the West Indies, there are Indo-Caribbeans, Euro-Caribbeans, and many mixed-race Caribbeans.

Appendix 2 Ideological eristic

Political ideologies are systems of justification for competing social groups having different interests and incentives for action. The policies of party X, whether advocated or implemented, must be justified in the face of counter-policies from party Y. Party X advocates a line of action as indispensable, while party Y thinks it disastrous. Each contention must be supported by convincing reasons which go to build up an alternative political world picture. As in a scientific theory, an ideology which cannot satisfactorily explain or justify a range of phenomena thought to fall under its jurisdiction is seriously flawed. Its weakness will be probed and exposed by those embracing alternative ideology. In metaphorical terms, ideologies must shield themselves from the thrusts of rivals and, in turn, attack them at their most vulnerable points. As a process, ideological discourse can be seen as a group's never-ending task of expounding new arguments to justify policies in the face of systematic criticism from other discoursing agents. New and more elaborate arguments develop in situations of weakness in the face of alternative, more persuasive views. This unfolding of discourse in response to other discourse is a socio-psychological phenomenon, but epistemological factors, e.g. the perception of contrary statements and fallacious argument, play an important part in deciding the line of development and acceptable discursive form.

From Greek times, philosophers have recognised the importance of debate in the development of new ideas, and in the pursuit of truth. The term 'dialectic' was applied to the method of seeking and perhaps finding truth by argument between different parties or from apparently irreconcilable positions. The Sophists were condemned by Plato for using argument to win conviction at the expense of truth. The search for truth rather than the teaching of techniques of persuasion came to be seen as the task of philosophy. Plato used the term 'eristic' (from the Greek ἐρίξ, strife) for false dialectic aimed at tricking audiences into agreement. As ideology's primary aim is persuasion, and not the search for truth, and its chief exponents make extensive use of rhetoric, its form of development might be better termed 'eristical', rather than 'dialectical'. Truth has also come to be

259

recognised as a property of statements of fact and not of evaluation and prescription. 'Eristic', then, is more applicable to the complex of description, evaluation, and prescription that constitutes ideology. Yet arguments are unlikely to be believed if they are not recognised to be valid or strong: successful eristic must be thought to have these characteristics, too. Many philosophers have, of course, recognised the political phenomenon of the development of ideologies through disputation, and have referred to it as 'dialectic'. Hegel (1952, pp. 34–5), for example, sees dialectic as 'matter's very soul putting forth its branches and fruit organically', but I have chosen to avoid the philosophic ambiguity of the term 'dialectic', in favour of the more appropriate 'eristic'.

The concept of 'eristic' must be developed for use in the analysis of actual political discourse. There is *general eristic* between individuals and groups within the population, and *party eristic*. It is clear that debate occurs not just between political parties, but within them, and between parties and the population in general through the media. There are formal inter-political eristical arenas, such as parliament and the local council chamber, in which the contending parties meet in accordance with formal rules of debate. There are formal intra-political eristical arenas, such as the party conferences, cabinet, and meetings of parliamentary parties. 'Formal' means here the publicly recognised political institutions bound by laws, rules, and conventions that play a role in the development and implementation of party and government policy. There are, of course, numerous informal meetings and exchanges in which ideas are developed at national, constituency, ward, or personal level.

For any debate, at least two positions, related in terms of common referent, must be posited in symbolic form. A difference of a synthetic or analytic kind must be recognised between the assertions. Traditionally, these have been called thesis and antithesis, but there is no need for the sentences to be contraries or contradictories. If, after examination of the assertions, a synthesised position (synthesis) can be agreed upon, the debate is concluded. If no such agreement is reached, the debate must continue, each assertion being defended and developed in response to the defence and development of the other. In the course of this elaboration, new assertions, drawing on further factual, evaluative, and prescriptive sentences, will emerge. We are referring here to the creative, ongoing, social process of producing new sentences, not to the static process of looking for formal logical properties of different arguments. There may be accepted procedures for resolving debate: at a factual level, empirical evidence may be produced, and, in the case of a prescription, a vote may be taken.

Formal ideological disputation has the same characteristics as outlined above, except that overall agreement between disputants is rarely achieved:

this would, indeed, herald the end of ideology. Limited agreement may, however, be reached between pairs of any of three kinds of sentence: description, evaluation, and prescription. There may be agreement of fact (belief) but not of evaluation (attitude). A particular prescription may be agreed between parties but given different justifications. The implication of this point is neatly brought out by J. S. Mill's account of Lord Mansfield's advice to the man of sound common sense who, without previous judicial practice or legal education, was expected as governor of a colony to preside in its court of justice. 'The advice was to give his decision boldly, for it would probably be right; but never to venture on assigning reasons, for they would almost infallibly be wrong' (Mill, 1961, pp. 217–18). A legally trained person might be able to 'justify' the decision after it had been made in accordance with the requirements of the law. Similarly, it may be possible for a competent politician to take some perverse policy forced upon a government, and to justify it, post hoc, by appeal to the mainstream of a political ideology. And different 'justifications', of course, might be produced for different audiences.

In social context, the disputants' perception of ideological boundaries is of major importance. There is a recognition that ideological frontiers must not be transgressed. Because the boundary is decided by group consensus it is never immutable. It may be hazy, but it is frequently clear which one of a set of ideologies is being called upon to justify a given policy, especially when party ideologies at opposite ends of the political spectrum are involved.

A distinction may be made between *antagonistic* and *non-antagonistic eristic* on the basis of ideological boundaries and the possibility of achieving synthesis. Antagonistic eristic contains more obviously contrary assertions for which the possibility of achieving synthesis is remote. If ideologies are conceived as having a core of basic assertions surrounded by concentric rings of assertions of decreasing importance, antagonistic eristic is likely to occur as a result of differences of central or basic assertions. Antagonistic eristic is usually to be found in the conflict between political parties in which basic premises are not shared.

Non-antagonistic eristic (although antagonism is more of a relative than absolute matter) consists of debate in which there is a proneness to seek reconciliation between assertions. Apparently contrary assertions are resolved by appeal to more central premises on which agreement already exists. Non-antagonistic eristic may be found in debate within parties, but not invariably so. Often dispute will arise in the process of discovering how a new situation is to be interpreted in terms of existing basic premises. Differences of prescriptive preference may be resolved by following procedures formally laid down. Once a common course of action has been agreed upon, there will be a need for justification in terms of the main ideological stream (but conformity here is not of such importance as the initial agreement itself).

The distance between assertions within a single party and between parties is crucial in any study of political ideology. Also of great interest is the way in which the formal context of political debate influences the form of discourse. In parliament, for example, Conservative and Labour members will speak in turn, each building his arguments and counter-arguments on the preceding discourse. The second reading of a Bill will be introduced by a Minister or Government representative and followed by a reply from a member of the Opposition. Finally, before the Bill is put to the vote, a Government spokesman will sum up and answer questions arising from the debate. Such formal procedure requires the speakers to consciously and systematically think out the justification for their respective positions in the context of interruption and counter-justification from the Opposition. Over time, each area of contention tends to become finely and delicately elaborated, and each argument balanced by counter-argument.

Arguments are not equally persuasive. But they are rarely judged in isolation, their acceptance depending upon the sophistication of the audience's already existing ideological framework.

The formal eristical arena of government, opposition, and people acting as audience, may be contrasted with the eristic of the common man as when, for example, he discusses a matter of common interest with a friend in the public house. Here, there is no decision to be taken at the end of the evening and no certain, or carefully balanced counter-argument. The audience may be involved or uninterested, or in agreement or disagreement. The unfolding of the discourse, the drawing out and systematic development of critical areas is by no means guaranteed. And there is a marked difference in the degree of stringency expected of an individual's private expression of opinion and that of a politician's views when he is publicly engaged in formal debate.

Appendix 3 Examples from colonial history of discoursive deracialistion

Discoursive deracialisation is not a new phenomenon. Huttenback (1976, p. 21) offers us a number of examples from nineteenth-century British white colonial policy arising from the conflict of two sets of principles:

> On the one hand marched the concept of what Burke had called 'the natural equality of mankind at large' which, under the influence of nineteenth-century liberal humanitarianism and the evangelical movement, had turned into the concept of trusteeship and the imperial philosophy of a nonracial empire, all of whose subjects were equal before the law. Emerging on the other hand was the determination of the British settlers in South Africa, Australia, New Zealand, and Canada that theirs must be a 'White Man's Country'.

One way to reconcile the desire to exclude non-whites from the colonies and the philosophy of the Empire was to pursue policies racialist in effect but to justify them non-racially.

In response to the 1854 anti-Chinese demonstrations in Australia in which the Chinese were 'injured, their property destroyed and their claims appropriated as they were driven from the mining communities', an ingenious way of limiting Asiatic immigration was devised (either intentionally or by accident). The Duke of Newcastle 'purported to be concerned about the conditions under which Chinese travelled to Australia' and suggested that legislation be introduced imposing penalties 'on all ships bringing immigrants to New South Wales in which it might appear that a sufficient proportion of space had not been allotted to the Emigrants or an adequate issue of provision made regularly to them throughout the voyage or that the Ship had left China in an unseaworthy state'. The subsequent Act introduced a ratio of one immigrant to ten tons of burthen, a landing fee of ten pounds, and further levies on immigrants to pay for the administration of the act. Huttenback adds that: 'To make the purpose of

263

the law absolutely clear, an immigrant was defined as "any male adult native of China or of an island in the Chinese seas or any person born of Chinese parents"' (p. 62).

Likewise, in Natal, the white colonists were fearful of non-white settlers, who were in this case the increasing number of ex-indentured Indians. At first, the colonial government attempted explicitly to exclude free Indians from the colony but met with resistance from the imperial authorities in London. However, the second attempt at legislation was more successful because, prima facie, it was non-racial. Entry requirements were introduced, based on property and a knowledge of a European language, the assessment of language ability being made by the immigration officer. The education test, which came to be known as the 'Natal formula', was 'administered in such a way that Europeans were judged eligible to enter Natal while all Indians were not'. Huttenback (1976, p. 141) describes how:

> The prime minister made its purpose quite clear when he told the legislature: 'It never occurred to me for a single minute that (the act) should ever be applied to English immigrants . . . Can you imagine anything more mad for a Government than that it should apply to English immigrants? The object of the bill is to deal with Asiatic immigrants.'

In Canada, the exclusion of Indians was attempted in yet another way. An order in Council of 8 January 1908, stipulated that whenever the Minister regarded the condition of the labour market as warranting it, immigrants might be prohibited from entering Canada unless they came from 'the country of their birth or citizenship by a continuous journey *and on through-tickets* purchased before leaving the country of their birth or citizenship'. Huttenback points out that 'There being no direct steamship service between India and Canada, the order in council provided an effective weapon to combat further Indian immigration to Canada' (p. 187).

These cases illustrate that by picking out features other than race and nationality – inhumane conditions of transport, language difference, the state of the labour market and type of journey undertaken – a racial group might be identified 'non-racially' and, in addition, its exclusion from a country justified on non-racial grounds. Evidence is provided of both the racial intent of the colonial legislators in that they sought to exclude members of other races and the discriminatory effects of their actions. The imperial ideology of equality before the law, however, forced the legislators to deracialise their legal prescriptions.

Appendix 4 Further examples of popular sanitary coding

By the late 1970s the number of black people who had lived in Britain for over a quarter of a century and the children that had been born to them here was beginning to make the term 'immigrant' appear inappropriate. A new term for the black population had to be found. It was supplied by social scientists who had rejected the biological connotations of the term 'race' in favour of what they regarded as the more scientifically accurate and culturally orientated expression, 'ethnic minority group'. In this way, Greeks, Italians, Indians, Pakistanis, and Jamaicans could all be distinguished and classified as ethnic minorities living among the British (or, rather, the English, Welsh, and Scottish?) ethnic majority. But, because the largest and most visible ethnic minority groups were black, and most attention was paid to them, 'ethnic minority' began to take on that specific connotation. Soon the term 'minority' could be dropped and 'ethnic' left to mean black – Asian and Afro-Caribbean.

Nowhere was this better contextually illustrated than in the draft of the 1979 Local Government Grants (Ethnic Groups) Act which, before it fell as a result of the 1979 General Election, was to have replaced Section 11 of the Local Government Act. The explanatory memorandum stated that the Bill's purpose was to enable grants to be paid to local authorities towards expenditure incurred by them in helping to remove disadvantages suffered by 'ethnic groups' living in their areas, of providing equally effective services for them, 'and of promoting good relations between ethnic groups or between ethnic groups and the rest of the community'. It was clear from this that the 'rest of the community', which, if it was to mean anything, presumably referred to the indigenous white British, was not regarded as belonging to an ethnic group, for the ethnic party to the relation was no longer limited by the term 'minority'. From the context, it was apparent that the native white population did not constitute what the authors of the Bill termed an 'ethnic group' and that the new expression referred essentially to the 'black British' – or to all those who did not constitute 'the rest of the community'.

Another example of sanitary coding is revealed in the use of the term

265

'mugging'. Hall *et al.* (1978) describe how the term was imported from America accompanied by the numerous private connotations that a recently established informal colloquialism is prone to carry. They give the conventional connotation as that of robbing or beating a victim in a particular way 'by petty professional operators or thieves who often work in touring packs of three or more' but stress that the term's significance lies in its considerable accretion of private connotations derived from the contexts in which it was most often used:

> By the 1960s, 'mugging' was no longer being used in the United States simply as a descriptive and identifying term for a specific kind of urban crime. It not only dominated the whole public discussion of crime and public disorder – it had become a central *symbol* for the many tensions and problems besetting American social and political life in general. 'Mugging' achieved this status because of its ability to connote a whole complex of social themes in which the 'crisis of American society' was reflected. These themes included: the involvement of blacks and drug addicts in crime; the expansion of the black ghettoes, coupled with the growth of black social and political militancy; the threatened crisis and collapse of the cities; the crime panic and the appeal to 'law and order'; the sharpening political tensions and protest movements of the 1960s leading into and out from the Nixon–Agnew mobilisation of 'the silent majority' and their presidential victory in 1968. These topics and themes were not as clearly separated as these headings imply. They tended, in public discussion, to come together into a general scenario of conflict and crisis. In an important sense the image of 'mugging' came ultimately to contain and express them all'.   (pp. 19–20)

It was with these connotations that the term 'mugging' came to Britain: it referred to street crime, to a breakdown in 'law and order', to black crime, and in its suggestion of recency, to a future of racial distrust and riot in the cities. With its use, the overt mention of race became unnecessary. Indeed, if the racial identity of the 'muggers' was unspecified in the news report, it might automatically be assumed that they were black. It is important to modify with 'it might' because 'mugging' maintains a defensive ambiguity. With the term 'mugging', the politician can refer to 'black crime' or to crime generally: the audience decides this in the context of widely established private connotations.

Critcher treats us to a further example of a term with extensive accretion of subjective connotation: 'the ghetto'. He claims crime, race, poverty, and housing are 'condensed into the image of the "ghetto"' (Hall *et al.*, 1978, p. 118). Certainly, 'ghetto' has come to mean more than an area of the city to which Jews – or other racial groups – are confined. It is now linked – in the same way as the expressions, 'inner city area', 'twilight zone', and 'slum' – with urban poverty and racial deprivation. The term may be an indicator of the existence of liberal theories purporting to explain the behaviour of the poor and the black in environmental terms and seeking to alleviate their troubles by resource reallocation. Alternatively, the ghetto might be seen as the place in which black immigrants prefer to live, as a pocket of hostile people who revel in their degradation, actively seek to maintain their exclusivity, and act as a Trojan horse within the 'host' society. I deal more fully with the force of the word 'ghetto' in the section on imaging.

Bibliography and references

Abbott, S. (1970) An approach to defining race. In *Some Approaches to Conflict and Race*, IRR/BSA/RAI Fifth Annual Race Relations Conference, 1970, at Queen Elizabeth College, London, pp. 5–6.

Abrams, M. (1969) Attitudes of the British public: the incidence of race prejudice in Britain. In Rose, 1969, pp. 551–604.

Ackerman, N. W. and Jahoda, M. (1950) *Anti-Semitism and Emotional Disorder: A Psychoanalytical Interpretation*. New York, Harper and Brothers.

Acton, J. E., 1st Baron Acton (1922) *The History of Freedom and Other Essays*. Figgis, J. N. and Laurence, R. V. (eds.), London, Macmillan.

Adorno, T. W., Frenkel-Brunswick, Else, Levinson, Daniel, J., and Sanford, R. Nevitt (1950) *The Authoritarian Personality*. New York, Harper and Row.

Allport, G. W. (1954) *The Nature of Prejudice*. Reading, Mass., Addison-Wesley.

Althusser, L. (1969) *For Marx*. London, Allen Lane.

American Labour Department (1965) *The Negro Family in America* (*The Moynihan Report*).

Amery, L. S. (*c.* 1945) *The Conservative Future: An Outline of Policy*. Conservative Political Centre, reprinted in Buck, 1975.

Attlee, C. R. (1937) *The Labour Party in Perspective*. Left Book Club, London, Victor Gollancz.

Bagley, C. (1970) *Social Structure and Prejudice in Five English Boroughs*. A Report prepared for the Institute of Race Relations Survey of Race Relations in Britain, Institute of Race Relations, London, pp. 59–89.

(1973) Race relations and the press: an empirical analysis. In *Race*, July 1973, Vol. 15, No. 1, pp. 59–89.

Balfour, A. (1924, 1925) On socialism (23 Oct. 1924), On class war (17 Feb. 1925). In *Opinions and Argument*, New York, Doubleday, Dovan and Co., 1928; extracts quoted in Buck, 1975, pp. 121–9.

Banton, M. (1969) What do we mean by racism? In *New Society*, 10 Apr. 1969, pp. 551–4.

(1969, rev. 1970) The concept of racism. In Zubaida, 1970, pp. 17–34.

(1977) *The Idea of Race*. London, Tavistock.

Barnes, L. (1939) *Empire or Democracy?* Left Book Club, London, Victor Gollancz.

Bealey, F. (ed.) (1970) *The Social and Political Thought of the British Labour Party*. London, Weidenfeld and Nicolson.

Beattie, A. (ed.) (1970) *English Party Politics*, Vol. 2, 1906–70. London, Weidenfeld and Nicolson.

Benewick, R. (1969, 1972) *The Fascist Movement in Britain*. London, Allen Lane, The Penguin Press, 1972.

Berger, P. L. and Luckmann, T. (1971) *The Social Construction of Reality.* Harmondsworth, Penguin University Books.

Berkeley, G. (1910) *A New Theory of Vision and Other Writings.* Introduced by Lindsay, A. D., London, Dent, Everyman Library.

Berkeley, H. (1972) *Crossing the Floor.* London, George Allen and Unwin.

Berki, R. N. (1975) *Socialism.* London, Dent.

Berkowitz, L. (1962) *Aggression: A Social Psychological Analysis.* New York, McGraw Hill.

Bernstein, E. (1961) *Die Voraussetzungen des Sozialismus und die Aufgaben der Sozialdemokratie (Evolutionary Socialism: A Criticism and Affirmation).* Introduced by Hook, S., trans. by Harvey, E. C., New York, Schocken.

Berry, B. and Tischler, H. L. (1978) *Race and Ethnic Relations.* Boston, Houghton Mifflin Company.

Bettelheim, B. (1970) *The Informed Heart.* London, Granada Paladin.

Beveridge, W. (1944) *Full Employment in a Free Society, A Report.* London, George Allen and Unwin.

Billig, M. (1978) *Fascists: A Social Psychological View of the National Front.* London, Harcourt Brace Jovanovich.

Birch, R. C. (1974) *The Shaping of the Welfare State.* London, Longman.

Blumer, H. (1966) United States of America. In *Research on Racial Relations,* UNESCO.

Bolt, C. (1971) *Victorian Attitudes to Race.* London, Routledge and Kegan Paul.

Brailsford, H. N. (1945) Socialists and the Empire. In Hinden, 1945, pp. 19–35.

Buck, P. W. (ed.) (1975) *How Conservatives Think.* Harmondsworth, Penguin.

Burke, E. (1910) *Reflections on the Revolution in France.* London, Dent, Everyman Library.

Butler, G. (1914) *The Tory Tradition, Bolingbroke, Burke, Disraeli, Salisbury.* London, John Murray.

Campbell, A. (1945) *It's Your Empire.* Left Book Club, London, Victor Gollancz.

Castles, S. and Kosack, G. (1973) *Immigrant Workers and the Class Structure.* London, Oxford University Press and Institute of Race Relations.

Cecil, Lord H. (1912) *Conservatism.* London, Williams and Norgate.

Christenson, R. M. *et al.* (1972) *Ideologies and Modern Politics.* London, Nelson.

Christie, K. and Jahoda, M. (1954) *Studies in the Scope and Method of the Authoritarian Personality.* Illinois, Glencoe.

Clarke, D. (1947) *The Conservative Faith in a Modern Age.* Conservative Political Centre, reprinted in *Conservatism 1945–1950,* Conservative Political Centre, 1950.

Clynes, J. R. (1948) Why a Labour Party. In Tracey, 1948, Vol. 1, pp. 13–28.

Cohen, S. and Young, J. (1973) *The Manufacture of News.* London, Constable.

Coleraine, Lord (1970) *For Conservatives Only.* London, Tom Slacey, reprinted in part in Buck, 1975.

Community Relations Commission (1977) *Reporting on Race: The Role and Responsibility of the Press in reporting on Race Relations.* CRC, Memorandum, Feb. 1977.

Conservative and Unionist Associations, National Union of, Conservative Annual Conference Reports (CACR): 1958, 1960, 1961, 1968, 1969, 1972, 1973, 1976, 1977.

Conservative and Unionist Central Office *The Conservative Approach:* The Faith We Hold, May 1949; We Believe in the Empire, July 1949; The British Empire, July 1951.

Notes on Current Politics (assorted): Two Years Work – World Affairs, 7 Dec. 1953; The Colonies – Conservative Record 1951–4, 12 Apr. 1954; Commonwealth and Colonies, 28 July 1958; Social Issues – Some Social Problems, 9 Feb. 1959; Social Policy Developments, 24 July 1961; Third Year Programme – Social Policy, 27 Nov. 1961; Immigration and Race Relations, 10 June 1968.

Imperial Policy – the Conservative Party's Policy for the British Empire and Commonwealth, 1949.

Election Manifestos/Programmes, 1959, 1966, 1970, 1974, 1979.

New Immigration Policy: Tough but Fair – Controlling Immigration. In *Conservative Monthly News*, May 1978.

Conservative Political Centre (1960) *Wind of Change: The Challenge of the Commonwealth*. London Conservative Political Centre.

Cox, O. C. (1970) *Caste, Class and Race*. New York, Monthly Review Press.

Creech Jones, A. (1945) Introduction to Hinden, 1945, pp. 9–18.

Critcher, C., Parker, M. and Sondhi, R. (1977) Race in the provincial press: a case study of five West Midland newspapers. In UNESCO, 1977, pp. 25–192.

Crosland, C. A. R. (1956) *The Future of Socialism*. London, Jonathan Cape.

Crossman, R. H. S. (1970) Towards a philosophy of socialism. In Crossman, R. H. S. (ed.) *New Fabian Essays*. London, Dent, pp. 1–32.

(1975) *The Diaries of a Cabinet Minister*, Vol. 1. London, Hamish Hamilton and Jonathan Cape.

Curtin, P. D. (1964) *The Image of Africa*. University of Wisconsin.

Curtis, L. P. Jr (1968) *Anglo-Saxons and Celts: A Study of Anti-Irish Prejudice in Victorian England*. Bridgeport, Connecticut.

Daily Herald, 30 June 1929.

Dawidowicz, L. (1977) *The War against the Jews 1933–45*. Harmondsworth, Pelican.

Deakin, N. (1970) *Colour, Citizenship and British Society*. London, Granada Panther.

(1975) Harold Macmillan and the control of Commonwealth immigration. In *New Community*, Summer 1975, Vol. 4, No. 2, pp. 191–4.

Dean, P., Douglas, J. and Utley, T. E. (1964) *Conservative Points of View*. Conservative Political Centre Publications.

DeFleur, M. L. and Westie, F. R. (1963) Attitude as a scientific concept. In *Social Forces*, Vol. 24, pp. 17–31.

Der Spiegel, Interview with Enoch Powell in *New Statesman*, 13 Oct. 1978.

Deutsch, K. W. (1966) *Nationalism and Social Communication: An Inquiry into the Foundation of Nationality*. Cambridge, Mass., MIT Press.

Dilke, C. W. (1869) *Greater Britain: A Record of Travel in English Speaking Countries during 1866 and 1867*. London, Macmillan.

Disraeli, B. (1872) Speech at the Banquet of the National Union of Conservative and Constitutional Associations, 24 June 1872; extracts reprinted in Buck, 1975, p. 70.

Downing, J. (1972) Britain's race industry: harmony without justice. In *Race Today*, Oct. 1972, pp. 326–9.

(1975) The balanced (white) view. In Husband, 1975.

Dummett, A. (1973) *A Portrait of English Racism*. Harmondsworth, Penguin.

Durbin, E. F. M. (1940) *The Politics of Democratic Socialism: An Essay on Social Policy*. London, Clifton New Jersey, Routledge and Kegan Paul.

Eden, A. (1961) Empire Day Address, 1951; extracts in *The Conservative Approach*, July 1951.

Ehrlich, H. J. (1973) *The Social Psychology of Prejudice*. New York, John Wiley and Sons.

Ellis, Havelock (1927) *The Task of Social Hygiene*. London, Constable.

Eysenck, H. J. (1971) *Race, Intelligence and Education*. London, Temple Smith in association with *New Society*.

Fanon, F. (1970) *Toward the African Revolution*. Harmondsworth, Penguin.

Farr, R. (1978) The modern lesson of Viking Greenland. In *Spearhead*, Nov. 1978, pp. 14–15.

Fischer, N. (1973) *Iain Macleod*. London, Andre Deutsch.

Foot, M. (1962) *Aneurin Bevan, A Biography*, Vol. 1, 1897–1945. London, MacGibbon and Kee Ltd, 1962; London, Four Square, 1966.

Foot, P. (1965) *Immigration and Race in British Politics*. Harmondsworth, Penguin. (1969) *The Rise of Enoch Powell*. London, Cornmarket Press Ltd.

Freeman, G. (1978) Immigrant labor and working class politics: the French and British experience. In *Comparative Politics*, Oct. 1978, Vol. 2, No. 1, pp. 24–41.

Galton, F. (1892) *Inquiry into Human Faculty and its Development*. London, Macillan; Eugenics Society, 1951.

(1905) Eugenics, its definition, scope and aims. In Sociological Society, *Sociological Papers*, London, Macmillan.

(1962) *Hereditary Genius*. London, Collins.

Gamble, A. (1974) *The Conservative Nation*. London, Routledge and Kegan Paul.

Genovese, E. (1972) *In Red and Black*. New York, Vintage Books.

Gibson, G. (1948) Labour and the British Commonwealth. In Tracey, 1948, Vol. 2, p. 269.

Gobineau, Count A. de (1915) *The Inequality of Human Races*. Trans. by Collins, A., London, Heinemann.

Goody, J. (1973) Evolution and communication: the domestication of the savage mind. In *British Journal of Sociology*, June 1973, Vol. 24, No. 2, pp. 1–12.

Gordon, I. and Whiteley, P. (1977) The political ideology of Labour councillors. In *Policy and Politics*, 1977, No. 5, pp. 1–25.

Gouldner, A. W. (1976) *The Dialectic of Ideology and Technology*. London, Macmillan.

Granada Television (3 July 1978) The National Front. *World in Action*.

Guiraud, P. (1975) *Semiology*. London, Routledge and Kegal Paul.

Gurevitch, M. and Blumler, J. (1977) Linkages between the mass media and politics: a model for the analysis of political communications systems. In Curran, J., Gurevitch, M. and Woollacott, J. (eds.) *Mass Communication and Society*. London, Edward Arnold Ltd and Open University Press, pp. 270–90.

Guttsmann, W. L. (1963) *The British Political Elite*. London, Macgibbon.

Habermas, J. (1971) *Toward a Rational Society: Student Protest, Science and Politics*. Trans. by Shapiro, J., London, Heinemann Educational.

(1972) *Knowledge and Human Interests*. Trans. by Shapiro, J., London, Heinemann Educational.

(1974) *Theory and Practice*. Trans. by Viertel, J., London, Heinemann.

(1976) *Legitimation Crisis*. Trans. by McCarthy, T., London, Heinemann.

Hailsham, Lord (1975) *The Door Wherein I Went*. London, Collins.

Hall, S., Critcher, C., Jefferson, T., Clarke, J., Roberts, B. (1978) *Policing the Crisis: Mugging, the State and Law and Order*. London, Macmillan.

Halloran, J. D. (1974) Introduction. In UNESCO, 1974.

Hare, R. M. (1963) *Freedom and Reason*. Oxford University Press.

Hartmann, P. and Husband, C. (1971) The mass media & racial conflict. Unpublished paper.

(1973) The mass media and racial conflict. In Cohen and Young, 1973, pp. 270–83.

(1974) *Racism and the Mass Media: A Study of the Role of the Mass Media in the Formation of White Beliefs and Attitudes in Britain*. London, Davis Poynter.

Hartmann, P., Husband, C. and Clark, J. (1974) Race as news: a study of the handling of race in the British national press from 1963 to 1970. In UNESCO, 1974, pp. 89–173.

Haxey, S. (1939) *Tory M.P.* London, Victor Gollancz.

Hay, J. R. (1975) *The Origins of the Liberal Welfare Reforms, 1906–1914*. London, Macmillan.

Hegel, F. (1952) *Philosophy of Right*. Trans. by Knox, T. M., Oxford University Press.

Heilpern, J. (1968) Down among Mr Powell's constituents – town that has lost its reason. *The Observer*, 14 July 1968.

Henderson, A. (1918) *The League of Nations and Labour, 1918*. London, Labour Party.

Hilferding, R. (1973) *Das Finanzkapital* (*Finance Capital*) 2nd edn. Frankfurt am Main, Europaische Verlagsanstalt.

Hinden, R. (ed.) (1945) *Fabian Colonial Essays*. London, George Allen and Unwin.

Hitler, A. (1974) *Mein Kampf*. London, Hutchinson.

HMSO Acts. Commonwealth Immigration Acts: 1962, 1968, London HMSO; Immigration Act, 1971, London HMSO; Race Relations Acts: 1965, 1968, 1976, London HMSO.

The National Plan, Sept. 1965, Cmnd 2764, Part 1, reproduced in part in Bealey (1970).

Parliamentary Debates (Hansard). Commonwealth Immigrants Bill, Second Reading, 1961–2, Vol. 649, pp. 678–820; Commonwealth Immigrants Bill, Second Reading, 1967–8, Vol. 759, pp. 1241–368; Immigration Bill, Second Reading, 1970–1, Vol. 813, pp. 42–174; Race Relations Bill, Second Reading, 1964–5, Vol. 711, pp. 926–1060; Race Relations Bill, Second Reading, 1967–8, Vol. 763, pp. 53–174; Race Relations Bill, Second Reading, 1975–6, Vol. 906, pp. 1547–670.

Report of the Committee for Housing in Greater London, Cmnd 2605 (1965) (*The Milner Holland Report*), London HMSO.

Report of the Royal Commission on Population (1949), London HMSO.

Report on Social Insurance and Allied Services, Cmnd 6404 (1942) (*The Beveridge Report*), London HMSO.

Third Report of the Overseas Migration Board, Cmnd 336 (1957), London HMSO.

Urban Programme Circular (1968), No. 1, Oct. 1968, London HMSO.

Hoare, Q. and Nowell Smith, E. (ed.) (1971) *Selections from the Prison Notebooks of Antonio Gramsci*. London, Lawrence and Wishart.

Hobson, J. A. (1965) *Imperialism: A Study*. London, George Allen and Unwin.

Hodge, J. L., Struckmann, D. K. and Dorland Trost, L. (1975) *Cultural Bases of Racism and Group Oppression*. Berkeley, California, Two Riders Press.

Hoogvelt, A. M. (1969) Ethnocentrism, authoritarianism, and Powellism. In *Race*, July 1969, Vol. 11, No. 1, pp. 1–12.

Huaco, G. A. (1971) On ideology. *Acta Sociologica*, Vol. 14, p. 245.
Hunter, I. M. L. (1957, rev. 1964) *Memory*. Harmondsworth, Penguin.
Husband, C. (ed.) (1975) *White Media and Black Britain*, London, Arrow.
Huttenback, R. A. (1976) *Racism and Empire: White Settlers and Colored Immigrants in the British Self-Governing Colonies 1830–1910*. Cornell University.
Jay, M. (1973) *The Dialectical Imagination, A History of the Frankfurt School and the Institute of Social Research, 1923–1950*. London, Heinemann.
Jenkins, Roy (1967) *Essays and Speeches*. Lester, A. (ed.), London, Collins.
Jenkins, Robin (1971) The production of knowledge in the Institute of Race Relations. Private Paper, Institute of Race Relations.
Jones, K. (1967) Immigrants and the Social Services. In *National Institute Economic Review*, Aug. 1967, No. 41, pp. 28–40.
Jones, K. and Smith, A. D. (1970) *The Economic Impact of Commonwealth Immigration*. Cambridge University Press.
Kant, I. (1952) *Critique of Judgment*. Trans. Meredith, J. C., Oxford, Clarendon Press.
(1964) *Critique of Pure Reason*. Trans. Kemp-Smith, N., London, Macmillan.
Katz, D. (1960) The functional approach to the study of attitudes. In *Public Opinion Quarterly*, Vol. 24, pp. 163–204.
Keynes, J. M. (1936) *The General Theory of Employment, Interest and Money*. New York, Harcourt Brace Jovanovich.
Kiernan, V. G. (1972) *The Lords of Human Kind: European Attitudes Towards the Outside World in the Imperial Age*. Harmondsworth, Penguin.
Krech, D., Crutchfield, R. S. and Ballachey, E. L. (1962) *Individual in Society*. New York, McGraw Hill.
Kuhn, T. S. (1962, 1970) *The Structure of Scientific Revolutions*. University of Chicago Press.
Labour Party, Annual Conference Reports (LPACR): 1946, 1948, 1949, 1953, 1954, 1955, 1956, 1959, 1960, 1962, 1963, 1965, 1966, 1968, 1969, 1970, 1971, 1972, 1974, 1976, 1977.
Election Manifestos: 1929, 1959, 1964, 1966, 1970, 1974, 1979.
Labour and the Nation, 1928.
Let Us Face the Future, 1945.
Towards Equality, 1956.
Lachenmeyer, C. (1971) *The Language of Sociology*. Columbia University Press.
Ladd, J. (1957) *The Structure of a Moral Code*. Harvard University Press.
Lane, R. E. (1962) *Political Ideology: Why the American Common Man Believes what he Does*. New York, Free Press of Glencoe; London, Macmillan.
(1969) *Political Thinking and Consciousness*. Chicago, Markham.
Langer, S. K. (1976) *Philosophy in a New Key: A Study in the Symbolism of Reason, Rite, and Art*. Cambridge, Mass., Harvard University Press.
La Piere, R. T. (1934) Attitudes vs Actions. In *Social Forces*, Vol. 13, pp. 230–7.
Layton-Henry, Z. (1978) The Tories: in two minds over race. In *New Society*, 24 Aug. 1978.
Lecky, W. E. H. (1899) *Democracy and Liberty*, Vols. 1 and 2. London, Longman.
Leigh, D. (1978) The Populists: Rhodes Boyson. In the *Guardian*, 28 Mar. 1978.
Lenin, V. I. (1966) *Imperialism, the Highest Stage of Capitalism, a Popular Outline*. Moscow, Progress Publishers.
(1969) Imperialism and the divided labour movement – 'Lloyd Georgism'. In

Social chauvinism, reprinted in Lenin, V. I., *British Labour and British Imperialism*. London, Lawrence and Wishart, pp. 142–9.

Lewis, A. (1968) What Britain can learn from America. *The Times*, 22 Apr. 1968.

Lippmann, W. (1922) *Public Opinion*. New York, Macmillan.

Luria, A. R. (1975) *The Mind of a Mnemonist*. Harmondsworth, Penguin.

McDermott, E. (1972) *Leader Lost: A Biography of Hugh Gaitskell*. London, Leslie Frewin Publishers.

MacDonald, J. R. (1907) *Labour and the Empire*. London, George Allen.

MacIver, R. M. (1961) *The Web of Government*. New York, Macmillan.

McKenzie, R. and Silver, A. (1968) *Angels in Marble: Working Class Conservatives in Urban England*. London, Heinemann.

Macmillan, H. (1938) *The Middle Way: A study of the Problem of Economic and Social Progress in a Free and Democratic Society*. London, Macmillan.
(1973) *At the End of the Day, 1961–3*. London, Macmillan.

McNemar, Q. (1946) Opinion – attitude methodology. In *Psychology Bulletin*, Vol. 43, pp. 289–374; referred to in Wicker, 1969.

Mannheim, K. (1936) *Ideology and Utopia*. London, Routledge and Kegan Paul.

Marx, K. and Engels, F. (1973) *Feuerbach: Opposition of the Materialist and Idealist Outlooks*. London, Lawrence and Wishart.

Mee, A. (c. 1953) *The Children's Encyclopedia*. London, Educational Book Co.

Miliband, R. (1973) *Parliamentary Socialism: A Study in the Politics of Labour*. 2nd edn, London.

Mill, J. S. (1961) *A System of Logic*, Vol. 1, Bk 2 (Ch 3). London, Longman.

Miller, S. M. (1978) The recapitalization of capitalism. *International Journal of Urban and Regional Research*, June 1978, Vol. 2, No. 2, pp. 202–12.

Minogue, K. R. (1967) *Nationalism*. London, Batsford.

Mullard, C. (1973) 'Community relations': a non-starter. In *Race Today*, Apr. 1973.

Murphy, J. T. (1930) *The Labour Government: An Examination of its Record*. London, Modern Books Ltd.

Myrdal, G. (1962) *An American Dilemma: The Negro Problem and Modern Democracy* (assisted by Sterner, R. and Rose, A.). New York, London, Harper and Row.

National Minority Movement (1929) *British Imperialism, An Outline of Workers' Conditions in the Colonies*. London, National Minority Movement, 38, Gt Ormond St.

New Society (1968) Is the working class really racist? In *New Society*, 2 May 1968, p. 627.

Newton, K. (1976) *Second City Politics, Democratic Processes and Decision-Making in Birmingham*. Oxford, Clarendon Press.

Nikolinakos, M. (1973) Notes on an economic theory of racism. In *Race*, April 1973, Vol. 14, No. 4, pp. 365–81.
(1975) Notes towards a general theory of migration in late capitalism. In *Race and Class*, July 1975, Vol. 17, No. 1, pp. 5–17.

Nisbet, R. (1961) The study of social problems. In Merton, R. K. and Nisbet, R., *Contemporary Social Problems*, New York, Harcourt Brace Jovanovich.

Oakeshott, M. (1962) *Rationalism in Politics and Other Essays*. London, Methuen.

Owen, R. (1972) *A New View of Society*. London, Macmillan.

Palme Dutt, R. (1936) *World Politics, 1918–1936*. Left Book Club, London, Victor Gollancz.

Panitch, L. V. (1971) Ideology and integration: the case of the British Labour Party. In *Political Studies*, June, Vol. 19, No. 2.

Pareto, V. A. (1963) *Treatise on General Sociology*, Vols. 1 and 2. First published in English, 1935; New York, Dover Publications.

Parker, R. A. (1970) The future of the personal Social Services. In Robson, W. A. and Crick, B. (eds.), *The Future of the Social Services*. Harmondsworth, Penguin.

Parkin, F. (1971) *Class Inequality and Political Order*. Frogmore, St Albans, Herts., Granada Paladin.

Parsons, T. (1970) *The Social System*. London, Routledge and Kegan Paul.
   (1966) *Societies: Evolutionary and Comparative Perspectives*. New Jersey, Prentice Hall.

Paul, Jimmy, and Mustafa Support Committee (1973) *20 Years*. C/o The Handsworth Action Centre.

Peach, C. (1968) *West Indian Migration to Britain, A Social Geography*. Institute of Race Relations and Oxford University Press.

Perelman, C. H. and Olbrechts-Tyteca, L. (1969) *The New Rhetoric: A Treatise on Argumentation*. University of Notre Dame Press.

Phillips, K. (1977) The Nature of Powellism. In Nugent, N. and King, R. (eds.), *The British Right*. London, Saxon House.

Plamenatz, J. (1971) *Ideology*. London, Macmillan.

Polanyi, M. (1958) *Personal Knowledge*. London, Routledge and Kegan Paul.

Poliakov, L. (1974) *The Aryan Myth*. Trans. by Howard, E., London, Heinemann.

Poulantzas, N. (1975) *Political Power and Social Classes*. London, New Left Books.

Powell, J. E. (1969) *Freedom and Reality*. London, Batsford.
   (1970) The limits of laissez-faire. In *Crossbow*, Spring, pp. 25–8, in Beattie, A. (ed.) *English Party Politics*, Vol. 2, 1906–70. London, Weidenfeld and Nicolson, 1970, pp. 488–94.
   (1972) *Still to Decide*. London, Batsford.
   (1978) *A Nation or No Nation*. London, Batsford.
   (1978) *The Common Market: Renegotiate or Come Out*. Kingswood, Surrey. Elliot Right Way Books.
   Speech at Wolverhampton, 25 Mar. 1966.
   Facing up to Britain's Race Problem. In *Daily Telegraph*, 16 Feb. 1967.
   Speech at Walsall, 9 Feb. 1968.
   Speech in Birmingham, 20 Apr. 1968.
   Speech to London Rotary Club, Eastbourne, 16 Nov. 1968.
   Speech at Northfield, Birmingham, 13 June 1970.
   Speech at Stretford, Manchester, 21 Jan. 1977.
   Interview in *Der Spiegel*, reprinted in *New Statesman*, 13 Oct. 1978.

Pritchard, A. M. (1964) *R. W. League's Roman Private Law*. London, Macmillan.

Pritt, D. N. (1963) *The Labour Government, 1945–1951*. London, Lawrence and Wishart.

Putnam, R. D. (1973) *The Beliefs of Politicians: Ideology, Conflict and Democracy in Britain and Italy*. New Haven, London, Yale University Press.

Race Relations Board and the National Committee for Commonwealth Immigrants Political and Economic Planning: *Report on Racial Discrimination* (1967).
   Report on Anti Discrimination Legislation (The Street Report) (1967).

Race Today Collective (1975) Editorial, *Race Today*, Sept. 1975.

Rawls, J. (1979) *A Theory of Justice.* Oxford University Press.

Reeves, F. (1982) *The Concept of Prejudice: An Evaluative Review.* SSRC Research Unit on Ethnic Relations Working Paper 17.

Reinders, R. C. (1968) Racialism on the Left: E. D. Morel and the 'Black Horror on the Rhine'. In *The International Review of Social History*, 1968, Vol. 23, pp. 1–28.

Rex, J. (1968) The race relations catastrophe. In Burgess, T., *Matters of Principle, Labour's Last Chance.* Harmondsworth, Penguin, pp. 70–83.
    (1970) The concept of race in sociological theory. In Zubaida, 1970, pp. 35–55.
    (1973) *Race, Colonialism and the City.* London, Routledge and Kegan Paul.

Rex, J. and Tomlinson, S. (1979) *Colonial Immigrants in a British City: A Class Analysis.* London, Routledge and Kegan Paul.

Richmond, A. H. (1955) *The Colour Problem: A Study of Racial Relations.* Harmondsworth, Penguin.

Rodgers, W. T. (ed.) (1964) *Hugh Gaitskell 1906–1963.* London, Thames and Hudson.

Rokeach, M. (1968) The Nature of Attitudes. Reprint from *The International Encyclopedia of the Social Sciences*, p. 450, London, Collier Macmillan.

Rose, A. (1948) *The Negro in America: A Condensation of an American Dilemma.* London, Secker and Warburg.

Rose, E. J. B. and associates (1969) *Colour and Citizenship, A Report on British Race Relations.* Published jointly by Institute of Race Relations and Oxford University Press.

Roth, A. (1972) *Heath and the Heathmen.* London, Routledge and Kegan Paul.

Russell, A. G. (1944) *Colour, Race and Empire.* Left Book Club, London, Victor Gollancz.

Ryle, G. (1949) *The Concept of Mind.* London, Hutchinson.

Sanders, E. (1972) *The Family, the Whole Charles Manson Horror Story.* Frogmore, St Albans, Herts, Granada Panther.

Seliger, M. (1976) *Ideology and Politics.* London, George Allen and Unwin.

Senior, C. and Manley, D. (1955) *A Report on Jamaican Migration to Great Britain.* Institute of Social and Economic Research, Kingston, Jamaican Government Printer.

Sennett, R. and Cobb, J. (1977) *The Hidden Injuries of Class.* Cambridge University Press.

Seymour-Ure, C. (1974) *The Political Impact of the Mass Media.* London, Constable.

Shah, I. (1968) *The Pleasantries of the Incredible Mulla Nasrudin.* London, Jonathan Cape; Pan Books, 1975.

Sharf, A. (1964) *The British Press and Jews Under Nazi Rule.* Published jointly by Institute of Race Relations and Oxford University Press.

Shaw, B. (1928) *The Intelligent Woman's Guide to Socialism and Capitalism.* London, Constable.

Shils, E. (1968) Ideology. In Sils, D. (ed.) *International Encyclopedia of the Social Sciences*, Vol. 7. Macmillan, 1968.

Simpson, G. E. and Yinger, J. M. (1965) *Racial and Cultural Minorities.* New York, Harper and Row.

Sivanandan, A. (1976) Race, class and the state: the black experience in Britain. In *Race and Class*, Apr., Vol. 17, No. 4, pp. 347–68.

Smelser, N. J. (1962) *Theory of Collective Behaviour.* London, Routledge and Kegan Paul.

Snyder, L. L. (1964) *The Dynamics of Nationalism*. New Jersey, D. Van Nostrand Company.
Socialist Challenge (20 Oct. 1977) The thoughts of Chairman Dobson, p. 8.
Sorel, G. (1950) *Reflections on Violence*. Trans. by Hulme, T. E. and Roth, J., Glencoe, Illinois, Free Press.
Spearman, D. (1968) Enoch Powell's postbag. In *New Society*, 9 May 1968, pp. 667–9.
Stopes, M. C. (1923) *Contraception*. London, John Bale, Sons and Danielsson.
Stubbs, W. (1906) *Lectures on Early British History*. London, Longmans Green.
Sudman, S. and Bradburn, N. M. (1974) *Response Effects in Surveys: A Review and Synthesis*. Chicago, Aldine.
Suhl, I. (1975) 'Doctor Dolittle': the Great White Father. In *Racist and Sexist Images in Children's Books*. Writers and Readers Publishing Cooperative, pp. 3–9.
Tajfel, H. (1973) The roots of prejudice: cognitive aspects. In Watson, P. (ed.) *Psychology and Race*. Harmondsworth, Penguin.
Tawney, R. H. (1964) *Equality*. London, Unwin Books.
Taylor, D. M. (1970) *Explanation and Meaning: An Introduction to Philosophy*. Cambridge University Press.
The Times, 17 Feb. 1964.
Thomas, J. H. (1920) *When Labour Rules*. London, Collins.
Tracey, H. (ed.) (1948) *The British Labour Party: Its History, Growth, Policy and Leaders*. Vols. 1, 2, and 3. London, Caxton.
UNESCO (1974) *Race as News*. Two general studies on attitude change by Klineberg, O. and Guillaumin, C. and a study of the British national press by Hartmann, P., Husband, C. and Clark, J., with an introduction by Halloran, J. D., Paris, UNESCO Press.
   (1977) *Ethnicity and the Media: An analysis of Media Reporting in the United Kingdom, Canada and Ireland*. Paris, UNESCO Press.
Utley, T. E. (1968) *Enoch Powell: The Man and His Thinking*. London, Kimber.
Van den Berghe, P. (1967) *Race and Racism*. New York, Wiley.
Warren, N. and Jahoda, M. (1973) *Attitudes*. Harmondsworth, Penguin.
Weber, M. (1964) *The Theory of Social and Economic Organisation*. Trans. by Henderson, A. M. and Parsons, T., New York, Free Press.
White, J. (1968) Rich Countries and Poor. In Burgess, T. (ed.) *Matters of Principle: Labour's Last Chance*. Harmondsworth, Penguin.
White, R. J. (1950) *The Conservative Tradition*. London, Kaye.
Wicker, A. W. (1969) Attitudes vs actions: the relationship of verbal and overt responses to attitude objects. In *Journal of Social Issues*, Vol. 25, 1969, pp. 41–78, reprinted in Warren and Jahoda, 1973, pp. 167–94.
Williams, F. (1949) *Fifty Years March: The Rise of the Labour Party*. London, Odhams Press.
Wittgenstein, L. (1963) *Philosophical Investigations*. Trans. by Anscombe, G. E. M., Oxford, Blackwell.
Wolff, K. H. (ed.) (1971) *From Karl Mannheim*. New York, Oxford University Press.
Wood, J. (ed.) (1970) *Powell and the 1970 Election*. Kingswood, Surrey, Elliott Right Way Books.
Woolf, L. (1945) The Political Advance of Backward Peoples. In Hinden, 1945, pp. 85–98.
Worsley, P. (1970) *The Trumpet Shall Sound*. London, Granada Paladin.
Zubaida, S. (1970) *Race and Racialism*. London, Tavistock.

Name index

Subject index

action, logical and non-logical, 66, 89
actor, social: account of social structure,
    45, 189; and deracialisation, 179, 181;
    and ideology 35, 359, 174;
    identification of racism, 183; and race
    relations terminology 255; racial
    intention of, 26, 29
Africa, 112, 113, 114, 116, 126; Central,
    113, 114, 116; East, 113, 116, 117–18,
    206; South, 115, 116, 125, 187, 256,
    264; Southern, 116, 125; West, 115
alienation, 48–9, 57, 63, 64, 65, 68, 69, 71,
    72, 77, 104, 152, 161, 246; square of,
    3, 48–55, 56, 246
analogy: argument form, 212; flux, 212,
    221; honey-pot, 156, 222–3; martial,
    212, 222; natural disaster, 219; and
    phoros, 212; proliferation, 222; run-
    on-bank, 223; statistical, 219, 220–1;
    and theme, 212; and trope, 212;
    ungrateful child, 223; volcano, 221–2
argument forms, 4, 210–39; abstracted
    social process, 218–24; agential,
    213–18; analogical, 212; dispositional,
    213–18; economic, 226–31; means-
    orientated 237–8; personalised,
    213–18; populist, 224–6; pro bono
    publico, 231–4; quasi, 238; reciprocity,
    234–6; symmetry, 235; typology of,
    210–11
anti-imperialism, 4, 88, 118, 122, 124
Anti-Nazi League, 73, 170–1
anti-Semitism, 153, 170–1, 186, 224; Jew as
    usurer, 183
Australia, deracialised immigration policy,
    263–4

black people, 25; as alien wedge, 107; as
    beneficiaries of immigration control,
    233–4; and brotherly love, 110, 111; in
    colonies, 46; community, 1; conditions
    experienced by, 93; conscientisation

of, 175; and crime, 139, 217–18, 247;
    as different, 216–17; discursive
    strategies of, 248; and education, 167,
    247; effects of capital on, 65; and
    equal opportunity, 134; and
    hierarchical arrangement, 130; identity
    groups, 50; ideology, 42, 248;
    immigration, 94; as inferior, 214, 216;
    and justice, 142–6; and the law,
    137–9; as lower class, 130–1; middle
    class, intelligentsia, 127; non-racial
    features, 209; perceived role of, 59; as
    potential communists, 114, 168;
    rhetoric, 248; suitability of term
    'black', 255–6, 257; as symbols, 55; as
    threat, 60, 108, 152, 217–18; as
    underdogs, 111–12, 144–5; and urban
    violence, 138–9; vote, 189; welfare
    contributors, 157; welfare entitlement,
    160; as welfare recipients, 156–9; and
    welfare stigma, 162
bourgeoisie, 48–53, 61–2, 245; national, 50;
    parties 71; reasoning, 132, 133
brotherhood of man, 94, 95, 108–12, 125

Canada, deracialised immigration policy,
    264
capitalism, 36, 40–1, 46–55, 61–2, 64, 99,
    103–4, 109, 111, 127, 132, 144, 149,
    152–3, 169, 171, 187, 245; and
    imperialism, 118, 120, 122–3, 126
colonialism: colonisation, 174; domestic
    neo-, 126–7; see also imperialism
colonies, 49, 52, 115–16, 118, 118n, 121–7;
    colonial immigrants to Britain 55–6;
    colonial proletariat 55–6; colour bar,
    abolition of, 126; Conservative policy
    towards 113–17; and deracialisation of
    policies 263–4; images of, 202;
    independence, 88; Labour Party
    policy towards, 95, 118–27; ladder of
    ascent, 121

286   Subject index

overseas aid, 111
ownership: private, 88, 96, 134, 146–50; social, 4, 88, 95, 99, 150–3

parties, political: difficulty of delineating party ideology, 82–5; discourse, 81–5; and eristic, 261–2; individual *v.* group pronouncements, 83; organs representative of, 83; poverty of theory, 83
party values, 82–8, 95–171; class-based nature of, 87; definition of, 84; difficulty of identifying, 82–5; extended to immigration and race relations, 87; typology of, 84–5, 88
paternalism, 92, 112, 114, 115, 119, 123–4, 126, 127, 154, 249
patriality, 92, 208
persuasion, 42, 62, 64, 65, 71, 75, 205, 246, 252, 259; persuasibility, 3, 34
philosophy: of intellectuals, 69–70; relationship with common sense, 70–1
pluralism, cultural, 94
police, 137, 139, 144, 146, 247
political apprenticeship, 74–5
Powellism, 72, 93; Conservative bogy, 169; Powell-mania, 185, 248; and sanitary coding, 202–3
practice, racial, 11, 51, 175, 179, 180, 181, 186, 206, 209, 242, 247, 253; belies words, 189; explanations for r.p. different from those for racial discourse, 68, 80, 242
prejudice, race, 28, 40, 50–1, 53, 72, 158, 161, 162, 224, 242–4, 251, 252–3; as attitude, 242–3; and education, 167; as empirically unfounded, 243; functions of, 244; inadequacy of concept, 5, 37, 208; as injustice, 243–4; as irrationality, 243–4; as natural imperfection, 164–5; as negative, 243
prescription, 37–8, 40, 75, 84, 89, 132, 252, 260–1; class orientated, 180; economic, 227; moral, 16–18; racial, 4, 13–18, 31, 87, 172, 183, 190, 204, 235, 241, 243, 249
primitive grunt, 75
private utterances, 18–19, 182, 247; and sanitary coding, 190–3, 250
proletariat, 48–56, 61–2, 245; colonial, 55–6; competition between proletarians 54; metropolitan, 55–6
public utterances, 18–19, 182, 188; and sanitary coding, 190–3, 250

race: definition of, 7–10, 172; perception of differences, 7–8

race relations; application of party values to, 96, 180; and empirical truth, 40; and square of alienation, 48–55; in structural context, 46; *see also* r.r. legislation
race relations legislation, 5, 43, 81, 99, 167, 183, 250–2; and brotherhood, 111; colonial paternalism, 126–7; equality, 131, 145; as favouring blacks, 130–1; and improvement through education, 166; l. in opposition to human nature, 164; l. in opposition to capitalist competition, 152; and minimal role of government, 148–9; as rationalisation, 103; and role of voluntary groups, 149
'racial', different from 'racist', 28–9
racial minorities, 1n, 2, 9, 42, 65; Jamaicans, 208–9; Kenyan Asians, 189–90, 206, 236–7; Muslims, 145; organisations, 146; Rastafarians, 52; Sikhs, 98, 145; suitability of terminology, 257; terminology used in relation to, 255–8; Ugandan Asians, 117–18, 130, 195, 224; West Indians, 53, 258
racialisation, 29, 173–6, 178, 179, 182, 248; anti-racialisation, 175, 176, 177; definition, 173–4; ideological or discursive, 174–6, 249; practical or actual, 174, 176, 249–50
racialism, 3, 11–12, 20, 24–6, 103, 152, 153, 175, 186, 187, 189, 241; distinguished from racism, 11–12, 241; racialist-effective discourse, 20
racism, 3, 11–24, 29, 37, 87, 88, 113, 145, 152, 182–6, 238, 241–2; argument forms seen as, 213; Banton's definition, 21–4, 209; defence against, 190; distinguished from racialism, 11–12, 242; and fascism, 171; folk, 22–3, 26; and folk imagery, 200–2; genetic, 213, 216; of head, 173, 184, 186, 204; of heart, 173, 184–6; 'I am not a r., but', 190; identification of, 184; as ignorance, 167; imputation of, 20–1; inverted, 196; jokes, 183, 183n; limitation of term, 26–7; medium, 12–13, 15; popular, 248; repressed, 185; scientific, 14–15, 22–3, 92, 112, 113, 176, 243; strong, 12–15; unwillingness to recognise own r., 184; verbally camouflaged, 184; weak, 12–15
rationalisation, 4, 87, 88, 95, 100–4, 247
referential meaning, 8–10
repatriation, 98, 139–40, 174
research methodology, 5